TABLE OF CONTENTS

INTRODUCTION
OF JUDGES AND OTHER SCOUNDRELS
SELECTED TV JUDGES

- Judge Alex E. Ferrer
- Couples Court – With the Cutlers
- Judge Marilyn Milian, People's Court

    ✓ Background From an Actual Participant
    ✓ The People's Court: Review
    ✓ The Men Behind the Woman

- Judge Jeanine Pirro

    ✓ Pirro, Conservative Politics and Donald Trump
    ✓ Jeanine Pirro and Her (July 2018) Appearance on "The View"

- Judge Lynn Toler, Divorce Court

    ✓ Lynn Toler: Mental Health Issues
    ✓ Reviews of "Divorce Court" with Lynn Toler

- Judge Karen Mills-Francis

    ✓ Judge Mills-Francis: Her Out-of-Court "Advice"

- Judge Faith Jenkins
- Judge Greg Mathis

    ✓ Background
    ✓ The Mathis Website
    ✓ Judge Mathis: Overview and Analysis

- Judge Joe Brown
- Judge Lauren Lake, "Paternity Court"

- ✓ Judge Lauren Lake and Paternity Court: Format
- ✓ "Paternity Court": Examples from 2018

- Judge Judy Sheindlin

  - ✓ Background
  - ✓ Review of "Judge Judy"

WHERE'S THE LOGIC IN THESE TV PROGRAMS?
WHO'S THE BEST? WHO'S THE WORST?
THE MINSTREL PRODUCTION MACHINE
CONCLUSION
REFERENCES

Judge not, that ye be not judged. For with what judgment ye judge, ye shall be judged: and with what measure ye mete, it shall be measured to you again. And why beholdest thou the mote that is in thy brother's eye, but considerest not the beam that is in thine own eye? Or how wilt thou say to thy brother, Let me pull out the mote out of thine eye; and, behold, a beam is in thine own eye? *Thou hypocrite*, first cast out the beam out of thine own eye; and then shalt thou see clearly to cast out th emote out of thy brother's eye. *Give not that which is holy unto the dogs, neither cast ye your pearls before swine, lest they trample them under their feet, and turn again and rend you* (emphasis added).

Matthew 7:1-6

PREFACE

If there is any doubt that there are millions of stupid people in America, then simply interject the variable of "television" and the offer of sitting in an audience or being on stage, and the total mind numbing ignorance of the American public will come to the fore. While entertaining, it is also evidence of how gullible the American public is and how exploitive these shows about "judges" can be.

Over the decades of television there have been clownish sitcoms and it is therefore expected that these people make asses out of themselves so that the canned laughter can ring out and in turn, advertising can be sold in the name of "comedic television." Long before cable, the major television stations – ABC, CBS and NBC – paved the way. When Fox came along later, they lowered the bar even more and added sleaze and racism to their comedy and, as can be expected, the hedonistic American public bought it hook line and sinker.

That is one thing when you have a script that tells you what to say and what to do, what marks to hit and what expressions to make. But the reason for this book is to make it clear that never before on American television as a genre of shows that are supposed to be about jurisprudence, dispensing justice, the law and the courtroom ever been the host of so many voluntary and clownish people.

According to one source, "As reported in late 2012, court programming is the second highest-rated genre on daytime television" (Wikipedia, 2018). And this book aims to show that the reason for that are those clownish litigants who appear, who spill their guts in front of millions, and who serve as fodder once that show is "in the can" and is distributed the world over. What could the motive be to make Americans look so greedy, pitiful, ignorant and vindictive? You do the math.

Whether you are talking Judge Joe Brown, Judge Faith, Judge Judy or any of the others that I will analyze, there is a trend: bring people before the camera who will sign away their rights to be judged and degraded and spill their guts about their foolish escapades. Many of them even get to the point where they openly admit guilt.

I am especially appalled at the black people who participate in these antics. White people have always been willing to perform stupid acts, from smashing pies in each other's faces, men putting on dresses and falling down stairs to opening slapping one another, calling each other names and so on. That is par for the course. But the concept of "black pride" seems to be lost on our community. They sign up for this bullshit, relinquish their rights and then allow themselves to be dogged and degraded in front of millions of viewers.

When you go to court you are at the mercy of someone who exercises a great deal of "discretion." America is a racist nation and therefore a black person in front of a judge, black or white, is always going to be viewed with some degree of disdain. Why then, do these coons come before the television cameras dressed like pimps and hookers? They come to court as if they are going out on a date. Or they dress like they are on their way to a rumble or some kind of gang intervention meeting. All of this helps to confirm the stereotypical views that whites have of blacks. As Woody Harrelson's character told Wesley Snipes in the movie, "White Men Can't Jump," "You would rather lose and look good than win and look bad."

What these people don't understand is that in this age of hi-tech, these shows are recorded. Not only by the station but at home. If you have a case pending and you go before one of these judges, that might not be the final word. That tape can be taken back home and used again for future lawsuits. And what about the ass whippings that can occur when black people get in front of their cameras and air their dirty laundry in front of a nation of peckerwoods who already deem us inferior and stupid?

Hence, the label of "minstrel." Not just for the blacks who appear on these outlandish insults to law and jurisprudence, but to the whites as well. A "minstrel" is defined as, one of a troupe of comedians, usually white men in blackface, presenting songs, jokes, etc., and portraying negative racial stereotypes."

So whether white or black, the people who are standing before these judges are there as targets. They are comic relief and charlatans. The fact is, the bias against them usually more on a "class" basis than on race, but both are definitely involved in the shows I am about to analyze.

The people who distribute these "legal shows," from "The People's Court" and "Judge Judy" to "Judge Greg Mathis" and the rest, send them all over the world. And not only to European countries; people in countries who may not even have running water but somehow have enough electricity to have television sets are watching us make asses out of ourselves. Is it any wonder that the confidence factor of America's enemies is sky high? They see the idiocy on these shows and assume that this is par for the course!

This book is a critical race analysis. If white people want to humiliate themselves, that is their business and right. My people should stop doing war dances on dance floor and take it out to the field where it belongs.

INTRODUCTION

In the case of the court TV shows that you are about to read about, why would anybody with even half a brain, go on national television and spill their damn guts about a lawsuit? Those shows that deal with TV judges are nothing more than a built in "snitch system" for the locals who are viewing the program. These people are on the air spilling their fuckin' guts and having everything they say professionally filmed. They make asses of themselves for the people back home to see, and in some cases, they are probably making enemies of the people who are waiting for them back home to "spank that ass."

Why would you do that? Not only that, but what you see is the product of meetings between plaintiff and defendant, television producers, writers, the assistants to whomever the judge is, and a room full of people who are making sure that you case is television worthy. And what does that mean? It means that the judge can say whatever he or she wants to say to you, insult you, demean your case or otherwise trample on your rights in the name of free speech while you are limited to kissing that judge's ass, staying quiet, acting as if you have nothing to say that is in response to that judge, and so on. In other words, you sign a document that states that you won't "talk back" and that you agree that the judge's decision is final.

How much more unfair can blind-ass "lady justice" be?

OF JUDGES AND OTHER SCOUNDRELS

If a person you meet tells you that he or she went to law school you are impressed for the most part because you think you know what they went through. You see late night study sessions, tests and exams, moot court and the like. You see them taking the bar, passing and then becoming attorneys. This is the way you see it because this is what the culture has been led to believe about these people who call themselves "attorneys" and "lawyers."

Let me tell you something.

I wrote term papers for a lot of these dumb bastards before they stumbled through the Law School Admissions Test (LSAT) and went to law school. My work helped their grade point average throughout college and in some case I even wrote the "entry essay" that goes along with the LSAT application which determines whether or not they get in or not. I've done that for three people in Omaha, one in Lincoln and another one at the University of Iowa. They paid me handsomely, but that's not the point I am making here.

Attorneys are just typical students who, somehow, made it through law school. They cram for the LSAT examination with a bunch of their pals or their parents, who may be lawyers themselves, help them for months in preparation. They then luck out and get into law school ("Oh good! Now mommy and daddy will get me that Porsche I always wanted!") and because they didn't put in the study that I did, they are then "programmed" in law classes as to how to format a legal brief, trained in how to present a case, robotically taught how to use a law library and the like. Most of them can get the degree in three years and come out knowing the language, knowing how to sound like they have a legal mind, but when all is said and done, still being dumb as a knot on a log.

So knowing this and having out-debated and out-argued lawyers in Omaha for over a decade, I have first-hand knowledge that most of them ain't about shit. Once they get in an office or lease an expensive one so that they can impress the people who stagger through the door seeking their help, they hire a secretary and a paralegal who do most of the typing and research. These receptionists also learn how to lie and stall time with such excuses as, "He's in court right now" or "I gave her the message."

At the same time, this "attorney" charges and accepts a huge chunk of change up front (a "retainer") and then takes his time. The key is that he or she may "consort" or "converse" with the attorney on the other side and, at least in the case of black clients, sell out the client to the other side. Even before that, these "attorneys" learn how to kiss some judge's ass and the females are experts at currying favor with these robed clowns. If you kiss enough ass or wear a skirt up to the crack of yours, the judge will make sure the word gets out that you're a "good egg."

At that point, you can win some cases, most of them slam dunks. If the client had a fuckin' brain, he could argue and win his own case, but the legal profession tries to keep smart people from doing that by circulating this maxim that, "A man who represents himself in court has a fool for a client." The fact is, most of the attorneys are the fools, but since they know more than the person that hired them, they get paid – win or lose.

Stripped of its pomp and rather impious ceremony, we have to see the judicial system for what it really is: the will and right of whatever white people want raised by LAW to the level of sacred observance. When peckerwoods didn't want to live next door to black people, didn't go to school with black people, didn't' want any black people in their movie theaters, hotels or restaurants, the law not only defended these actions, but punished anybody who tried to oppose or resist them. It is the law and the judges that uphold it that justified slavery, paved the way for racial zoning, made it clear that black people ride on the back of the bus, provided rationale to stop interracial marriage and so on.

If the law ain't shit, then the people who are paid or elected to enforce ain't shit, either. Always remember that.

And it is with this in mind that we come to a kind of stratification of judges. Some of them just go along to get along and pick up the paycheck or station themselves for re-election or re-appoint. But from among these, as in any occupation, are people who have stellar records and who have not only background in law, but have worked as district attorneys, sat as judges on Superior and/or Municipal courts, and maybe even worked as cops at one time (ala Judge Alex Ferrer). At least one – Judge Jeanine Pirro – was an elected official in addition to serving on the bench. Hell, Mills Lane was a big time boxing referee and is the one that threw Mike Tyson out of the fight with Evander Holyfield after Tyson bit part of Holyfield's ear off.

So these ain't no lightweights as far as their representation in the legal system. But television does strange things to people. First of all, they're flattered to be approached for a show. Then there are all those contracts and all that money that they can make. Third, the publicity and now they can tell all their friends and the inference is that this judge must be "incredible" in order to be asked to have her own show. Fourth, you have people tripping all over themselves to get you ready for the show: the promotional tapes that are shot, the bios that have to be distributed, and then there's the fifth point: the people on the set putting you in makeup, doing your hair and "prepping" you for the show itself. You feel like a star, not a judge. And if you watch most of these people, they are placing their performance above the decisions that they render. Not all of them – just most of them.

Point number six are the papers that the plaintiffs and defendants both sign. There is no doubt in my mind that if there weren't some kind of "protection order" in those papers that defends these judges against unsatisfied people cussing them out or charging the bench, several of them would end up getting their asses kicked, namely Judge Judy, Judge Lake, Judge Joe Brown and more likely than not, Judge Mills Lane. But Lane has boxing skills so I doubt anybody would fuck with him.

At any rate, most of these shows are about the plaintiffs and defendants getting paid one way or the other. According to one source, participants agree before the show begins to drop their small claims case and have it decided by arbitration through the show. The winner of the case is awarded from the show's budget, so the loser doesn't actually "pay back" the winner. The losing party is usually also compensated for their appearance.

The following shows that are being evaluated and analyzed are properly referred to as American arbitration-based reality court shows. These "judges" sit in as mediators and have to make decisions that usually revolve around cases of civil law. Some deal with paternity, others deal with business disagreements, but all of them have one thing in common: their shows, the people who appear before them and everything involved is pre-scripted. It's arranged and if money is involved it may or not be paid by the TV show itself. These programs may have some tidbits of law, but most of it is about entertainment, and the zanier the plaintiffs and defendants, the better.

SELECTED TV JUDGES: CRITIQUE AND COMMENTARY

JUDGE ALEX FERRER

Of all the judges, Ferrer comes off as being the most competent, the most prepared, and, along with another judge (Judge Mathis) appears to be the most committed to getting to the crux of the issue minus the primping and playing around for the camera that affects several other judges (Toler, Sheindlin, Milian, etc.) He is also the most experienced, having worked as a cop on the touch streets of Miami.

Judge Alex's show is also the most professionally done, from the opening credits and overview to the graphics. The introduction makes it clear that this guy has the experience and background. The narrator lets us know, "As a cop, he stood up for the law; as trial judge, he stood up for the truth,; as a criminal court judge, he commanded authority." Now, according to the introduction, he "returns to preside over America's courtroom." This is what I call a resume; and it's probably why his show is the most well-articulated of all the court shows on television.

For instance, during one episode, he said that he didn't miss working in family court at all because "in family court, you see the best people at their worst (in court) and in criminal court you see the "the worst people at their best." That's so true. On one segment a black man and black woman wanted to break up because he wanted one kind of chicken and she wanted another. On another episode, a black couple got into a fight in a supermarket over the size of a can of beans. She wanted to purchase the large number 2 size cans – known as restaurant size – and he wanted to purchase small cans. After all, he argued, "there was only three of us, me, her and her daughter." She said, "I like to buy in bulk." Country muthafuckas.

Moving on, Ferrer has a black bailiff, a brother named "Mason." Isn't ironic that it is a white man (Ferrer), a Jewish woman (Sheindlin) and a Latina (Milian) who have black male bailiffs and the "sister Judges" do not? Toler's is Joe Catalano, a barrel-chested Latino brother, a holdover from the days of Judge Mablean. Just a thought.

But back to Mason: he's probably the biggest "coon" out of all the black men on reality television. Bald and dressed more like a cop than a bailiff, all he does is laugh at Judge Alex's jokes (whether they're funny or not) and his laugh is one of those bellowing laughs. During one show the issue was these fat black women who put out a calendar called "Thicken Women." One of them sued, although they all posed in lace panties and nothing else. LaToya gave her a photo that she didn't want to have published by Na'Kisha Cole, the organizer of the calendar photo shoot, because "it was just a picture that I wanted in my bedroom." Bullshit.

These fat bitches had no business posing in semi-nude photos for a calendar or anything else. You should have seen the photo that was selected of this fat bitch. On the cover of the calendar they were all fat, a "thick girl calendar," all twelve posing, tits exposed. They couldn't show it on television but you can use your imagination and when you do, make sure you've got a barf bucket.

Another fat bitch, Miss Annie Thompson (who tells the judge that she goes by the name "Unique") walked up as a witness for LaTonya. Tall and light skinned, this hefty bag had bright red (and I do mean "red") hair and a giggle like some boney white bitch that had just seen a dick for the first time. At one point Alex has to pause and ask her, "Are you flirtin' with me?" She keeps on giggling, looking and sounding silly with that insane giggle, and said, "No."

Yet another fat bitch, this one with a dyke haircut, came up as a witness for the defendant. Fat ass is suing for slander in addition to being embarrassed by the picture and loss of income. The Defendant's witness/dyke stood there and didn't say anything, but remember that this is the second calendar that LaToya did: the first one was a calendar of women who dressed up like men! How can you slander a bitch that's doing shit like this?

Let me conclude by nothing that at one point during the segment, when Judge Alex asked LaToya what she was posing in, she replied, "lace panties." Alex cracked up and then turned and said, "That's the same thing Mason wears on weekends." Laughs at the expense of his trained coon who serves as his bailiff. Not even the twisted Judge Toler, the monotonous Judge Joe Brown or the frustrated and wicked Judge Judy would or has cracked on their bailiffs in such a callous manner. But it's not Alex' fault: They have staff meetings and Mason should be letting it be known that he's going to be treated with dignity. Evidently, he doesn't.

"COUPLES COURT" WITH THE CUTLERS

I was channel surfing one late morning and I came across this show. At first I thought it was a skit from Comedy Central. Here you had two obese black people sitting with judges robes on. The name of the show? "Couples Court with the Cutlers." A more appropriate name would have been "Meat Loaf Court with the Cold Cuts." Of all the shows on the air, of all the racial insults and innuendo I have witnessed during the years of analysis for this book, this was the only show that truly embarrassed me. Not the drunken conclusions of Judge Joe Brown, not the hair extensions of Laura Lake, not the dyed and laid to the side honey blonde hair of Judge Karen Mills-Francis, or even the effeminate "crack joke obsessed" litanies of Judge Greg Mathis.

This show hit the spot.

The promo tells us that this show is "Where modern-day technology meets every day cheating." The real cheating took place when these two whales were able to finagle their way onto the airwaves! According to the snippet, "Dana and Keith Cutler are television's first married couple to preside over a courtroom program. Highly respected for their legal expertise, the Cutlers combine their knowledge of the law with their own marriage experiences to dispense."

Of what use are their own marriage experiences? Those experiences are unique to them. They are so different from the average Joe. First of all they both went to and graduated from law school. Secondly, they both must have some background in the judicial system. So they've always been middle- or upper-middle class. How in the hell are they going to relate when it is crystal clear that a large portion of their paychecks goes to food?

What a joke. During one show I caught (I don't want to get ahead of myself, but this is worth sharing with the quickness), they were sitting in judgment and the subject was marriage. She said that "no marriage is one hundred percent. Sometimes you give ninety-nine and he gives one percent." Then she looked over at the male tubster and said, "Not Mr. Cutler."

I have never met Mr. Cutler but here is one thing I know. He needs glasses and he needs them NOW. This woman is obviously someone who spends a great deal of her time in the kitchen and at the grill. And at the local Burger King. He is no better. This is no joke but I'm willing to bet that the two of them together, on a scale, must tip the balance at close to 550 pounds. I ain't bullshittin'!

Their website tells us what we get from the show: "Real advice. Real justice and real solutions …" If a person cannot give themselves justice or continue to stuff their bodies with mayonnaise sandwiches, then how in the HELL are they going to give out anything even remotely approaching a "solution"? Their very presence, in their current shape, is evidence of *injustice!*

The following article provides a preview of what the show is supposed to be about and who is involved. My analyses will filter in and out:

> LOS ANGELES (June 27, 2017) Orion TV Production, a subsidiary of Metro-Goldwyn Mayer Inc., began production on the first season of the new syndicated, half-hour weekday strip, Couples Court with The Cutlers in Atlanta, GA. this week. The series comes from David Armour, the creator and executive producer of Orion Television's two-time Emmy-nominated daytime court show, Lauren Lake's Paternity Court. (Booker, 2017)

Whose idea was this? How did they come across these two obese black people and come up with the idea that they would be television material? Was this for laughs or what? There are no obese white people on the bench rendering judgments on the American public and in fact, they are thin as hell. The society we live in knows now that a fat person is a sign of someone who is out of control on some level and is in need of help. And yet the Cutlers, who are married, appear on television with the gall to give marital advice along with what little legal insight they administer.

This white man, David Armour, has one show that is hosted by a black person (which I address elsewhere). But not only is she a star with a voice who backs up famous music groups, but she is average sized, through flawed with those hair extensions.

So now Armour is the creator of two "black freak shows. Continuing:

> Award-winning trial attorneys Dana and Keith Cutler will be the first-ever married couple to preside over a television court show. This fresh series **will use cell phone forensics, GPS tracking, DNA evidence and other high tech tactics to tackle relationship disputes head-on and help uncover the truth**. The husband and wife team who have been married and practicing law together **for nearly three decades**, will bring their legal expertise and guidance to **these couples in crisis** throughout each episode. Couples Court with The Cutlers debuts in fall 2017 and **has been picked up in over 85% of U.S. markets**. (Booker, 2017 – emphasis added)

How ridiculous. These people are most likely not "current" in their thinking and the couples they sit in judgment of. Using cell phones and DNA information is no guarantee because both of these have proven to be flawed. This society's reliance on DNA is going to be exposed in the years ahead because Israeli scientists have found a way to manipulate DNA as was reported several years ago. Look at all the people being released from prison because a previous DNA "test" was found to be contaminated or otherwise flawed.

The idea of the Cutlers being married doesn't mean a damn thing. You can be married for thirty years and merely "tolerate" the other person. They have law school in common so that gives them something, but it is clear that if she cared about him and he cared about her they would have told one another to put down the fried chicken or to cut back on having seconds and thirds at the family reunion. Reliable studies show that the more money black people have the more likely they are to be obese or morbidly obese because so many grew up in poverty and in family settings where food was scarce.

If eighty-five percent of households carry the show, then that is for a reason. The people doing the distributing don't care about outcomes, they only care about ratings. Most of these court shows are aired on Fox Network, a station that is white nationalist in its base and it not afraid to humiliate black people or anyone else. The owner, Rupert Murdoch, is not even an American. Their big hits are the professional football games that they air on Sundays. These court shows have a large following because the people who appear in front of these courtroom judges, as I will show, make complete and utter asses out of themselves.

Some background on the Cutlers is in order:

> Dana and Keith Cutler earned undergraduate degrees from Spelman College and Morehouse College, respectively, and continued their education together, graduating from the University of Missouri-Kansas City School of Law in 1989. Dana practices education law focusing on charter schools, and Keith is a civil defense trial attorney. Together, they are members of their family's law firm, James W. Tippin & Associates, where they practice with Dana's father and another partner. (Booker, 2017)

So they both attended black colleges and, in case you've never been to Atlanta, Spelman and Morehouse are right across the street from each other. Spelman is an all-female institution and Morehouse is for all-males. The fact is, their families had money, so they grew up rather sheltered of this there is no doubt. They must have fallen for each other and then worked together to head to Missouri for law school.

Their family has a law firm where they practice. So again, they haven't missed many paychecks. And judging from looking at them, they also haven't missed many meals. It must have been great being in love and growing increasingly fat together. But they are accomplished according to the background info:

> Both Dana and Keith Cutler have been named "Missouri Super Lawyers" **multiple times** by the legal publishing company, Thomson Reuters. **Dana is the first African American female to be elected President of The Missouri Bar, and Keith was the first African-American to be elected as the President of the Kansas City Metropolitan Bar Association Young Lawyers Section**. The Cutlers have been married for 28 years and have three adult sons. (Booker, 2017 – emphasis added)

There are a lot of coincidences taking place in their lives. I find it rather odd that they win awards with similar titles. I find their entire life off. And nowhere in these awards and all this money and family status do I see where they have the background to sit and rule over couples who are in trouble. People who have never been in trouble or conflict cannot judge others who are involved in situations where trouble and conflict are a part of their environment. Upper middle class "negroes" who probably never lived near low-income people sitting in judgment of the average Joes that appear in front of them. This is beginning to smack of a black version of "elitism."

Next we find other elements of the show that are worthy of analysis and correction:

> Couples Court with The Cutlers **offers litigants the chance to resolve their differences, and make it through some of the most the emotionally charged moments in relationships.** The Cutlers also give **heartfelt advice** to help the couples integrate the court's decision into their lives. The show is produced by David Armour's 501 East Entertainment and distributed by Orion TV Productions (Orion Television). Executive Producers are: **David Armour, Myeshia Mizuno, Angela Smith and Barry Poznick. The show will be directed by Stacie Saugen** (Booker, 2017 – emphasis added)

This is not really a court of law. It is a mediation court or a resolution forum. If the litigants could "resolve their differences," they would have done so already. Furthermore, how are the show decision-makers notified? Does someone write a letter spilling their guts? Are these litigants even real? Are they flown in and put in hotels the way the litigants who appear in front of Judge Judy and the others are? How do the decision makers "rate" which differences are worthy?

The snippet claims that the litigants are helped to make it through "some of the most emotionally charged moments in relationships." How can the bourgeois Cutlers relate to that? What could be emotionally charged about two upper class people living the life and whose major decision is deciding how many layers to place on their mayonnaise sandwiches? "Emotionally charged moments"? These sound like issues that should be in front of a criminal or civil court. And yet, thanks to the people pulling the strings (white folks), this show got the "green light" and is actually being watched during mid-day by housewives and the unemployed.

Check out the names listed above as the "executive producers": A Japanese, a Polish person and a couple of Jews (whites). What this should teach a gullible American public is that just because it is dark in hue doesn't mean that it is dark in point of view. Everything that's black ain't black.

As ridiculous as it is informative, Christal Jordan offers another article about the Cutlers, this one titled, "'Couples Court' TV Judges Say Having a Prenup is Like Health Insurance."

The viewpoints of this married couple are their views, views based on personal perspectives and their upper class lives. Their opinions are skewed because they cannot relate to the people who stand in front of them. They appear to be sitting up high on that bench, staring down at litigants, hurrying through their cases so they can get up and go around the corner and cut their respective farts. They look extremely uncomfortable and they come off as being divorced from reality.

According to the article,

> "Couples Court" TV stars Dana and Keith Cutler stopped by *rolling out*'s Reality Check to talk about the hit show on Atlanta's CW, **the importance of prenuptial agreements, cheatingspouses, and how they've managed to stay married for 35 years.** On "Couple's Court with the Cutlers," attorneys Keith and Dana Cutler **hand out verdicts to couples seeking justice after alleged infidelity**. As with most court TV shows, the cases and litigants themselves **are outrageous with extreme circumstances.** The Cutlers apply their legal backgrounds **to determine who's running game and who truly wants to save their relationship.** (Jordan, 2018 – emphasis added)

What was just described makes the program sound like a veritable freak show! If these people need and require prenuptial agreements, that would solve most of their problems right there. Marriage vows are basically testimonies in bullshit; the people taking those vows know that they can't "forsake all others" or comply with the other sick crap that the preacher has them agreeing to! A prenup, which means my shit is mine and yours is yours unless otherwise stipulated, would be a rockstrong beginning.

Furthermore, the "cheating spouses" thing has already been done with "Divorce Court." In fact, that is what this show sounds like. Why else would couples come to court to get some kind of "verdict"? A verdict? That means a judgment or decision. Who are these overweight negroes to sit in judgment of others? And if the infidelity is "alleged," that means that it may or may not have even taken place. These people were interviewed before they were flown in. They were rehearsed backstage before they went on the air. The Cutlers know who was unfaithful and who was not. It is therefore up to them to do as Judge Judy does: get the litigants to spill their guts as much as possible, knowing that the decision has already been made, and then when time allows (a commercial break), they render the verdict.

Third, "outrageous with extreme circumstances"? This is where my freak show allegation comes in. Who judges what is outrageous and what is not? Is a man with three mistresses in an outrageous situation or is it the wife or girlfriend who allows it to continue? Whoever wrote the skillet must be black because there is a reference made to "running game" as opposed to "who wants to save their relationship."

You can do both! Being married IS a game – a game that women control from the outset. They manipulate the situation to "choose" whose money they will take. After a few dates (prostitution), they decide if it is long term of a "friendship." The dating process is legalized prostitution and marriage confirms it. The old rap song by Dr. Dre, "Can't Turn a Ho Into a Housewife" is wrong on all counts because they are one and the same. The marriage merely legitimizes being a ho to a man who is a hound. Being a housewife merely means that they have a place to stay so they can save money on hotel rooms!

The snippet refers to "running game." The game is being run on the viewers who take the advice of the Cutlers without researching their background. They talk about relationships like they are reading from sociology textbooks. For instance, note the following excerpt from the article:

> **"An affair is not a deal breaker in a relationship," Keith says adamantly**, "in fact if a couple uses the hardship to develop more effective communication and listen to each other it **can be the opposite."** As on the show, his **wife chimes in** with advice that **complements her husband's initial statement.** "Both sides have to be willing to **forgive and then implement new behavior moving forward,"** she explains. (Jordan, 2018 – emphasis added)

Such bullshit and contradictions. If an affair can help develop more effective communication, then why doesn't everybody just go out and have one? If the affair has such positive outcomes, then why even have this show or, for that matter, "Divorce Court"? Everybody's fuckin' everybody so everybody should be happy.

Moreover. Notice how the male's wife on the bench "chimes in." Do you know what that means? It means "to join in about something" or to "offer your thoughts." This makes it sound like he's the one who is the leader, although the attempt is made to make them sound like legal equals. Also to "chime in" means to "complement" something as in "your findings in this case really chimes in with Keith's ideas toward the verdict." Mockingbirds sitting on the bench wasting time, waiting for lunch time so they can probably have a hot dog eating contest.

With this in mind, why is there a need for "forgiveness" or "new behavior" aimed at moving forward? The litigants have been rewarded with the trip to midtown Atlanta, meaning that if they're coming in front out of town they have to endure that long-ass interstate or the busiest airport in the nation. They get free hotel rooms and food. Then they get to come on television and do their best to live up to those "extreme circumstances" that the show revolves around and depends on. Everybody wins whether the relationship is resolved or not, because there is nothing "legal" or "binding" about the findings!

But it's not just cheating and infidelity. The Cutlers give out marital advice to litigants. In the article about the "prenup," here is what these bulky barristers have to say:

> While cheating is the hottest topic on the show, the Cutlers had some additional advice for couples looking to tie the knot in the near future. "Of course, celebrities should have prenups **but sometimes a person with less needs a prenup even more.** If you only have ten dollars to your name, you don't want to go through a divorce and end up with five," Dana warns. She went on to liken a prenup to having health insurance. "You don't go through life thinking you are going to get cancer, but you keep health insurance anyway just in case something like that happens. **A prenuptial agreement should be looked at like insurance.** Neither side should be offended **because they both should have their own**." (Jordan, 2018 – emphasis added)

Prenuptial agreements – another reason for understanding the inner workings of marriage in America and how closely it is linked to financial well-being.

For instance, if a person with less needs a prenuptial agreement even more, then that means that there is a question about "trust" in the relationship. Look at the traditional Roman Catholic vows and what they require:

> I, ____, take you, ____, to be my (husband/wife). I promise to be true to you in good times and in bad, in sickness and in health. I will love you and honour you all the days of my life. I, ____, take you, ____, to be my lawfully wedded (husband/wife), to have and to hold, from this day forward, for better, for worse, for richer, for poorer, in sickness and in health, until death do us part.

If these words are true, then why the prenup? If you are going to be "true in good times and in bad," and if you vow to have and to hold "for better, for worse, for richer, for poorer" then why the prenup? I'll tell you why: because the people taking these vows KNOW that it's bullshit! The preacher talks about "by the powers invested in me" and then he names the state that the marriage is taking place in. Invested in you by what power in the state? Where did that power get the authority? If a person with less needs a prenup, then that goes against the whole concept of the economic bases for being married in the first place!

Moreover, the claim that a prenup should be looked at like insurance because "both sides should have their own." Again, more autonomy. So what good is a wedding? If "I got mine and you got yours," then why get married at all? So that the children will have a last name? Is that all there is to it? You don't need a prenup for that, do you?

> Unlike some relationship experts, with 35 years under their belt, **the Cutlers have proven to be a living example of what a successful, functional marriage looks like.** While they don't claim to be perfect, Keith says **"practical realism" has kept their marriage and family life successful.** Besides meeting and falling in love at Morehouse and Spelman college respectfully, **the two agree a secret to their success has been keeping family and friends out of the middle of their marriage**. "We decide what we are going to do and pretty much that's it," Keith says. (Jordan, 2018 – emphasis added)

If the Cutlers are "a living example" of what a successful, functional marriage looks like, then there is no wonder that the divorce rate hovers near sixty percent! Well off, financially secure, obese and out of touch with their family, they are no role models of any kind. Keith has the nerve to talk about "practical realism" – what other kind is there? But what's practical for a 350 pound oaf like him and his equally elephantine wife may not work for a couple that truly cares about their long-term health!

And going back to keeping friends and family "out of the middle" of their marriage – that's just common sense. If they're in the middle, how are the Cutlers going to have sex? Of course I'm joking. But the marriage vows, once again, make it clear that each person should interact with that one person. Maybe the Cutlers just don't want to share any of their food with outsiders!

Now that we've shared Keith's idiotic beliefs, check out what his "better half" has to say:

> Dana also believes that **her parents' successful marriage gave her a firsthand perspective of a healthy relationship.** But even with all those things in their favor, the two admit they have something special that holds all that together. **"I'm not sure if he's my soulmate, because I don't know if we only have one, but there's something that happened here. We just fit, and we always have,"** Dana says. (Jordan, 2018 – emphasis added)

She said it all! They "just fit" alright. Two balloon-like human beings bouncing off one another – that must be a barrel of fun! Not only that, but take note about the role that her parents' marriage played. They had money and they told her to marry someone who had or would make money. His family has a law firm, so he was ripe for the pluckin'. Both went to schools that were single-sex institutions and the schools are in Atlanta, a mecca for bourgeois negroes who look down their noses at black people who are less fortunate.

"Couples Court With the Cutlers" is an overweight version of "Divorce Court." How can you even look at these people whose collective weight is obviously out of control and think that they can give you tips on how to control YOUR life?

Back in the day there was a group called "3 Tons of Fun." The three women hailed from South Africa and the group consisted of three beautiful but large black women who wore flamboyant costumes. The name of the group, minus one of them, would be a perfect name for the Cutlers: TWO tons of fun.

JUDGE MARILYN MILIAN

One of the great loves of my life was a beautiful and intelligent *Cubana*, so I know what a great women many of them grow up to be. It is not just because of their nationality, don't get me wrong. It's because of their history of struggle against various forms of discrimination, and because of their strong family bonds. They are loved and therefore know how to give love. My ex is now a full professor at one of Chicago's great educational institutions, and works around the clock for the defense and development of Latinos in general and Cubans in particular. She has authored a number of books on Latino poverty, directs a major Latino institute and is respected throughout the academy.

In the case of Judge Marilyn Milian, she lives in Florida but was born in Queens, New York on May 1, 1961. After graduating from the University of Miami she went to Georgetown where she got her law degree. From there she worked at Harvard Law School and also taught as an adjunct at her alma mater, the University of Miami. As it relates to her show, "The People's Court,' one source informs us that, "By the end of the show's 28th season (2012–13), Milian had completed twelve-and-a-half seasons presiding over *The People's Court*, making her the longest-presiding arbitrator on the series" (Wikipedia, 2016)

She's got an impressive resume:

> Milian worked as an **assistant state attorney** for the **Dade County State Attorney's Office**. She was appointed to the position by **Janet Reno**, who was then the state attorney for the county. In 1999, Florida governor **Jeb Bush** appointed Milian to the **Miami Circuit Court**, where she served in the Criminal Division. Prior to that, she spent five years in the Miami County Court in the Domestic Violence Court, Criminal and Civil divisions. In 2001, she replaced Jerry Sheindlin as judge of *The People's Court,* and became the first Hispanic judge on any television court show. Milian is listed as an adjunct faculty member of the **University of Miami School of Law**, teaching Litigation Skills.(Wikipedia, 2016).

Being that beautiful for so long, despite her intelligence, is inevitably going to sway her toward some rather deviant ways. According to another source:

> She has been caught swimming topless while on a Caribbean vacation and is accused by critics of flirting while ruling on her hit show, The People's Court. But Judge Marilyn Milian has also sparked the ire of both defendants and plaintiffs because of her acerbic tongue. In 2012 freelance paralegal Claudia Evart wanted to block the episode she appeared in from even airing, telling the New York Post: "She [Judge Milian] didn't let me speak." Evart added: "You have the right to be treated with dignity." (Millar, 2014).

The swimming nude in the Caribbean is no big deal; from where I sit she has perfect breasts because her body is tight as evidenced by those tight fitting dresses that she parades around in during promotional "breaks" in her TV show. But that "acerbic tongue" issue is part of the ruse, in my book.

Furthermore, during a March 9, 2017 episode, she admitted she was a ho! It was a case where this Latina had been dating this older white boy and he brought her a car. She didn't make the payments and he wanted the car back. After prodding from Judge Milian, we find out that the guy purchased the car after knowing the woman only two weeks. Milian snapped: "Two weeks! I went out with a lot of guys … and I also used to be a hot tamale!" The crowd cracked up and the woman said, "You still are." By the way, this was the second or third time that Milian had used the term "hot tamale" in reference to a Latina – the plaintiff in the case.

But she admitted it. You can see it all over her. She's gorgeous and has a body that won't quit. Sure, she has on a robe and sits behind a bench, but during some of the promo snippets aired during the break they show her talking with the audience, skin tight dresses on, fuck me pumps and breasts that are incredible.

"Acerbic" is more than just being loud or insulting. According to the dictionary it translates to mean, "expressing harsh or sharp criticism in a clever way." In simple terms, Milian is a smart-ass. She knows it and she makes sure that the people standing in front of her know it. And that is the hook on the show: not only is she gorgeous but she's unbearably loud – an affirmation of both the red-headed woman stereotype and of the boisterous out of control Latina. The producers therefore kill two birds with one stone.

This woman has changed over the years, but one thing remains constant. She is a beauty with one of the baddest bodies on daytime television. In recent years they show clips of her talking with the audience before her show is aired, and she's always wearing some stilettos and some tight fitting dress and blouse. She is built like a brick shithouse – and she knows it. But there's one more thing about her because all pretty girls have a flaw that they can't cover up because they're used to getting attention.

Her fatal flaw – if you want to call it that – is that she talks loud. No, the fact is, she shouts. Now I don't know if this bitch is on some kind of medication or what, but she goes on these conniptions where she points her finger, raises her voice and I've heard her call those standing in front of her liars on more than one occasion. Personally, I think she's being "handled" by the Jews who promote these types of shows because she's knowledgeable and has an impressive track record. But I find it more than a coincidence that she is conforming with the stereotypes that many people (whites) have about Latinas: loud, emotional, red-headed (dyed, of course) and confrontational.

During an August 22, 2016 airing of the show she told one defendant, "There is nothing that makes me angrier than when I am out of control as when someone tells me to calm down." So she admits that she gets out of control – as if we can't see that during one of her conniptions during the show. Again, she's affirming what white people already think about redheads and what they have always stereotypically believed about Latinas.

But as I say, for the most part she's a beauty and is not ashamed to throw in a Spanish (she's Cuban-American) phrase or two and talk about her daughters, her husband and some personal bullshit like the fact that she used to be a landlord. *But she must enjoy the job because she's transformed since her early days on the show, a point I alluded to earlier and one that I will elaborate on in this section.*

According to the research,

> **Judge Marilyn Milian is the first Latina judge to host a nationally syndicated television court show**, and in 2012 she returned for a 12th season of the show. On the show, Judge Milian **decides actual small-claims court cases**. The highly successful court series takes viewers inside a television courtroom **where Milian dispenses her own unique brand of justice daily ...** (People's Court website, 2018 – emphasis added).

It should be noted that over those years she has changed from a mild-mannered family court decision-maker to a walking stereotype of the red hot Latina, a term that she often uses in references to some of the litigants. She knows she's beautiful and she acts the part: the casual flipping of the dyed red locks (obviously using henna to make sure it stays right red), the lip stick and the casual references to her black bailiff, Douglas, who I believe is screwing her.

In lock step with stereotypical Latina behavior, she screams most of the time and will revert to Spanish clichés and sayings to make her point and to prove to her handlers that she's a "real" Latina. She's built like a brick shit house and during some of the commercial breaks when they are promoting the show and inviting people to come in and sit in the audience, they show her, skin tight dresses, huge breasts, small waistline and the classic "fuck me" pumps.

The previous snippet says that Milian "dispenses her own unique brand of justice daily." What is unique about it? Justice is justice and right is right. We know what they mean. They mean "Latina justice," and she has a saying she uses from time to time: "tough justice." That shit comes from the days of the wild west when white boys were lynching Latinos and yet here she is, trying so hard to be the hog with the big nuts, screaming and cracking on people nearly as badly as Judge Judy.

Pay close attention to the following:

> Judge Milian explains Americans' fascination with the court show genre: "We are a fast-food nation. People love to see resolution, they want to watch someone who has done wrong confronted and see justice prevail … all in an hour."
> (People's Court website, 2018)

And it doesn't hurt when the person doing the dispensing of the justice is a gorgeous red head – a younger version of Judge Judy. Much younger.

Background from an Actual Participant: Critique and Commentary

Since Marilyn claimed earlier that people love to see justice prevail, that we're "fast food nation" and that wrong gets "confronted," I felt it necessary to share with you some background about the show, coming from an actual litigant. The statement, which can be found on the internet, begins as follows:

> I attended a taping a few months back, at the studio where The People's Court is filmed. Ask me anything about the experience. A few things that some people on reddit might be curious to know: The music they play while the parties walk down the aisle is indeed played in the studio. The voice over is also done at the time, only the typewriter noise is added in in post-production. (Reddit, 2016)

To begin with the voice over itself is insulting. When this Jewish man "introduces" the litigants, he insultingly describes their charges and counter-charges with as much drama as possible. For instance, if the plaintiff is suing because the defendant didn't refund money on a car repair. The voice over may say something like, "The plaintiff says the defendant ripped him off and he's not going to take it any more." The music itself is also dramatic, that kind of deep theme music you might hear during a suspenseful period in a creature feature or some scary flick at the movies.

Continuing:

> Yeah signed a **contract so I can't be sued again**, even if I talk shit on the girl or the case. I also signed an agreement that they couldn't use my business name on the final airing, just my first name no last. Since the case involved my business I was afraid of it tarnishing our reputation. The chick who sued ended up looking like a jackass and I barely even talked on the show so it wouldn't have been a problem for them to use my name anyway. (Reddit, 2016 – emphasis added)

So a contract is signed, and you can believe that the contract also includes a clause where the litigants can't talk shit back to Milian. As in the case of Judge Judy, insults and name-calling frequently flow out of the judge's mouth. With no contractual agreement, litigants would be teeing off on this bitch, especially the black women.

The witness continues his rather crass description of events:

> I'll be the idiot here and admit I never understood how those shows worked. People tried telling me that the rulings are actually real. Can someone explain how that works? **It's a form of binding arbitration.** In other words, the Judge was originally a Judge (hence the title), **but no longer performs in a real court** (which should explain why the set is missing a wall, if you look at the photos). The participants agree that they **will go by whatever judgment the Judge sets out for them**, and they also agree to other conditions, like **not being able to sue each other after the ruling.** (Reedit, 2016 – emphasis added)

It's a televised form of a mediation or intervention. And what it actually accomplishes is that the presentation provides comedic fodder for viewers. If these people are stupid enough to appear as litigants on national television and spill their guts over petty bullshit, then they deserve to be viewed as jesters and in doing so, become the butt of jokes all over the country and the world.

These "judges" like Milian just sit there and make decisions about who is right and who is wrong. She's eye candy for the most part, a stereotype of the hot-blooded Latina (she's used the slang term "hot tamale" in reference to several litigants in the past) and the show's title, the "people's court" seduces people into thinking that programs like these are representative of what people's problems are and what the solutions of those problems should be. In my view it's a legal version of the "bait and switch" con.

The participants are willing thralls, more or less. They agree to forego their rights and then sit in silence as this beauty on the bench cuts their shit to shreds, fast talks most of them, and puts on a show for the viewers by casually flipping her red hair and making a joke or two in response to something stupid that a litigant might say.

And this show and others like it accomplish something else. The decisions are "final." You can't sue once you leave. This clears the real courts and it also increases the likelihood of street justice once these people, if not satisfied, get back to their respective cities and become the butt of jokes, ridicule and scorn. You sacrifice you day in a real court in order to save a few bucks (for an attorney), appear on television with no legal defense, get a free round trip ticket and then where are you when it's all over? Worse off than you were before.

It is explained that,

> People are likely to do this, **as it allows self-representation**, and the show pays both parties a fee for appearing. Also, in the event that you win, **you don't need to collect money from the person, the show will just write you a cheque for the judgment**. And yes, **the Bailiff is an actor**. He even has his own IMDB page: http://www.imdb.com/name/nm1214546/ (Reddit, 2016 – emphasis added)

You call this "self-representation"? All you're doing is spilling your guts and hoping someone else sides with you. How is that representation of any value? You stand there and tell this woman why you are suing, although she already knows because you filled out a form before the appearance. The plaintiff states their case after being constantly corrected because most of them can't remember what they wrote. Then the defendant gets a chance to say something, again under the guise of "self-representation." If there is no autonomy, there can be no freedom of expression. This is a clear cut checks and balance system employed in full view of millions of viewers.

Judge Milian determines the outcome in terms of money. If the plaintiff is asking for too much, she whittles it down. If she gets pissed at the defendant then she'll tack on some extra bucks. In other words, she determines the financial outcome. How in the hell is this "self-representation" when the people involved are not even acting independently?

The bailiff is an actor alright. He's this clean shaven, buff young brutha who you just KNOW got that ass from Milian. Her on-going references to her younger days, how this "isn't her first rodeo" and references like that lets me know that when they're in that back room, that young brutha is telling her that he has an apartment/condo right down the street. Her schedule is flexible enough and her kids are all grown. You do the math.

Moving right along:

> **The loser has no 'out-of-pocket' expenses to pay. That's why people go on these shows**. The winner is guaranteed to get their money once they win, and the loser **doesn't need the money to pay the winner.** The show gives both parties **an appearance fee, no matter what happens**. If one or both of them win, they can receive up to an **additional $5000 from the show**, paid for by the producers. The loser 'wins' no matter what. The winner also wins, because they receive the money even if the loser is broke and has no assets. The legal system won't give you money if the person you're suing has none, but The People's Court will. **That's why people agree to go on it; you get paid in exchange for acting like a fool on TV.** (Reddit, 2016 – emphasis added)

In other words it's a scam. If you lose the case you still get paid meaning that you didn't lose. If you win the case the show pays you and the loser doesn't suffer. That means that the verdict is "no harm, no foul." What kind of bullshit is this? The deal, as the previous passage makes clear, is to agree to make an ass out of yourself. Now I see why these litigants take so much shit from Milian, take so many insults from her and allow her to yell at them at the top of her lungs. They want that money and they will undergo anything to get it: like the true prostitutes that they are.

The story about an appearance continues:

> My friend went to one of these shows and **said the judge was allowed to re-do their lines,** but not the participants. Did this happen during your taping? I don't know if she is allowed to, but she didn't. I imagine that she might occasionally re-do them, but in six cases (two episodes worth), she didn't need to re-do anything.
> (Reddit, 2016 – emphasis added)

I don't know why there would be a need to re- do any lines. There is an application that is filled out and these judges read it and know the case beforehand. Why should they re-do anything they say? Was there an insult they could have lodged? Did they miss out on a chance to make a litigant look like an ass?

The article continues by stating,

> I just realized that it's possible that she might be re-doing her lines. She didn't re-do anything while I was there, **but I can imagine that after a show is done being edited, they could get her to re-do certain things if they didn't like the outcome in the episode.** This is the most likely situation, given that the camera is on her when she's talking, and nobody else is visible in the courtroom. It's quite possible that every couple weeks or so, **someone gives her a list of phrases to read off, but I wouldn't know anything about that.** (Reddit, 2016 – emphasis added)

I've been on television scores of times as part of news casts addressing community issues. This is live television. But they reserve the right to edit for time and since I'm a black nationalist, they usually edit out the things that deal with race and racism. In the case of "The People's Court," why would they not end a show and then carry it back to the editing bay and take out what they don't like? This is a part of the history of television and these shows are distributed all over the world. The key is to make the system in America look as fair and impartial as possible. You can't do that if you come off on the air sounding drunk (like Judge Joe Brown) or insane (like Judge Jeanine Pirro).

As for that "list of phrases," I discussed earlier how Milian will toss in some long sentence in Spanish and truthfully, it sounds sexy. Then she translates it for the audience. This is to ensure that she sounds Hispanic and to add some cultural flavor to the show. If there was going to be something added, I would think it would be one of these phrases, since most of the time she prefaces the Latin phrase as being something "my mother used to tell me" or "my father used to say."

But for the most part,

> Everything was done in one take. I assume that it's easier, and cheaper, for them to not use a case (1/3rd of a show) than to have to write a script. The only thing that was done in more than one take was the walking down the aisle. If someone wasn't dramatic enough, or their timing was off, they would be asked to do it again. (Reddit, 2016)

One take, meaning there was some kind of rehearsal beforehand. They meet behind closed doors and go over the material. Marilyn reads it over before that and is smart enough to ask intelligent questions when she meets them. All that introduction at the taping of the show is all bullshit – she's met them before. It's all staged as the previous observer bears out. The key is "drama," and it is important that shows remain thought-provoking. The more insults, the more anger and ire, the better.

The recollections shared on Reddit continued:

> I was in the studio for around four hours. This included over half an hour of waiting to be seated, as they get everything ready. There's also a large amount of time spent between cases, as they set everything back up again. **I'd say each case probably took around 25 minutes, with the rest of the time being 'prep-time' for the cast and crew.** They don't tend to edit much, if the case is under 20 minutes or so long. In the episode of the show I've seen that I was in, the only thing removed was some useless 5 minute anecdote, about how a lady contacted an expert on something for a pointless opinion. **They also cut down a lot of time by only using one take of people walking down the courtroom, as opposed to the couple they might do if it isn't dramatic enough**. (Reddit, 2016 – emphasis added)

All staged. And probably includes that crowd of clowns outside the studio that Harvey Levin (a backbiting asshole in his own right) gets to "interview." He fast talks them by asking loaded questions, and the returns it back to the studio only after getting the comments and replies that he hopes for.

Continuing:

> I was bored, and had time to kill during a trip. There is absolutely no skill required to get tickets for the show, **you literally just need to call ahead of time and show up when they want you.** They don't check attendance or ask for ID or anything, so **you could show up whenever you wanted without advance notice**, if you were certain they'd be taping that day. I called about a week in advance, and was told to show up whenever I wanted on a handful of days. They tape **twice per day, three times a week, every other week,** and you can come and go essentially whenever you please. **I could have stayed for the afternoon taping as well (another 6 cases), but I didn't have time.** (Reddit, 2016 – emphasis added)

The mass production or warehousing of television programming. The highlight is the chance to be on national television and appear in front of one of the most beautiful women on daytime television. In addition, you get paid if you get to become a litigant and it's free to sit in the audience and pretend to be interested. And again, let me explain: these shows are distributed all over the world. What could the purpose be other than to present the image that Americans are stupid but that the court system is fair? What other purpose could such productions intend than to show how disgruntled, disjointed and petty Americans are? What better way to show enemy nations that they need not worry because when all is said and done, Americans are egocentric, confused assholes who couldn't fight their way out of a wet paper bag.

Moreover,

> The audience is entirely made up of fans, tourists, and the elderly. Nobody there gets paid. I believe Judge Judy pays people though, because it's easier to hire actors than to deal with people off the street. (Reddit, 2016)

The audience for Judge Judy is made up of some beautiful women, all aligning the front row and all who seem to think her stale jokes and quacky quips are funny. Only someone who is paid could make such an ass of themselves. But I am not sure on that point. But I am sure that the people in Judge Milian's court are not paid. Their joy lies in meeting her between takes and taking a gander at that state of the art body. Her charisma mesmerizes them so they dare not speak out or do anything but show appreciation for being there and hoping that they can get their faces on television.

Of "Judge Judy" the observer adds,

> Judge Judy is definitely a crock of shit, two of my friends **literally made up a case in their head, took some bullshit pictures, and then got a free plane ride to tape the show**, all because of some clever social engineering. Definitely one of the cooler social hacks I've ever witnessed. I usually can't stand judge shows, but The People's Court is the only one I kinda like, and it seems more real for some reason. (Reddit, 2016 – emphasis added)

I got the hint that some of these Judge Judy shows were fake. Two people get together and make up a fake case, pretend to hate each other and then they split the settlement money after the show. I thought about that and it seems easy to do. Why? Because Judge Judy is a frustrated old Jew. She makes an occasional reference to her forty year marriage but she doesn't mention that Jerry was fucking around behind her back with some blind Jew while she was out of town, they divorced, and then got re-married. She looks down her nose at people reminding them that her job "has already been applied for" and that she's the only star of her show. In the middle of such megalomania, it would be easy to scam someone who is so busy patting themselves on the back that they can't see the forest for the trees.

I don't see much difference between Judge Judy and the egomaniacal Marilyn Milian. She's always been a beauty and had a wild streak back in her younger days, much of it involving nudity. She owns rental properties and seems to know her way about contracting and construction issues, courtesy of her father and husband. But it's her presence that is the star of the show. Judy's gimmick is "old

Jew who insults people" and Marilyn's is "hot Latina who screams a lot while administering some semblance of justice."

More evidence of "The People's Court" being rigged can be found in the following excerpt:

> **There are only a handful of rows (four, I think), and they didn't appear to prioritize people's location based on attractiveness.** That being said though, they did arrange people as they entered the courtroom, to ensure that **demographics were accurately represented.** In other words, if a tour bus of old ladies showed up, they wouldn't all be in the front row, as then it would look weird on TV, so they would place groups of people around the seats. I imagine they also adjust for other things, like height, to prevent anyone from having to strain during the cases to see the Judge, and prevent anything from looking awkward. (Reddit, 2016 – emphasis added)

When you start having seat placements then you know the show is rigged. That is why I said earlier that I think that Judge Judy screens for good looking women. They have lovely faces, many are large breasted, and the sit near the aisle and always well within range of the television cameras. Even during the breaks when the camera pans the entire room, you can see tight-skirted women interacting and it seems to be mostly women in Judy's courtroom. The same can be said for the courtroom of "The People's Court."

The information provided moves on to add some important tidbits about the show:

> **Did you get to meet judge Millian after the show?** I went to a taping of Jerry Springer and after the show he meets and greets all his audience members. A really nice guy as well. **She and the bailiff usually do a meet and greet / Q and A before each session,** but they were pressed for time and started taping immediately. At the end of the morning session though, as they were about to go for lunch, **she came off the bench and did a mini-Q and A. She seemed really nice in person, and much less scary than on TV**. (Reddit, 2016 – emphasis added)

Of course they call it a "question-and-answer" period but she takes off that black robe and is showing off that ass! She's got on a tight dress that is above the knee and her legs are perfection. She's got on a pair of "fuck me pumps" and her breasts are the star of the show. This is what the cameras are cued on when there is a break and they are promoting the address to the show and how to apply for tickets if you live in another city. But those few seconds of seeing Marilyn Milian are just like seeing an under dressed woman in a night club. It might not lead to anything, but you can see enough to know that this women has seductress potential.

As for Curt Chaplin, the guy in the hall following a Milian decision, the article claims the following:

> Did you get to talk to Curt Chaplin (the guy who does the post-interview)? **I literally watch the show JUST for him because on some rare occasions his comments are so underhanded and passive aggressive and condescending that it's HILARIOUS.** I'm surprised there are no fan sites out there for him compiling his zingers. (Reddit, 2016 – emphasis added)

Put another way, Chaplin is a chickenshit muthafucka. It seems as if his goal is to get the people walking out of the court to do one of two things. If they won, which means they walk out last, he tries to get them to promote the need for court justice and to take any grievance you may have to the courts. If they lose, which means they come out first, that is when he's making he kind of under handed jokes that are inferred in the previous paragraph. He even goes so far as to refer to the loser's arguments as "stupid." Then after he gets in his digs, he quickly dismisses them to go around the corner and sign some papers.

The People's Court: Review

The show is worth watching because Judge Marilyn Milian is smart and knows her craft. But they surround her with these two Jewish guys (whose backgrounds I will address later) who seem more committed to and concerned about insulting the guests than with offering up supplemental law-related material. This is what makes the show as insulting as "Judge Judy" in many regards;" it is clear that Judy insults people because she's a Jewish curmudgeon who's not getting any dick. But in this case, it seems as if Milian, Chaplin and Levin sit around a table before the show is aired and say, "Let's say this," or "let's call this guy that." Let me show you what I mean.

During a show aired on July 11, 2013, this Middle Eastern fellow sold a house to this African brutha. However, mold had been painted over and began to seep through the paint. The camel jockey kept denying that he had anything to do with it, that his contractor did it. Milian was all over his ass, saying that he had to see the mold before it got painted and even if he didn't his contractor did and had an obligation to report it in order to get permission to paint. Then there's this law in New York that says that the jockey had to fill out a form with a bunch of questions regarding the condition of the house or, if he doesn't want to, he can pay the purchaser $500.

The spear chucker got the $500 but still wants to sue because he ended up buying a house filled with mold. The jockey never lived in the house and only owned it for about 6 months. What is Milian's decision? Milian says it's the chucker's responsibility for knowing what he's buying. He didn't answer questions which shows something. There's a disclaimer in that contract that says you have to make that decision based on your own expectation and not on anything the seller says to you. If I think if its' "active concealment," it's a different story. Was it possible that between July 17th and August 8th, could this mold have happened? "There is more than mold," she observed. " I'm looking at calcification, mushrooms are sprouting. I gotta tell you. When I look at this stuff makes me kind of feel that it is your goal is to flip and make as much money as possible and then pass it on to the next guy. Could this have happened during that time. I find in favor of the spear chucker in the amount of five thousand dollars."

The jockey denied it during the post interview and claimed he didn't know what happened. He said that the guy must be an opportunist. It was this bruthas life savings and was on the verge of tears. He said he's going to move as soon as possible. You can still sue the seller for fraud or for active concealment if he tries to hide it from the buyer that would cause the buyer damage.

Milian always finds a way to work herself into her statements. For instance during an August 14, 2014 airing, the issue was a vintage table from the 1980s. As she looked over the picture of the table, she remarks that, "This table reminds me of a hairdo that I wore in the 1980s." What? Judge Milian is proud of her Cuban heritage and often uses phrases from her grandmother when addressing litigants. "No sabes ni adobar la mentira... You don't even know how to season the lie to make it palatable," Milian admonishes a litigant who is trying to lie in her courtroom.

During an October 10, 2104 segment, the Plaintiff, an elderly veteran was suing the Defendant, for work that was shoddy. Forget about the details: at one point Milian and the old dude start talking about his service in World War II, after she asked him his age. Then she talks about having a husband whose uncle also served. The senior plaintiff replies that he had a brother who was a prisoner of war after being shot down, and was detained in Stalag 17. Obviously moved, Milian gets up off the bench and says that, "this has nothing to do with the case," walks over and shakes the old man's hand. She goes back to the bench, repeats her statement about her actions having nothing to do with the case, and adds, "the greatest generation." Then she rules AGAINST the defendant!

What kind of nationalistic shit is this?! It DID have something to do with the case because the people who filmed and approved this segment allowed it to be aired. Perhaps it was an appeal to the veterans who view her show, I don't know. Nor do I give a fuck. Those veterans, black and white, bombed and shot people of color and are still doing it. Even when they fought white folks, their own ranks (American) were racially segregated and they treated black soldiers like shit, and were aiding and abetting in the incarceration of 110,000 Japanese-Americans during World War II.

Speaking of hairdos, during the August 22, 2014 show, some young yellow sister with ahead full of fake ass here came in flipping it all around and Milian DOGGED her. "I'll just wait until you finish what you're doing. You come sashaying in here as if this is fun and games and I tell you, it is not." After that the young sister, who was being sued, kept shaking her head and smiling, while the plaintiff was talking. This bitch must have been high; she had a Thrifty rental car that she (the plaintiff) wrecked (but it was in the yellow girl's name) while supposedly returning it to the airportx. In turn, the yellow girl told her to take it to a "friend" who would fix it. But the auto repair shop didn't really exist on GPS. While the plaintiff was talking, Milian had to tell the yellow bitch to take a seat, and she (the girl) just kept on waving her hair around, enabling Milian to do the same shit (mockingly) and wave around her red locks.

Meanwhile we find out that some guy comes over to her and says yellow girl sent him. She handed him the keys and he said he was taking it to the auto body shop. He didn't give her a name or anything. This yellow girl is seated and has a dress on up the crack of her ass (looked like a hooker). The plaintiff didn't know where the car was, but the girl wouldn't tell her for at least two weeks. She finally called and told the plaintiff that the car was in the shop.

No information was shared. There was no rental insurance taken out, the yellow girl is obviously protecting this guy, so the plaintiff sues her – but the Defendant won, even with all the hair flipping.

During the September 1, 2014 episode, we have a real story. Four days after he bought this woman a 55-inch television, a kitchen set and a living room set, an older brother is suing the woman to get his shit back. He bought her earrings and other jewelry. He wanted to know where the relationship was going and she told him, "Let's start all over." He got $43,000 from an accident he was in and spent it, more or less, on her. Right on the spot he says he no longer wants to sue her. She said that they were "friends with benefits." This ugly four-eyed bitch said, "He wants all of me" as if she is some beauty queen.

In the meantime, Marilyn laughing and joking with Douglas McIntosh, her bailiff (who I think fucked her) during this particular episode. The man says he doesn't want to sue. Milian says, "You were right to say that you didn't want to sue because I was going to rule against you anyway." She gives him a piece of advice: "Figure out what you want, because I don't think you want her … if you want a serious relationship, then you don't want her." The sister dropped her "counter-claim" and they leave the courtroom. During the post-courtroom activity in the interview, she came out with two women who looked like stone dykes. Hmmmm. When Milian said she "wasn't for him," maybe that's what she meant.

Judge Milian was hyped up during a September 1, 2014 show. The plaintiff was suing defendants for not fixing a leak in his roof. He said the rain was coming in through the skylights and he called and they didn't respond at all. Milian went off: "the roof wasn't fixed in the first week, the second week, the third week," and she went on and on and on. She was screaming and shouting and riding the members of the homeowners association about the problems (the residents were paying $5000 a year for mandatory membership in that homeowners association – that's how white folks keep blacks out). She was screaming and banging her open hand on the table.

Personally, I think Marilyn Milian has got a bipolar disorder. Because one minute she can be as sweet as apple pie, and the next minute, the bitch is trying to smash a cream pie in your face! She seems to be amped up much of the time, almost trembling to get in her word, to get her face on camera and to "put on a show" ala Judge Judy.

For instance, during a December 11, 2015 program, the issue was soy sauce stains, where an Asian woman was suing some Middle Eastern guy. The woman had problems with English and at one time the woman referred to small claims court as "small court." Milian cracked on her. "Small court? I never heard of that. I often have delusions of grandeur but where is small court!?" Delusions of grandeur is nothing to joke about and I think there's more to it than viewers are willing to concede – I think she really does suffer from it.

What are delusions of grandeur? According to one internet source, "Grandiose delusions (GD) or delusions of grandeur are a subtype of delusion that occur in patients suffering from a wide range of mental illnesses, including two-thirds of patients **in manic state of bipolar disorder**, half of those with schizophrenia, patients with the grandiose subtype of delusional disorder, and a substantial portion of those with substance abuse disorders" (emphasis added). Now here is where Milian may be affected.

The definition goes on to say that, Delusions of Grandeur " are characterized by fantastical beliefs that one is famous, omnipotent, wealthy, or otherwise very powerful. The delusions are generally fantastic and typically have a supernatural, science-fictional, or religious theme." Now it is clear that Milian is a beautiful woman and she knows it. Her hair is bright orange and she's gorgeous and even the promo just before her show shows her walking in front of a camera, posing with her hands on her hips, with wind blowing through her hair. What the fuck does this have to do with the fact that this intelligent woman has a law degree, was obviously successful, and now as a national television program?

So the promo itself shows an exhibition of grandeur on the physical level. I don't know if Milian is bipolar, but her rants, regular screaming at the court and her apparent mood changes would tend to indicate that there is something amiss.

In an August 22, 2014 case, a white private eye is suing some Middle Eastern dude for $151 owed on his private investigation fees. The Indian dude's attorney hired the private eye . "He's a robust, temperamental kind of guy," the Defendant said. Milian retorts, "Well I'm a robust, temperamental kind of gal, but I can't take a swing at you." She admits it (read my allegation regarding bipolar disorder) The Indian dude wanted the detective to dig up some information, but found out that the private eye and the lawyer were related. The Indian's former partner was a rough guy and the Indian was afraid of him.

The detective was charging him $150 per hour and the Indian had paid $1800 thus far.

Admitting that she consistently insulted the plaintiff, during a January 25, 2016 show Milian was listening to a case. I don't know if the "hot Latina" stereotype is what she's going for, but she continues that screaming and sounds as if she's on the border of conniption. At one point she told the Plaintiff who told her that he wanted his woman to take a lie detector test, "I've been married over 20 years and if my husband asked me to take a lie detector test he'd find himself on the ground." Say what? Who does this bitch think she is, and why say that shit on national television? As they ask in the drama business, "What is her motivation"?

During the same show, she told the Plaintiff, "I think you're a nut!"

During a show aired June 1, 2016, the subject was the plaintiff asking the female defendant to take a lie detector test. Do you know what Milian said to that man? She said, "I've been married for 23 years and if my husband ever asked me to take a lie detector test, he'd find himself on the floor." What?

Although his case did border on obsession and stalking, was it necessary for her to say this shit the way silly ass Judge Judy Sheindlin would do? The show is called "The People's Court" and as the years go by, Judge Milian doesn't seem to be very representative of "the people." She's proud of her Latina background and heritage and she's gorgeous; she has a sharp mind and a great wit. But her show is also aided by Harvey Levin, this wise cracking Jew who has a small audience outside in an alley that he asks questions to. Actually, they're not real questions because it is clear that he doesn't give a fuck about what they think. He asks them questions and he has an answer that he ends up imposing on them. When he can, like most Jews on television, he takes a shot.

During a show aired February 8, 2016 we learned two things out of the lovely mouth of Milian. First, she quipped that the Defendant's business 90 Second

Fitness is an interesting name and suggested that the only 90 second fitness she knows of is a glass of scotch that is guzzled in ninety seconds. This tells me this bitch is a drunk. Secondly, she tells the Plaintiff that she is "familiar with back issues because I have back issues." Why would this lovely woman's back be hurting? Perhaps she threw it out of socket fuckin' Douglas during the break.

By watching the show we learn that her father was into construction contracting and that she, herself, is a landlord. This speaks volumes in terms of the kinds of things that are on her mind. In fact, during the airing of the show on June 7, 2016, she told the plaintiffs that, "I've spent the last two years in renovations." I interpreted this to mean that not only was she a landlord, but she was also into "flipping houses," which means even more income for her. In simple terms, this bitch ain't broke, and she has a husband who has money as well. She talks the talk, but it doesn't appear that she's got much of a track record, when it comes to the low- and middle-income people who appear on "the people's court, that she has "walked the walk."

During one segment a defendant attempted to approach the bench to give her some papers, and she told him to stop and that Douglas would retrieve it. She then added after Douglas got the papers and gave them to her, "He's very protective of me," she says. It is almost as if she was saying that he was jealous and possessive of her. His job is to do what he did: how could she draw an emotional motive out of it unless Douglas and she had been intimate behind the scenes? That is what the word "protective" implies.

Marilyn Milian is a beauty as morphed before our very eyes. Not in terms of her beauty but I do notice that in recent shows she appears to be dying her hair increasingly blonder. But one thing remains constant: her screaming at the top of her lungs over what appears to be the most simple or mundane of issues. She's a screamer because I believe the Jews who are in charge of production and distribution of this show have, as an ulterior motive, they need to perpetuate stereotypes about these judges. Just look at the record:

Judge Judy, the Jewish curmudgeon; Judge Mathis, the former thug and dope dealer who turned his life around; Judge Joe Brown, drunk on the bench rendering decisions; Christina Perez, another "hot tamale" Latina; Judge Mills-Francis, a street wise "sistah" with hair dyed blonde; Lynn Toler, a beauty who used to have mental issues; and Jeanine Pirro, an angry white woman who will do whatever it takes for a "break."

In the case of Milian, it's the stereotype of the hot-tempered red head and also of the over-emotional Latina. And Milian plays it to the hilt. Her screaming for apparently no reason only adds to the stereotype that Latin women are emotional and out of control. Watch the show and you will undoubtedly see a walking stereotype in action.

This woman has changed over the years, but one thing remains constant. She is a beauty with one of the baddest bodies on daytime television. In recent years they show clips of her talking with the audience before her show is aired, and she's always wearing some stilettos and some tight fitting dress and blouse. She is built like a brick shithouse – and she knows it. But there's one more thing about her because all pretty girls have a flaw that they can't cover up because they're used to getting attention.

Her fatal flaw – if you want to call it that – is that she talks loud. No, the fact is, she shouts. Now I don't know if this bitch is on some kind of medication or what, but she goes on these conniptions where she points her finger, raises her voice and I've heard her call those standing in front of her liars on more than one occasion. Personally, I think she's being "handled" by the Jews who promote these types of shows because she's knowledgeable and has an impressive track record. But I find it more than a coincidence that she is conforming to the stereotypes that many people (whites) have about Latinas: loud, emotional, red-headed (dyed, of course) and confrontational.

But as I say, for the most part she's a beauty and is not ashamed to throw in a Spanish (she's Cuban-American) phrase or two and talk about her daughters, her husband and some personal bullshit like the fact that she used to be a *landlord. But she must enjoy the job because she's transformed since her early days on the show, a point I alluded to earlier and one that I will elaborate on in this section.*

According to the research,

> Judge Milian explains Americans' fascination with the court show genre: "We are a fast-food nation. People love to see resolution, they want to watch someone who has done wrong confronted and see justice prevail … all in an hour."

The show is worth watching because she is smart and knows her craft. But they surround her with these two Jewish guys (whose backgrounds I will address later) who seem more committed to and concerned about insulting the guests than with offering up supplemental law-related material. This is what makes the show as insulting as "Judge Judy's;" it is clear that Judy insults people because she's a Jewish curmudgeon who's not getting any dick. But in this case, it seems as if Milian, Chaplin and Levin sit around a table before the show is aired and say, "Let's say this," or "let's call this guy that." Let me show you what I mean.

She's laughing and joking with Douglas McIntosh, her bailiff (who I think fucked her) during this particular episode. The man says he doesn't want to sue. Milian says, "You were right to say that you didn't want to sue because I was going to rule against you anyway." She gives him a piece of advice: "Figure out what you want, because I don't think you want her ... if you want a serious relationship, then you don't want her." The sister dropped her "counter-claim" and they leave the courtroom. During the post-courtroom activity in the interview, she came out with two women who looked like stone dykes. Hmmmm. When she said she "wasn't for him," maybe that's what she meant.

Judge Milian was hyped up during a September 1, 2014 show. A man was suing two men for not fixing a leak in his roof. He said the rain was coming in through the skylights and he called and they didn't respond at all. Milian went off: "the roof wasn't fixed in the first week, the second week, the third week," and she went on and on and on. She was screaming and shouting and riding the members of the homeowners association about the problems (the residents were paying $5000 a year for mandatory membership in that homeowners association – that's how white folks keep blacks out). She was screaming and banging her open hand on the table.

Personally, I think she's got a bipolar disorder. Because one minute she can be as sweet as apple pie, and the next minute, the bitch is trying to smash a cream pie in your face! She seems to be amped up much of the time, almost trembling to get in her word, to get her face on camera and to "put on a show" ala Judge Judy.

During a show aired February 8, 2016 we learned two things out of the lovely mouth of Milian. First, she quipped that the Defendant's business 90 Second Fitness is an interesting name and suggested that the only 90 second fitness she knows of is a glass of scotch that is guzzled in ninety seconds. This tells me this bitch is a drunk. Secondly, she tells the Plaintiff that she is "familiar with back issues because I have back issues." Why would this lovely woman's back be hurting? Perhaps she threw it out of socket fuckin' Douglas during the break.

By watching the show we learn that her father was into construction contracting and that she, herself, is a landlord. This speaks volumes in terms of the kinds of things that are on her mind.

We also learn during a February 12, 2016 airing of the show that the first job that this beauty ever had was that of a collections person. How'd she get it? She claims it was because she had a deep voice and added, "They would never let me do it personally because I was only 18 at the time."

She thinks very highly of herself, indeed. During a June 26, 2018 airing of the show, a 51-year old Latina, still in good shape, is being sued by an old white man who she met on the "Our Time" website. He bought her a car after a few months knowing her and she never made the payments, which was part of the deal they made.

At one point Milian tells the man that he did it because the woman was "a hot tamale." After getting that racist stereotype out of the way, she adds that it is clear that the man was paying for sex. Milian screams, "I didn't get married until I was over 30 and I had plenty of men!" Then she adds, "And not one of them ever offered to buy me a car, *and I was also a hot tamale!"* The woman tells her, "You still are!" There is no doubt in my mind that Milian more likely than not screwed her way through law school – and beyond.

The Men Behind the Woman

Working on the set with Marilyn Milian must be a day well spent. She's easy on the eyes but it is clear that she's a handful. She gets to manipulate situations and become a star on television at the expense of "the little guy." When her discretion is added to her backing by a major television enterprise, it is clear that this woman must think that she's Queen of the May.

She works with three men. Most notably they are Curt Chaplin (now replaced by the man he replaced, Doug Llewellyn), listed as the "court reporter." This asshole insults the people after the case has been decided after they walk into the foyer, where he is standing microphone in hand. He asks loaded questions and then steers the unwitting folk – who are ever so happy to have appeared on TV – into making asses out of themselves. First he does it to the losers and then once they walk off, the winners come forward, all smiles and unbeknownst to them, are walking right into a nationally televised setup of ridicule. Of Chaplin the "People's Court" website offers the following:

> Curt Chaplin brings more than 30 years of broadcast experience to his role of in-court reporter on "The People's Court." Chaplin outlines each day's cases and interviews litigants after decisions have been rendered in their cases.

That is not totally true. The person who outlines the cases is Harvey Levin, a Jew who I will deal with momentarily. At any rate, the website adds that Chaplin's travels in broadcast journalism have taken him from Yankee Stadium to Yugoslavia, from the crime beat to City Hall, with stops in Moscow, Berlin and Lake Placid where he covered the famous "Miracle on Ice" hockey game. As a newsman and sports reporter Chaplin worked with the giants of radio, including Howard Stern, Don Imus, John Madden and Howard Cosell. New York listeners remember Chaplin's six hilarious years as the unpredictable, tell-it-all sidekick/sportscaster on WNEW-FM's top-rated morning show (The People's Court, 2016).

Enough about Chaplin because he replaced Doug Llewelyn for some reason but now Llewelyn is back, and picked up where the insultingly inane Chaplin left off. Earlier in this text an excerpt outlined Chaplin's crassness and it was so close to fitting Llewelyn in its accuracy and on-the-button I am going to reprint it here:

> Did you get to talk to Curt Chaplin (the guy who does the post-interview)? **I literally watch the show JUST for him because on some rare occasions his comments are so underhanded and passive aggressive and condescending that it's HILARIOUS.** I'm surprised there are no fan sites out there for him compiling his zingers. (Reddit, 2016 – emphasis added)

Llewelyn goes a little deeper than just "zingers." He actually gets people to say that they lied or tells them that what they did "could be considered stupid, wouldn't you agree"? And then he, like Chaplin, sends them on their way to go sign some papers.

Next is Harvey Levin, the host of TMZ where once again Jews get to spy and insult people, most of whom are celebrities, and a show that is promoted on "The People's Court" since Levin is also the guy who gets to do the lead-ins and also post-decision analyses.

The show is then wrapped up by Harvey Levin, the Jew who loves to instigate mess and who is also the host of "TMZ." Listed in the credits as a "host and legal reporter," he's an even bigger piece of shit than Chaplin/Llewelyn. As each case is introduced, his voice narrates those introductions and they are replete with puns and oftentimes below the belt quips that are, admittedly, funny every now and then. But again, if this is "The People's Court," Levin, Milian and Chaplin combine to ridicule the people to the point where they should be traumatized by the time they leave the courtroom; not so much from the decision, but from the on-going subtle and not-so-subtle insults that are hurled at them from both in front of and behind the camera on an on-going basis.

Of Levin's actual involvement the website makes the following claims:

> A prominent producer, investigative reporter and attorney, Harvey Levin is no stranger to "The People's Court," having served as the behind-the-scenes legal consultant and as Co-Executive Producer for 19 years. As the show's host and legal reporter, Levin introduces the cases to viewers, and then literally takes "The People's Court" to the people by **polling fans who watch cases via monitor**. These **spirited discussions and debates regarding the cases and Milian's decisions** are then incorporated into the show. Levin also examines and explains the legal issues introduced in each case. (People's Court website, 2018 – emphasis added)

If Levin is involved with producing the show, then has total control. That "co-producer" label is nothing but window dressing. Secondly, the snippet claims that he "polls" the fans who watch the show on an outside monitor, but then turns around and more truthfully calls it what it is: spirited discussions and debates." But since Levin holds the microphone, and since the segments usually last less than a minute, he is the one in control, he asks the loaded questions and he goes from fan to fan until he gets the answer that he wants to hear.

Jews award each other and since the public doesn't notice, perhaps they should. This is why you see no-talent hacks, usually Jews, getting awards for everything from their acting to their behinds-the-scene management work. Because Jews control Hollywood and the Fox Network, the following should be no surprise:

> Before reuniting with Ralph Edwards and Stu Billett, Executive Producers of the original "The People's Court," Levin spent more than a decade as the investigative reporter for KCBS-TV in Los Angeles. He has also served as a legal reporter covering high-profile court cases for a number of top CBS stations across the country, including the affiliates in New York and Chicago. **Levin has received nine Emmy Awards and numerous other local and national awards.** (People's Court website, 2018 – emphasis added)

So he benefits from his ethnicity and climbs the ladder, comes up with his own show by green lighting someone's idea and all of a sudden he's a qualified "legal analyst"? There is a term for such a history of raw luck: "white privilege."

The snippet also claims the following:

> Levin, a graduate of the **University of Chicago Law School**, began his career as a litigator **at a prestigious Los Angeles law firm** and has been **a professor of law at three universities**. He has also served as a **consultant for the American Bar Association** and testified before Congress on behalf of the organization. For seven years, Levin was a legal columnist for the Los Angeles Times. Additionally, he has hosted radio talk shows for KABC-AM and KMPC-AM in Los Angeles. (People's Court website, 2018 – emphasis added)

An impressive resume, but his ego wants him on TV and behind that microphone. In that way he gets to "direct" what is taking place instead of having to merely report on it.

Finally, there's the somewhat buff bailiff, Douglas. As black people we can often tell what's going on behind the scenes. And I've got a sneaking suspicion that Douglas has fucked Judge Milian on more than one occasion. Oh sure, like most cute bitches she can mask it on the camera when she accepts the paperwork from him. But it's the way she refers to him as "Douglas" and the vibes between them. All I can say is what Eddie Murphy's character Guido said to Detective Justice in regard to his partner Detective Rita Veder (played by Angela Bassett), in the movie' "Vampire in Brooklyn: "Yeah you beast fucked her. You did it."

Douglas McIntosh serves as Court Officer on "The People's Court." His duties include assisting Judge Milian in maintaining courtroom order, as well as serving as an intermediary between the Judge and the litigants. McIntosh's popularity with "The People's Court" audience has led to recurring roles as police officers on the acclaimed daytime dramas "One Life to Live" and "All My Children."

I suspect that something is taking place behind the scenes when it comes to Douglas and Marilyn. During a show aired on October 18, 2016, two women were in front of the judge over a catering issue. But the defendant took the time to pardon her comment, "not to influence the court," but told Milian that she was truly beautiful and that "your bailiff is very good looking" or something to that effect. Marilyn replies, "Thank you – and I know he is." It was the way she said it kind of matter-of factly and yet those of us who understand the game know "play" when we hear it.

There is no way that this brutha could be "working" with someone as fine as Marilyn Milian, a woman who has in her past swam nude in public, someone who is fiery and impulsive, and not screw her at least one time. Sure, she has a husband, which is a point she makes quite regularly. But that don't mean shit. This is Hollywood and these television personalities are treated like kings and queens and have entire staffs of people who can cover for them. I'm sure Douglas has an apartment or an American Express card to charge a hotel room. And I bet he tore that ass up.

JUDGE JEANINE PIRRO

This bitch is borderline crazy and most definitely politically motivated. But, like Milian and Judge Faith, she is also a beauty. I never knew who she was when she was doing the TV judge thing, but once she joined Fox News and I heard some of her views and opinions of President Donald Trump, I knew she had some serious mental issues. More on that later.

She started off as the average white woman. Lombardi (2000) writes,

> WHEN Jeanine Pirro was named one of the 50 Most Beautiful People in 1997 by People magazine, she was asked how -- as a wife, mother and hard-working district attorney known for championing the causes of battered wives and abused children -- she managed to look so great."Gallons of eye concealer," she said. (Lombardi, 2000)

She's laughing it off but she knows she's fine. As I share later she's won a beauty contest and since her divorce from her husband (he was screwing around behind her back), she's made her way into the beds of several well known men (the ones we know about) and that is solely because of her beauty. Because if her seductions were personality based, she's be one lonely bitch.

And one on-line snippet offers the following:

> **A tempestuous marriage,** federal tax evasion and illegal taping are all part of this TV judge's colorful past. Until 2013 the host of Fox News Channel's Justice With Judge Jeanine was married to Albert Pirro – a **lawyer who was once disbarred for a tax fraud conviction and whose adultery resulted in an illegitimate daughter**. In 2006 Judge Jeanine was under federal investigation for an alleged plan to **bug her husband's boat to see if he was cheating on her**. (Millar, 2014).

In other words, the bitch cray-cray! There is no doubt in my mind that the problems between her and her husband included some knock down-drag out brawls. This guy was probably tied up with organized crime and she knew about it and wanted her cut. She is also smart enough to know that men like that always have "a piece on the side."

As beautiful as Marilyn Milian, as articulate as Judge Ferrer and as cruel and cratchety as Judge Judy, Pirro is an interesting person to watch and has an impressive legal background as a former prosecutor, judge and even an elected official from New York. The fact that she ran for the position of New York State Attorney General in 2006, as a Republican, shows you how fucked up her politics are. If more proof is needed, keep in mind that she works for Fox News and has a show called, "Justice With Judge Jeanine." It came on in January of 2011 and was later nominated for an Emmy. A few months later, in September of the same year her court show was cancelled due to low ratings.

Boasting that she's known Donald Trump for 25 years, she sounded like it when she interviewed him during a September 5, 2015 Fox News rerun of her show, "Justice With Judge Jeanine." She kissed his ass at every turn and apparently is a part of the FOX channel political apparatus: anti-Obama and pro-conservative. Asking leading questions all the way, she let Trump talk at great length, babbling with a single policy idea.

Like Sarah Huckabee-Sanders, Omorosa Manigault, Ann Colter and Sarah Palin, Pirro is just what the conservative white man like Trump ordered. "You're so on message," she told Trump while referring to President Obama as a "paper tiger." Trump added to her insults by referring to the administration as "truly stupid leadership."

Pirro was at one time a TV judge. As one source reminds us:

> On May 5, 2008, The CW announced that Pirro would host a weekday television show to be named Judge Jeanine Pirro, part of the network's CW Daytimelineup, with two episodes airing daily. The show was distributed by Warner Bros. Domestic Television and was carried by default on all CW affiliate stations … Judge Jeanine Pirro was cleared for a second season beginning in fall 2009. Unlike its first season, the second season, which began in the fall of 2009, was not exclusive to CW affiliates … In May 2010, the show received its first Emmy nomination, and in 2011, received the daytime Emmy Award. In September 2011 the show was canceled due to low ratings.

The Emmy nomination must have been a token one, probably revolving around her physical appearance (ala Marilyn Milian) because other than that, the show was lackluster and bland. That show gone, she got another chance with Fox News, the pro-Trump station that is about as conservative as they get. Wikipedia (2018) explains that, "Pirro is now the host of Fox News Channel's "Justice with Judge Jeanine," which premiered in January 2011. The program airs on weekends and focuses on the big legal stories of the week." It may have focused on legal stories, but it did so from a right-wing position and one that was both critical and supportive of Donald Trump, both before and after the election.

Her version of "Justice" got more and more attention as she continued to take positions that could only be deemed "right wing." For instance,

> After Trump's election, Pirro was known for delivering fiery defenses of the president … *The Washington Post* described her show as "almost universally positive about Trump … According to *Politico*, "From the outset of the administration, she has used her TV platform to hammer the president's critics and to ding his allies, including Sessions, as insufficiently loyal …(Wikipedia, 2018 – emphasis added).

It soon became common knowledge that President Trump was a cable news addict and really loved Fox News, since his friend, Roger Ailes, was the owner. Even after Ailes got fired for sexually harassing a number of women at the station, Trump because super-tight with Sean Hannity. But Pirro was busy carrying her bucket of water up the stairs of oppression.

There was no doubt that she continued to have political aspirations:

> Pirro has called for arresting individuals who work for the special counsel, Robert S. Mueller III, who is leading the investigation into

> Russian meddling in the election of President Trump … Pirro called
> for "cleansing" those government agencies of people critical to the
> president … These sorts of attacks on the FBI and Justice
> Department have been criticized as dangerous, "despicable", and
> strictly out of place with US traditions of constitutional democracy …
> (Wikipedia, 2018).

Whatever position Trump took, Pirro took; whatever she said, Trump would watch television and mimic what she and Sean Hannity said. Her right wing views and incredibly conservative views were catching on:

> In May 2018, Pirro said that Trump had "fulfilled" a "biblical
> prophecy" by moving the US embassy in Israel to Jerusalem … In
> June 2018, *Politico* reported that **Pirro had repeatedly since late
> 2016 told the Trump administration about her interest in
> becoming the Attorney General** … On her show, Pirro had referred
> to current Attorney General, Jeff Sessions, as "the most dangerous
> man in America …." (Wikipedia, 2018 – emphasis added).

According to her website on Fox News, "Jeanine Pirro currently hosts Justice with Judge Jeanine(Saturday, 9PM/ET). She also serves as a legal analyst for FOX News Channel (FNC) where she provides legal insight across the network's programming. She joined the network in 2006 and is based out of New York.

<u>Jeanine Pirro, Conservative Politics and Donald Trump</u>

Her politics are becoming increasingly aggressive and overt, and now with her position on Fox News, she can work with and for Trump to promote a conservative (and racist) agenda.

Pirro is one of those women I wrote about in my book "Transformers," where the white woman is the new white man; she doesn't care about him getting off of the throne of oppression, she merely wants him to scoot over, make room for her, and then she can show him how it's done. In this case the "king" of oppression is none other that President Donald Trump. Dawsey (2018) informs us of the following:

> President Trump and Chief of Staff John F. Kelly do not regularly
> give on-the-record interviews. **But both men recently sat down with
> Jeanine Pirro, the fiery Fox News host whom Trump adores, for
> her upcoming book on the Trump presidency,** White House
> officials said.The White House communications shop arranged the
> 30-minute interview with Pirro and the chief of staff in the West

> Wing, two White House officials said. **Trump gave her an even longer interview, one of these officials said.** (Dawsey, 2018 – emphasis added)

This woman tows the conservative line better than Sean Hannity and Chris Matthews ever could. She's sharp-tongued but smart, and she won't let you get a word in edgewise if you have anything negative to say about Donald Trump.

The ass kissing is therefore two way. Trump probably screwed her because she seems to be the type that is "open" for advances even from an ugly bastard like him. After all, look at her life: her husband screwed around behind her back, ended up going to prison and then to top it off, had a kid behind her back while they were married. This had to hurt someone as beautiful as she was. Such an act sends a message to the public, and that message has something to do with sexual prowess and the spouse's choice based on which "love interest" has the most skills.

Another reason why I alleged that there was a tryst between Pirro and Trump is that all you have to do is appeal to his ego and you can make him do whatever you want him to do. She must be massaging his ego (or something else) with the utmost skill because he appears to be obsessed with her.

For instance,

> The president has also encouraged other advisers to interview with Pirro, officials said. The cooperation with Pirro **further illustrates the inordinate power of the conservative-leaning Fox cable channels on the Trump presidency.** The president usually begins his morning with the "Fox & Friends" show on Fox News, often sending tweets that correspond with the show's headlines and programming. The show even partially fueled his decision this week to call for sending National Guard troops to the U.S.-Mexico border. (Dawsey, 2018 – emphasis added)

Pirro is an opportunist and she has her eyes set on the Attorney General slot, the one currently occupied by Jeff Sessions. Slowly but surely, insult after insult, Trump has berated sessions to the point where the public is waiting for Sessions to resign as a result. Who, pray tell, could be instigating such insults and hoping to get in next to "the boss"? I suspect it would be Jeanine Pirro.

Furthermore,

> But aides say there are few shows the president fancies as much as "Justice With Judge Jeanine," a Saturday Fox News show that **Trump makes sure to watch live or record,** whether he is in the White House or at his Mar-a-Lago resort in Florida. Pirro, formerly a prosecutor in New York, **often delivers strident defenses of the**

president and scores high ratings, which the president notes to advisers. (Dawsey, 2018 – emphasis added)

Trump was tight with Roger Ailes, the fat white boy who was the head of Fox News but who got fired for sexually harassing female employees. Pirro is still at the station and has said nothing at all about that or about on-going allegations about Trump, his affair with porn "star" Stormy Daniels or the host of other affairs he's had behind his wife's back. She is his stiffest (no pun intended) supporter, and to think it all started off with a lackluster TV court show.

And so it goes:

> In the White House communications shop, officials rotate going on Pirro's show because they know Trump will be watching — and partially to prevent him from calling in himself, several officials said, as he did earlier this year. "Someone has to be on the show every week," an official said. **Pirro has given the president legal advice** in the West Wing about the investigation into Russia's role in the 2016 election **and has shared some of his grudges**, particularly about Attorney General Jeff Sessions, in her frequent conversations with Trump, advisers say. (Dawsey, 2018 – emphasis added)

When you get to the point where you give the president legal advice, and you see the plethora of instances where he has scoffed at or over stepped legal bounds, it is clear that the information she's giving him is how to BREAK the law. And who would know better than a woman who was married to a man who was put in prison or a woman who, herself, had a very messy and public divorce from that same man?

It says that Trump has shared some of his grudges. I'll bet he has – as in pillow talk! In fact, according to the article, "You know who," Trump said when he called into her show earlier this year, implicitly criticizing Sessions for not investigating his opponents. *"I think I know, Mr. President," she said, grinning.* (Dawsey, 2018 (emphasis added). This is more than playful banter – this is flirting. She's available and so is he (Melania seems not to give a shit what he does). And don't say she's not capable of it.

According to Dillon (2018):

> Robert Durst's Los Angeles murder case took an unexpected turn Wednesday, veering into the love life of former Westchester County District Attorney Jeanine Pirro. Writer Lisa DePaulo was called to the witness stand during a special pre-trial hearing **and put on the spot about Pirro's rumored romance with Cody Cazalas, the Texas homicide detective who investigated Durst for the 2001 death and**

dismemberment of neighbor Morris Black. (Dillon, 2018 – emphasis added)

Pirro will screw anybody to get a "scoop" or an advantage over other people who are into delivering what she calls "news." Continuing:

"Did you become aware Detective Cazalas and Jeanine Pirro had a romantic relationship?" Los Angeles County Deputy District Attorney John Lewin asked. "Yes," DePaulo replied. "Did you inquire when that relationship started?" Lewin pressed. "She was vague," DePaulo replied, referring to Pirro, who split with her husband in 2007. (Dillon, 2018)

Pirro "split with her husband" in the same way that Joe Frazier allowed Muhammad Ali to knock him on his ass. Pirro's husband was playing her all the time with another woman that he felt comfortable enough to relax and not use any protection when having sex. And Jeanine didn't even see it coming. She was hurt because she's always thought she was top dog and believed that her beauty and brains would pull her through. That incident scarred her and once freed from the man who had made an utter ass out of her, she felt free enough to dive into other areas that would bring her access to power and fame.

The story about DePaulo's recollection of Pirro continues:

DePaulo said she knew the two were lovers because she spent many nights at Pirro's house while working on the ex-prosecutor's 2015 Durst book "He Killed Them All." She watched them retire to the same bedroom, she testified. Under cross-examination by Durst's defense lawyer David Chesnoff, DePaulo was grilled again. (Dillon, 2018)

In the house that she and her husband probably shared. Perhaps the same bed that she had slept with while married. This is akin to President Trump's having prostitutes urinate on the same bed at the Ritz Carlton in Moscow that Barack and Michelle Obama had slept in. Trump's hatred and jealous of Obama runs so deep it is almost homoerotic and in my view akin to what Jeanine must have felt for her husband.

In other words, Pirro will do what it takes to be associated with powerful men. This explains why,

Her show is almost **universally positive about Trump**. The president was frustrated recently when conservative commentator Ann Coulter sharply criticized him on Pirro's show, saying that one reason Trump signed a spending bill that did not include enough money for a border

> wall was because he wanted to go to Mar-a-Lago. **"This guy is the hardest-working guy who has ever been in the White House,"** **Pirro said. "He doesn't sleep, and he works day and night."**
> (Dawsey, 2018 – emphasis added)

The station she works for is Fox News. It is filled with sexually abusive men who do not hide their actions. Their most famous broadcasters and even their former president, Roger Ailes, were fired because of sexual harassment. The fact that she can survive in such an environment shows what kind of bitch she is. And to add to that lack of moral character is the fact that she supports the biggest asshole of all time, the man who has abused women as a way of life, none other than President Donald Trump.

The lies she tells above indict her. He is not even CLOSE to being the hardest working guy who has ever been in the White House. He's too busy watching television and visiting his other house in Mar-A-Lago, avoiding his wife who he never screws, and flying around the world pissing off America's allies. Hard work? He's on the golf course twice as much as Obama ever was and yet before he ran he lambasted Obama about the time spent on the greens. Ever since Obama humiliated him at the 2011 White House Correspondents dinner (for five long minutes), Trump was never the same. He wanted revenge and he is now getting it. And people like Jeanine Pirro support his every effort.

She lies and claims that he doesn't sleep. Of course not: he's hyped up on Diet Coca Cola. Paranoid schizophrenics rarely sleep and he's not doing anything but flipping through recordings of the day's news shows so that he can hear his name being uttered. Pirro is lurking and looking for something from Trump, perhaps a place in the administration. At any rate, one writer offers the following:

> But Pirro, who recently went on an expedition to Chappaqua, N.Y., to mock Hillary Clinton, even lurking in the woods on a whimsical hunt for the 2016 Democratic candidate, is unlikely to disappoint Trump. **The book is called "Liars, Leakers, and Liberals: The Case Against the Anti-Trump Conspiracy." It is due out in June.** (Dawsey, 2018 – emphasis added)

There you have it. A television judge who then went on to become some kind of news pundit, and now an author with a book she's pushing in an attempt to shield Trump from the legitimate criticisms of the millions of people he's pissed off. The book's title is filled with the labels of the three groups that Trump hates the most: liars (of which he is the biggest of all time), leakers (giving out information on how he fucks up all the time while waddling around the White House) and liberals (those who are on the left side of the political scale but in my book, a peckerwood is a peckerwood.

Her defense of Trump was never more apparent than when she made an appearance on ABCs morning talk show, "The View."

Jeanine Pirro and Her Appearance on "The View"

More evidence to show that Pirro is no stranger to controversy can be found during a July 2018 appearance on ABC's talk show, "The View". The following article, including my analyses, explains what took place when Pirro went up against "The View's" fiery and weird co-host, Whoopi Goldberg.

Here's how it all went down:

> Pirro visited the set of "The View" on Thursday morning to promote her new book, "Liars, Leakers and Liberals: The Case Against the Anti-Trump Conspiracy." **But there wasn't much discussion about the upcoming book after Pirro made a comment to Goldberg, who had been trying to ask Pirro a question about the president.** "You suffer from Trump Derangement Syndrome," Pirro said, pointing at Goldberg. The term, which stemmed from "Bush Derangement Syndrome," has been used by Trump supporters to suggest **that those who do not support the president are unable to think clearly and logically about the state of the country.** (Yasharoff, 2018 – emphasis added)

Whoopi came into the situation with an ulterior motive. "The View" is a show comprised of four women who spew their opinions in front of a female audience of idiots. The viewers, mostly women, get their "political tips" from this show for the most part. So this is no panel of experts: it's a panel of women with axes to grind and grind them they do.

Whoopi is the most politically astute of them all, but her life shows she's also a chameleon. When this bitch was dating Ted Danson and accompanied him to the a Friar's Club event back in 1993, and allowed him to get up on that stage in blackface, that tore it for me. I already considered her to be an Aunt Jemima because of her past exploits, but this incident took the cake. On the view she is the voice of "all women" but seems knowledgeable about black people. That makes her water-carrying attitude all the more hurtful.

For those of you who don't remember the Danson incident, here is how reviewer Roger Ebert reported it for his "Robert Ebert's Internet Journal":

> It's a tradition of the celebrity roasts at the Friar's Club that everything goes - that no joke is in such bad taste that it cannot be told. Friday, that tradition may have ended, **as a roast for Whoopi Goldberg turned into such a tasteless display that some audience members hid their faces in their hands, and others left.** (Ebert, 1993 – emphasis added)

This woman brought this man to a roast and he used the opportunity to skewer black people. Before you say that it was "all in good fun," continue reading the account of Roger Ebert, who was there on the scene:

> They cringed in disbelief during the opening monologue by actor Ted Danson, Whoopi's lover, **who appeared in blackface** and **used the word "nigger" more than a dozen times** during a series of jokes that drew smaller and smaller laughs, until finally the audience was groaning and Danson faltered as he tried to plow through his written material. (Ebert, 1993 – emphasis added)

The black men in attendance should have kicked Danson's ass. Montel Williams, whose wife is white, got up and left. Yeah, he doesn't want to piss off the white man because he's a long-time military "boy" and he stands for all that America stands for. And that would include Danson's name-calling.

Now we fast forward 25 years to Whoopi's role with the women on "The View." Remembering what you just read about her ex boyfriend Ted Danson, check out the following:

> "Let me tell you what I have," Goldberg began. **"I'm tired of people starting a conversation with 'Mexicans are liars and rapists.'** I'm 62 years old. There have been a lot of people in office that I didn't agree with. **But I have never, ever seen anything like this. I have never seen anybody whip up such hate.** I have never seen anybody be so dismissive." She continued: **"Clearly, you don't watch the show, so you don't know that I don't suffer from that. What I suffer from is the inability to figure out how to fix this."** (Yasharoff, 2018 – emphasis added)

Say what??? That is why I shared the details of the Friar's Club incident with you. This bitch believes that most people have short memories. I'm not one of them. You read about what she "allowed" when the racist doing the dividing and the "dismissing" was a white man she was screwing. But what does she do when she's on a show a quarter century later? She hypocritically turns the table and becomes the champion of race relations!

She says she never saw anything like what Trump has done and is doing. She says she never saw anybody whip up such hate. The examples she uses are the insults against Mexicans and yet Trump has also dogged out and degraded black people. Goldberg is black. Where is her defense of her own race? Nowhere to be found.

Moving on with the Pirro incident:

> **The morning after her segment on "The View" turned into a shouting match with host Whoopi Goldberg**, Fox News personality and former judge Jeanine Pirro made an appearance on "Fox and Friends" to explain her side of the story after the segment ended. "Whoopi got angry, and what the viewing audience didn't see was they popped up the cover of my book and (after cutting to commercial) **she pushed off the desk, unplugged her mic and stormed off the set**," Pirro said. "I'm there saying... 'I don't think the segment's over'... So I take off my own mic, and... **go down the stairs and she's right there."** (Yasharoff, 2018 – emphasis added)

Upset about a book about Trump? Is she fucking Trump? No. Goldberg is supposed to be interviewing a woman about her book, and just because she doesn't agree with Pirro doesn't give her the right to act like some black militant and throw a hissy fit on live television. It was just a front anyway: most black people know Goldberg is an Uncle Tom and she'll do anything for a role on TV or in the movies. Pirro continues her explanation:

> "I said something like, **'Whoopi, you know I spent my whole life fighting for victims,' because we had talked about rapes and all that**. And she said to me -- she got up in my face... she said "(expletive) you, (expletive) you.'" Pirro denied doing anything to provoke Goldberg: "You can ask the people I was with. She was nuts going off the set, and then... as I started walking out the building, **this woman is yelling behind me, 'get the (expletive) out of this building.'**(Yasharoff, 2018 – emphasis added)

Whoopi snapped – and what for? She isn't going to do a damn thing about what Trump says or does. She's all talk. She couldn't control Danson, could she? She just sat there and took it. Danson even took a few jabs at her and their sex life. She didn't say shit. Now a quarter century later, she's cursing out a guest who is supposed to be peddling her book – probably an appearance that Pirro paid for.

Pirro said in regard to Whoopi's conniption, "I've been a judge and prosecutor for 30 years, I can go toe-to-toe with anybody," Pirro said. "But that was abuse. It was a sad moment. She was triggered and I never understood triggering." (Yasharoff, 2018) Abuse? What does this bitch think she does when she's spouting off that conservative, pro-Trump rhetoric, including backing him when he called black athletes "sons of bitches"? Pirro still wants to play the role of victim, probably still stinging from her husband's infidelity. But she got as good as she gave on that day. Lucky for her what she got came from a woman who is equally as pitiful and duplicitous as she is.

But the feud ain't over. Check it out:

> Later Friday morning, Goldberg responded to Pirro's comments on "The View"."There's a lot of spin that she's doing, and I can't do anything about that, but I can tell you what went on," she said. **"She was upset when she got here because Ana Navarro was here instead of Joy (Behar).** And after the segment, which ended when it was supposed to -- it was not early, it was not late. **She then called everybody at the table a name I cannot repeat on TV and said it in front of the audience."** (Yasharoff, 2018 – emphasis added)

This is Whoopi's version and it sounds believable. But so what? Did that give Whoopi the right to go out into the hallway and stalk Pirro? Where is the so-called "professionalism" that negroes like Goldberg are always talking about, lecturing on and striving for? When the shit hits the fan, it's time for some "nigga shit," huh?

Moving on with Whoopi's claim:

> She continued: **"When I came off stage, I went over there because I was a little hot. She came off, she could have just passed me. She didn't need to stop, but she stopped. She put a finger in my face, and yelled, 'I've done more for victims than you ever will.'** Then I said some few choice words that I cannot repeat. Yes, I did say it. But I did not spit on her, I did not intimidate her, no one chased her out of here saying 'get out.' **But she did leave here cursing at the people who booked the show, cursed at the guys who do security for the show**. (Yasharoff, 2018 – emphasis added)

Two angry bitches, both of them representing the white way of life, although only one of them will admit it. There can be no winners in a situation like this. Pirro left cursing but take note that she was "booked" for the show, meaning that she got PAID. Therefore she had a legal and financial right to be there to promote the book, even if Whoopi didn't like the subject of that text. The fact is, the contract was violated so the question is, which side is most liable?

Following is how Whoopi attempted to get out of it:

> "For 20 years, this show has always had people on with different views, like Newt Gingrich, Corey Lewandowski, Charlotte Pence, Sarah Sanders. Jeanine, good luck with your book," Goldberg concluded. "Look, you can come to this show. We treat everybody with respect. **But you cannot come and call people names."** (Yasharoff, 2018 – emphasis added).

Oh – like Danson did back in 1993 as you sat there looking like some powerless slave? What can be more insulting than some of the movies you've made? Did you give a shit about the black audience or you just wanted to pick up a check?

The article closes out thusly:

> Goldberg then attempted to switch topics to the "deep state." Instead, a shouting match erupted as both women debated what is most horrible about the country today: Pirro claimed those entering the country illegally were killing U.S. citizens; **Goldberg countered that the president's rhetoric was inciting violence toward minorities**. "Say goodbye. Bye. I'm done," Goldberg said, ripping up her cue cards. "Wow," Pirro replied, shaking her head and rolling her eyes. The show cut to commercial, after which Goldberg addressed the camera directly for closing thoughts: **"So you saw me do something I very rarely do. I very rarely lose my cool. And I'm not proud of it. I don't like it. But I also don't like being accused of being hysterical. That's one of the things I try not to be on this show. So have a great day."**
> (Yasharoff, 2018 – emphasis added)

Jeanine Pirro is a piece of work. Like Marilyn Milian she's gorgeous and very loud. Like Judge Judy, she's insulting and can't take it if someone gives her back what she gives. And like her role model Donald Trump, she embellishes facts, lies when necessary and really doesn't give a damn about anything any one else has to say about it.

JUDGE LYNN TOLER

I have watched this show, not so much by choice, but for a few months I was without cable television, so I had to watch Fox because it also had shows like Judge Alex, Judge Joe Brown and Judge Judy. Of all the shows, I dislike this one the most and it because of Lynn Toler. "Divorce Court" went from being my favorite show back in the day to, as I say, being one that I might listen to while I'm writing, but just looking at Lynn Toler is quite a sickening experience.

By her own admission during a segment that aired on June 13, 2013, "I make a great first impression, but I'm hard to live with." That's no lie. No, it's not because she's ugly. In fact, she is a beautiful woman. But the problem is that she KNOWS it. Ever meet one of those women whose been told that she's "fine" so many times that now she assumes it, flaunts it and lives by it? That is Lynn Toler.

While spilling her guts during an October 9, 2013 episode, the people who were in court were having problems and the plaintiff, Mr. Katzky (male) shared that when his woman left to go to Florida on a girls vacation with her friends, he felt she was gone for good. The woman says that three weeks later he had another woman living there – he says it was "about three months later." Toler started laughing and acted like she didn't understand. She said that three months was not a long time because it was three years from the time she got out of law school to the time she was married was "like three years." Bullshit. Maybe it was three years before this guy decided to ask her to marry him (remember her admission that she was hard to live with), but that bitch was more likely than not fuckin' before law school, during law school, and afterwards. She knows it and if you get a look at her and that "attitude" she's got, you'll know it, too.

During an October 10, 2103 rant, she was in one of her civil rights moods when some young brother gave her the wrong answer to the question, "do you have a job"? He said something like, he didn't have a job because there were "limitations to how much he could take …" or something like that. This bitch went OFF! She told him to shut up and then started talking about Martin Luther King, Jr. and all the stuff that black people had to take. You should have known there was some self serving aspect to her concern about black people, so she then shifted to her father, who she claimed was in the same group as King. She said that her doctor had a doctorate in law, and couldn't get a job because no law firm would hire him, so he worked in a linoleum factory! No wonder she's always pissed off about something!

The pre-show promo says that she's "intense with common sense." What in the hell does that have to do with matters of law? In fact, aren't these two things – intensity and common sense – the antithesis of what most judicial decisions are rooted in? She's supposed to be making decisions based of the law, legal precedents and so on. She goes off on her own as if she's some kind of family counselor or therapist and that is why things are not going well as far as I can see. OR she'll come up with some simplistic shit like she did at the conclusion of the June 13, 2013 show: "Decide to decide." Say what???

And she has ruined "Divorce Court" and turned it into the Lynn Toler opinion show. Now, the show is requesting that if a viewer needs some marriage BEFORE they get married, to call the number for that show. So it's not so much about divorce – it's about preventing marriages that might not work. This is not what the show was intended for and the title of the show proves that. It is a televised version of the "bait and switch" and when you tune in and see this beauty on the bench, you are going to keep the channel in place – that is until she opens her mouth and shows how sophistic her concepts are.

The promos claim that "Divorce Court" ratings plummeted. One respondent asked, "Could that be because they're now pulling stunts like "Before the Vows" week? Huh?! I recently watched an episode of a married couple who, after the episode, wasn't sure whether they were going to get divorced afterwards.)"

Whoever wrote this, I believe it. She's confused and gives out nothing more than common sense advice, which shows you how dim-witted the litigants are.
Now we have another review, which goes back a ways, to the 1950s. This one, penned by Brian Rathjen (briguy_52732@yahoo.com), offered these insights:

> An updated version of the 1957-1969 series, "Divorce Court" presented a new divorce proceeding each day. Though some cases revolved around standard divorce issues (abuse, adultery, irreconcilable differences, etc.), many stories seemed to involve unusual circumstances or those with "shock value" (e.g., in one story, a wife accused her husband of involving their sons in "accidents" so he could collect on the insurance). Judge William B. Keene rendered his decision by the end of the show and also resolved other divorce issues (e.g., child custody, alimony, division of assets, etc.). In later years, some divorce proceedings were played out over multiple shows.

Again, these were law-based, but I believe that the litigants were real. People were learning about "Divorce Court" and divorces were actually granted following the judge's decision.

Not any more.

Read about Judge Mablean and you will see that she took it to another, more positive level: she offered street savvy and the law. Like Toler, there were references to her mother's "rules," but all of this was done within the confines and context of the courtroom.

Let's take it back for a minute.

Think back to the old days of "Divorce Court" when you could actually learn something about law, precedents and the like. It was about marriage and the deterioration of same – not about Lynn Toler's views, perspectives, opinions, and homespun assumptions – and, of course, the shameless peddling of her bullshit psycho-babble books. If she's got mood disorder issues, which she has admitted to having, then how in the hell is she going to give out free tips to people?

I found an interesting synopsis on a website, Fiberbit.net, and got a short review on the history of the show to buttress what I've shared (I was a fan back in the early 1980s). Here is what the excerpt, written by Jean-Marc Rocher, stated:

> An early successor to "The People's Court" (1981) and precursor to later 'reality-based' shock-TV shows. Actors portraying litigants in divorce proceedings presented their stories to a judge who gave his judgement based on the merits of the case. Accusations of infidelity, dishonesty, incompetence and insanity were frequent.

Now take notice: there were actors posing as litigants and there was a reason for that: it was an education in family law. You could learn things. As the preceding excerpt makes clear, you could deal with all of those emotional issues, but it was within the framework of law.

Now it's degenerated into street slang ("you go girl," and "he's a playa!", "no more big ballin'" and one brother came on and introduced the term "bourgetto" – that's somebody who acts "bourgeois" but also acts "ghetto.") Then, of course, Lynn Toler's beautiful face, pouting that sexy mouth every single chance she gets.

Lynn Toler and Mental Health

A website called Black Doctor.org carried an article about Toler under the headline, "Judge Lynn Toler: Putting Her Own Mental Health on Trial." Following is a transcript from that website article and my analyses of the contents. Let me say beforehand and make it clear: this woman is out to lunch and should not be allowed to carry sharp instruments, let alone sit in judgment of litigants who don't know their asses from a hole in the ground.

The website article, which offers us some background information on Toler's childhood, begins thusly:

> Judge Lynn Toler runs a tight ship on TV's popular "Divorce Court." She helps couples navigate and work through some of the worst marital issues including infidelity, domestic violence and miscommunication. She's honest, thoughtful, fair, concise and even funny at times. She pretty much has it all together. **But, growing up, she had to deal with and is still sometimes coping with a rocky childhood spent living with her mentally ill father.** She had to go on the medication **Zoloft and had severe depression**. Toler credits her mother for **helping her survive**, and shares her wisdom in a new book, *"My Mother's Rules: A Practical Guide to Becoming an Emotional Genius."* (Black doctor.org, 2018 – emphasis added).

How can you run a tight ship when, as a captain of that ship, you are one can short of a six-pack? In other words, how can someone who is most likely taking meds for her mental state be "in control" enough to "steer" a show without snapping? That's the risk these white boys take when they see this gorgeous black woman with the pouty mouth and a law degree and they figure "why not make her a courtroom judge on TV"?

The previous snippet is packed with bullshit and fluff. For instance, where it claims, "She's honest, thoughtful, fair, concise and even funny at times." Oh sure – that's the way bipolar disorder works. On one hand or one day you're the personification of "the great human being." And the next minute or day you can be slapping the shit out of someone for stepping on your feet. You never overcome that shit once you've been diagnosed with it and these white men know that. They probably use it as a gimmick (e.g., Judge Judy's Jewishness, Judge Mathis' street background, Judge Milian's Latina fire and emotion, etc.). So Judge Toler has one too: a nut with a gavel!

The snippet says, "But, growing up, she had to deal with and is still sometimes coping with a rocky childhood spent living with her **mentally ill father.**" What? There's no telling what this man did to those kids and her mother that she never speaks about! Mentally ill? Are there some bodies lying around the neighborhood that we don't know about? And now Toler's genetically predisposed to be a nut as well. There's no two ways about it because the snippet quickly adds that "She had to go on the medication Zoloft and had severe depression."

What?! Do you know what Zoloft is prescribed for? Let me tell you what the medical professionals on the internet site WebMD have to say.

Can you say walking time bomb? According to this site Zoloft is derived from Sertraline and "Sertraline is used to treat depression, panic attacks, obsessive compulsive disorder, post-traumatic stress disorder, social anxiety disorder (social phobia), and a severe form of premenstrual syndrome (premenstrual dysphoric disorder).

These are major problems. How Toler made it through law school one can only imagine. Her beauty certainly didn't hurt, but it sound like something that only a psychiatrist could prescribe. This drug, the website claims, "works by helping to restore the balance of a certain natural substance (serotonin) in the brain. (WebMD, 2018).

Are there side effects? Of course there are. According to the website Drugs.com, some of the side effects include decreased sexual desire or ability. Less common side effects include Aggressive reaction, confusion, fast talking and excited feelings or actions that are out of control, inability to sit still, restlessness, or sudden loss of consciousness.

And Toler has the gall to write a book about the concept of "emotional genius"? That's like Al Capone writing a book about "the benefits of Christianity"! According to the Black Doctor.org website interview with

> **"An emotional genius is a person who doesn't have everything under control, but knows how to manage their emotions and get things better under control day after day after day."** At home,

> Toler's dad's manic attitude swings clashed with daily life. He would rage over mispronounced words, misplaced eyeglasses, carpet dust, or imperfectly aligned window shades. In general, his tendency to exaggerate everyday things turned into ugly outbursts. (Black doctor.org, 2018 – emphasis added)

What was just described is what a person can become if they take Zoloft or some other drug! If a person is bipolar they cannot become an emotional genius because they lack control and how to manage those emotions on a consistent basis! Without the drugs, Toler would be hosting a show called "Zombie Apocalypse!" Furthermore, whose definition of "emotional genius" is this? I ask because it really doesn't make sense, and I've just shared a reason or two as to why this is the case.

Continuing with the Toler interview:

> In the book, she writes, **"Daddy was an ongoing event. At our house, a mispronounced word could have us running for our lives. A dirty carpet could lead to gunplay."** As Lynn approached junior high school age, she recognized that her father's acting out affected her own moods. She became angry and began acting out, breaking light bulbs, wetting herself in public, and reacting hysterically to minor frustrations. Anxiety and depression dominated her days. When Lynn was about 10 years old, a pediatrician and close family friend attributed her mood disorder to her father's erratic, combative behavior. (Black doctor.org, 2018 – emphasis added).

Check out what she says about her father? Pot, meet kettle. How can she talk even in retrospect about her father being a nut who had mood swings when there is no doubt that she has them herself. The girl was traumatized as a child. That's like having post traumatic stress syndrome and a lot of kids don't get over it. By her own admission "anxiety and frustration dominated her days." And of course they blamed it on the father, which anyone would have done because it was genetically transmitted, like an alcoholic or a dope fiend giving fetal alcohol syndrome or addiction to a child.

And she has a show claiming to be solving other people's problems when she had to use drugs to solve her own.

Moving right along:

> **"I had two nervous breakdowns by the time I think I was 12** – mom's not quite sure," confesses Toler to NPR. "The first one I had in the fourth grade. And I was, as my mother often said, someone who fell a little too close to her husband's emotional tree. And that's why I found my mother's way of doing business so important, because she helped me

> walk from an emotional mess to one in which I can control how I feel and what I think." (Black doctor.org, 2018 – emphasis added).

Yeah: scapegoat the father, leave him out of the equation, teach that all men are dogs and that you (Toler) has to "do it all on her own." Yeah, that sounds like the typical female in America to me. And as she grew up she was as erratic as Greg Mathis was. Check it out:

> As an adolescent, "my emotions changed and defined my life," Lynn says. "It was so overwhelming…" In her book Lynn says, " … my fears would cascade on me. **Daddy would break out a window and I'd wake up convinced that I was going to die in an automobile accident that day."** By the time Lynn reached high school age, her depression had morphed into anger and headaches, and she withdrew from social gatherings and people. (Black doctor.org, 2018 – emphasis added).

That's what SHE says. Somebody that fine, with a mental problem, would have been put in "special classes" and moved on by every brutha in the neighborhood. She talks about withdrawing from social gatherings and people but what does she do? She goes to college and law school, two places where, if there is nothing else, there are huge gatherings of people. In her book and during the interview she reflects on her concerns. Here is the lie she tells:

> "While I was on the bench, there were so many immensely ill people coming in my courtroom, and that we were their first line of defense. I know one guy – I remember one guy [that said]… "…please put me in jail so I can get back on my medication. And I thought to myself, this failure to deal with mental illness, I believe came twofold. One, because, you know, it's just economics, money, and all that. And two, nobody wants to raise their hand and say I'm mentally ill, because it had such a stigma to it."(Black doctor.org, 2018)

The question is, how did she get the opportunity to sit on the bench? Don't they have a vetting process? What did she put on her applications to the undergraduate school? When the application asked her if she had medical problems did she truthfully write down, "I'm a fuckin' nut who could go off any minute"? of course not, and that is the fault of the system and to the people who were supposed to be her mentors and role models. Knowing what you know about Lynn Toler's mental state, isn't it clear how far her good looks have gotten her?

She claims further, "Now if I'm going talk that talk, how can I not say my father was bi-polar and I struggled with issues myself? And I'm not embarrassed. I'm not ashamed. I've done very well in life. My father's done very well in life, and it is what it is." (Black doctor.org, 2018). It depends on what you consider to be "doing very well." If you mean "doing very well despite the thousands of dollars of property he tore up and had to pay for," then that's one thing. But if you mean doing well and he's cured, that's bullshit. You have to keep on taking those meds because that's how the white man makes his money: he cures you and puts enough chemical into the med to hook you on it. And that is the major side effect.

A recovering mental case with a national television show. And she has the gall to give out advice about marriage and divorce. According to her interview,

> So getting back to what she does every weekday in her TV divorce courtroom, Toler shares one of the biggest reasons for divorce that we can all learn from."Money is always the big problem. People don't even know how they feel. They never sit down and have the conversation. How do you feel about money? What do you want out of money? So if you have different concepts of money, it's going to be very, very difficult to have a calm, cool and meaningful relationship without a lot of trouble." (Black doctor.org, 2018).

Toler also has another book, *Making Marriage Work: New Rules for an Old Institution.* She's been married 22 years to a brother who bought four kids into the program and since then, she's had two more. Her simplistic advice is that you treat marriage like a job. She's giving out bullshit family philosophy and counseling, the show is granting what they call "a dissolution of cohabitation," she gets to sticking those lips out and cutting those eyes and people and looking, at times, like some skank off the streets. Cute, but a skank nevertheless.

She says she brought four kids into the program? This bitch is crazy! Then she turned around and had two of her own? She doesn't strike me as the motherly type based on the advice that she gives to the litigants who appear on "Divorce Court." If you want evidence, check out the following section as I go deep undercover and break down some of Judge Lynn Toler's "antics" on the court show, "Divorce Court."

Lynn Toler, "Divorce Court": Reviews

Most of her shows are about what we would call "nigga shit." The kind of shit that the old bruthas used to talk about on the corner over swapping a bottle of wine, The kind of shit the sistahs used to talk about in the beauty shop. It is also the thing that borderline nutty women talk about just before they go out and purchase a .38 "just in case." Can you say "homicide"?

During the October 31, 2013 show, she told one sorry ass nigga, "Obligations come before aspirations." What? This nigga left his fat ass woman and his job as a welder, went to L.A. with 15,000 in his pocket, then came back 3 weeks later, broke, and wearing the same clothes he had on when he left. His plan was to buy some clothes and then sell them. Toler is shouting out, "Those clothes were hot, weren't they?" as if she has street savvy.

Then something truly weird occurred.

The fat ass plaintiff asking Toler to award her a thousand dollars. Toler said, "you didn't ask for it in your paperwork." This bitch says, "I'm asking for it right now. Send a message to the men out there that they can't do that! No I mean make him give it to me right now! Make it two thousand!" This same guy was selling a home-made sex tape with her knowledge!"

This bitch sounded as nutty as Toler. And yet what did Toler recommend? Toler told the woman she presented a powerful case and concluded, "I do have the right to assess compensatory damages but also extraordinary damages for outrageous conduct." Toler continues: "Just for the sheer wrongness of it. Miss Noble: two thousand dollars!" Ain't that a bitch?

Not only that, but Toler puts words in the mouths of the people who are testifying. And she does it throughout the show. She only asks questions so that she can lead these nitwits toward assumptions that Toler has already arrived at. She told one man, "one of the gears isn't working right." She even peddles her damn books (one is called "My Mother's Rules") on the air (as does Judge Judy, by the way). She gives her opinion on marriage as if everything she has done has been a cultural universal worthy of emulating.

For instance during one show, *Charles Wilson v. Melissa Sykes*, the brother was the plaintiff and his wife was the defendant. Judge Toler goes so far as to tell the wife what she should be saying to her husband in order to make him feel needed. She told the woman, "repeat after me," and then went through this thing where she said, "Charles – Friday night belongs to you. You pick out something what you want to do, and I will do it with you …" and so on and so on. "Men like to kiss a little bit," she says. "Don't sit in front of the television, she's offered you her Friday night," Toler says.

During this same show she told the plaintiff that if his wife's brother died that he should go with her all the way to Indiana to attend the trial. Now he works and he's supposed to ask for time from from his job to attend a trial even though neither person is contributing to it. If her brother got gunned down, then she can attend funerals the way black people seem obsessed with doing, and go to the trial. But why does he HAVE to go as if he's obligated?

She tells him to pull the car over and "touch that leg, then pull it back." This bitch is giving out fuck tips while she's on the bench. I'm gonna give you a copy of my book Making Marriage Work, it's got two thousand rules – none of which I obey …" What kind of bullshit is this. "I'm going to leave you two to fix this marriage, there will be no recovery in this marriage." So 30 minutes was wasted while she ego tripped.

During one show which featured a male named Anthony "Pimpin'" Augustus, you saw true "nigga shit" in action. This nigga told the court and Judge Toler that he had 15 children. The stupid bitch that had taken him to court – Mary Augustus -- looked like she was straight off the street: fake ass hair, too much blue mascara, long ass fake eyelashes – somebody who should not be trying to attract attention to herself. He supposedly "cheated on her" while he was locked up in jail, having one of his "babies mama" coming to see him. He had tattoos of the girls names on his ankles. To dumb muthafuckas who shouldn't even be carrying sharp instruments, let alone appearing in public to spew forth their specious bullshit.

During one show aired in April of 2013, a couple came forward with their marriage certificate. They left it up to Judge Toler, who they turned the certificate over to, to decide if they should continue and get married or, if the Judge didn't deem them worthy, they gave her permission to tear the certificate up! During the airing of a June 3, 2013 show, she told the black male plaintiff, "Do you know what one of the sexiest things in the world is? For a man to do all the house work that a woman does for one day." This is a sexist statement! There is no such thing as "women's work" or housework: just work that needs to be done and the gender of the person doing it makes no difference! And yet on another show she told a woman, "You're a hot mess, with your triflin' self!"

During one show, plaintiff Jasmine Cotton was divorcing this brutha who was a walking baby-making machine. The man was an idiot, and this is the kind of story that white people love to watch because it confirms the stereotype of "the irresponsible black father." Jasmine- met him when he was living across the street with his kids mother. She said she walked her daughter to the bus stop and he would joke around with her, she gave him the digits and he told her he was going to marry the woman he was living with. He then came over and did her eyebrows and she fell for him She knew him about a year and a half before she married him. She got pregnant. Now get this: he was bringing his kids to her house while he cut hair. When asked how many kids he bought over, she said "about eight." "It was probably more than that your honor," he said. He had 12 sons and 15 daughters – 27 kids all together. He bought a chart with him to show how he keeps the kids straight. Four women with more than one child with him, and 16 babies mamas altogether. This bitch still married him.

She was 20 years old and a single mother and had a child with cerebral palsy. He has five kids that are the same age. Jasmine got all emotional and lectured, "you don't play with nobody like that especially after I took care of your damn kids!" Talk about the pot calling the skillet black: here's a bitch that set him up with a kid and knew that he had other kids. She was the one that was looking for a sugar daddy. Nobody told her to marry a nigga who cuts hair for a living.

During the same show the woman claimed that she found some names and messages in the man's phone. Toler says that this is something she could not understand, how people can hide something from their spouse or would-be spouse, on their phones. She told them, "I have my husband's security code and he has mine." I ask, so what? Why the need to "share codes" in the first place? His phone is his business and her phone is her business. Women want to pry, and just because there are men out there who are stupid and weak enough to surrender their Fourth Amendments rights (protection against invasion of privacy), that doesn't make it right.

During a show aired on July 15, 2013, it was pure "nigga shit." A couple – get this: "Michael "Greedy" Jones (that's real name) was the defendant and plaintiff was, "Leonora Jones." Before we get into the gist of this case let me just say right here for the record that whoever this nigga's mother is needs her black ass kicked. What parent, in his or her right mind, would give a child the name "Greedy"? And even if it wasn't his birth name, it was a street name that he adopted for some reason! And even worse, why tell these people at the studio of "Divorce Court" that your middle name is "Greedy"? What's wrong with these black muthafuckas? It's one thing to do it on the street and in the 'hood, but why you wanna go on television in front of millions of people with that nigga shit?

These embarrassing country ass niggas were on here and Jones came right out and said that, "she wouldn't give me no booty. She got on them booty shorts and wants me to scratch her back but she won't give me no sex." This nigga got some initials cut into the side of his head, she got some extensions in her hair and is wearing it slung to the side like Latinas do on one side, with braids to the back on the other.

And the stories were straight out of a backwoods swamp/inner city text book. Simply put: niggas that ain't never had nothing. The true country truly coming out. She admits that before they got together, "I choked him up." If this bitch would have called herself hemming me up in a corner, grabbing my collar and shouting at me, I would have kicked her ass right there. That's why I tell my boys don't let ANYBODY put their hands on you, not even in jest. Whatever they do to you, do it to them – regardless of gender.

When the lights were turned off he was sitting his ass up in the house with candles on and partying nonetheless. Anyway, he says she quit her job so that she could watch him. HE was playing ball in the park playing ball. He hands his phone to a woman to hold, she drives up and confronts him about why this woman has his phone. He says he sleeps on the couch or goes and sleeps in another room. She's going to be 43 and he's 37 and she says "I ain't gonna spend no more years wondering when King Greedy over here is going to get it together. "You don't want to get it together, you just get some." He will, according to her, "jump out my car while it's movin'. You know what I do? I speed up!"

Even sorry ass Judge Toler told him, "You are too old to be having designs cut in your hair."

What did this bitch expect from a nigga named "greedy"? Even if it was a street name, it's a descriptor. It says something about him. These same niggas that go around talking about how "religious" they are (he didn't) are the same ones that answer to these names. He's called greedy because somebody regards him as such! He didn't pick that name – he just accepted it once somebody picked it FOR him! Jones moved one bitch into the house who was living right down the street! When his old lady left town for a while, he moved this woman in! Mrs. Jones says she owes him $3,300. She said he wasn't working. "He likes to drink so I was buying drink. Cognac every day, all the time." She spent all that money buying this nigga some cognac.

He had a counter suit for defamation of character, he said. She shouts, "What character??!" He explains that she cusses him out. He had no case. All they did was entertain Toler, the audience and the viewers. "It was hilarious and horrifying all at the same time," Toler says. He couldn't prove shit. They left there angry after not receiving any money. According to the post-show analysis, they got back home and the arguing got worse and then they decided to do what Toler recommended, which was go their separate ways.

During a segue section between commercials she promotes, "Are you having problems with baby mama drama or baby daddy drama and you want to get a divorce? Call us at (phone number not relevant – I don't want to promote this bitch any more than I have to)." Peddling the white man's wares (promoting goods and services) so that black people (and poor whites) can come on television for their fifteen seconds of fame and humiliate the hell out of themselves and each other. For most of them it only takes an appearance or the opening of their mouths to expose their ignorance, to demonstrate that much.

Aisha Thomas v. Richard Thomas was another joke of a show. These two people have twelve children between them and have been married four years! She was pissed because the woman and her "man" couldn't have an adequate wedding. She wanted a big wedding and not done before any justice of the peace. Judge Toler tells the plaintiff and defendant that a wedding is HER day and "The wedding day is all about her (the woman)." Ain't that a bitch?

"We would have had a perfect wedding if you would just man up," Aisha says. One day, Aisha claims, she went to the store and was gone three or four hours. He calls her up and she's around the corner at a friend's house. She stopped to talk while not even thinking of him enough to at least bring the groceries home first. She says she went to get her nails done and it took two and a half hours. He says it doesn't take that long. "It was a weekend," she says. There was a nail shop around the corner but she went to a different one. "What's the problem?" she asks. She said she just wanted "to get out of the house." (Don't we all).

At one point she says, "It was stamp day," which is what they call the day when food stamps are available on their electronic cards. Spilling her guts showing how stupid she is, and the man is still kissing her ass even though it is clear that she is a drama queen. "You'll never get along with any man you get as long as you've got all those tornadoes running' around in your head." The show concludes that the two of them are "working hard to stay together for the children's best interests. Say what??

A wedding when you've got all those kids. She didn't think about marriage when she was doing all that fuckin'! Toler sat up there and listened to this woman and then had the nerve to tell her that the wedding day is the woman's day. Then why doesn't the woman marry herself? If it's the woman's day, then why does the father of the bride have to pay? (according to the American tradition).

On another show Judge Toler came clean and admitted she couldn't cook and added that her husband just "chokes down whatever is on the plate." You know, I could look at her and the way she talks and could tell that she was this kind of person, that she was someone who never worked to refine her craft unless it was of some benefit to her. There are a lot of women like that out there, who ask you when you're hungry, only because they are; who ask you how you feel because they feel a particular way; who ask you if you were bored and would like to go to a movie because they have a movie that they want to see.

It might not be a bad idea to re-name this show, "Country Nigga Court," because as of late, this is what the tendency seems to be as it relates to plaintiffs and defendants. Oh sure, there are a few white couples every now and then, but that's to make it a show that appears to be "balanced" when, in reality, it is a show about black men and women going on television and making complete asses out of themselves, mispronouncing words ("street" becomes "skreet," "your honor" becomes "ya onna," "act" is "ack," "this" becomes "dis," "that" becomes "dat," "texts" becomes "texes," "hair" becomes "her," "care" becomes "ker," "corner" is "ko-nuh," "never saw" becomes "never seen," "supposedly" becomes "suppose-ubly," "numerous times" (or "number of times") becomes "numerous of times," "liked it" becomes "liked-ed it," and so on. I haven't seen or heard such an incomprehensible mish-mash of linguistic shit like this since the days of Stepin Fetchit and Buckwheat!

During one show she told a Latina, Mrs. Kimberly Sanchez, that she was "irritating" her. The woman did talk a lot, but then Toler added, "you are over the top and under my skin." She added that, "no man wants a woman who tells them what to do," and the concluded the dogging by telling the plaintiff, "there will be no recovery."

She appears to have a bias against black men. During one show, Tawanna Wiseman versus Devon Clark, she told a black male defendant that, "I'm going to give you a chance to saying something because we (she and the plaintiff) have been talking about you like a dog." This means that she was aware of what she was doing, but continued doing it anyway. If a white women said the things about black men and women that Toler says in court, they would be charged with "racism" right off the bat.

This nigga was spending money on designer end clothes and shows while Ms. Wiseman was taking care of the kids, hosting black kids after school and working with them, and he was acting like he was pissed off. He wanted her to dress like Li'l Kim and was pissed when, after they had kids, she stopped doing it. She told him, "You are façade, you are a storefront somebody." He took the money that she loaned him for a house and spent it on himself. So what I'm wondering is why this nigga would agree to appear on Toler's show, knowing his woman was going to humiliate him. They claim, at the end of the show, that they are receiving counseling and are dedicated to making their relationship work.

What do those people who sponsor this show expect the conclusion to be? Toler is screwing up in the ratings and is listed as being a "legal consultant" in the credits. And I think I recently found out why.

The "Ricki Lake Show" has returned to television (don't ask me why), and it airs on CW33 weekday mornings at 8:00am. On the June 7, 2013 there was a show that featured different types of marriage: elderly, lesbian and so on. Guess who was sitting on the front row of the audience commenting as a "relationship expert"? None other than Judge Lynn Toler. What? *This is a woman who admitted that she's been under psychiatric care for clinical depression before!* She admitted it! Who is she to be giving out advice on relationships when she's a borderline nut herself?

During another segment of the Rickie Lake story, Toler was on the front row as a relationship counselor. This bitch told a story about women knowing the "culture" of their in-laws. She said that she was in the shower and her husband needed a razor. So she got the razor and walked out of the bathroom and handed it to him. Now she was at her in-laws house at the time and his father was there. Both the husband and father saw her nude and she thought nothing of it. She told the audience that her husband later said something to her about it and the moral was "walking around like that is okay in the Toler household." What? This bitch as teenaged and grown sons. Are you telling me she parades around naked? I see why she had clinical depression issues!

Furthermore, it seems that she's willing to do whatever it takes to stay on the air, so they keep turning her onto a "legal mammy" and she obviously doesn't care. And then there's the race-degrading bullshit that she utters and yes, I believe a black person, in a certain position, can act in a "racist" manner. Let me explain.

In my book, just because the person saying it is black doesn't mean it's alright; it may not be white racism, but it sure in the hell is cruel and it is racist. Racism, according to Karenga (1994) is, "an ideology, a violent imposition, and an institutional arrangement." So then, if a black person represents a racist system such as the judicial system, and imposes her personal views on black people rather they be legal or biased, and uses an institution in order to validate those findings and decisions – this makes that black person racist!

For instance, during one of these types of shows with a couple, Chris and LaToya Sharpnack, true hillbilly "niggerisms" were in abundance and Toler was right there in the middle of it. For one thing, he was the plaintiff, weighed about 400 pounds and was in a wheelchair. He wanted $400 for long distance phone calls that she made on a phone he bought for her. He also charged that she was unfaithful, having come back into the house one night with, get this, "no draws on." Furthermore, one night in the early morning she left the house with a girlfriend that she was supposedly taking to the store. LaToya, hardly attractive and rather obese herself, said that it wasn't true. He added that he walked out on the porch at 3 in the morning and there she sat in a van with another man. She denied it.

LaToya countered by saying that he had a girlfriend and that he wanted attention. She said he was jealous of her friend and wanted all the attention. At one point she charged that once he called her and told her that he had been shot and stabbed. She raced home to find him leaning against the car, nothing wrong. These are the kinds of case that Toler gets embroiled in, uses ghetto slang when possible, and pushes one of her bullshit books at every opportunity.

During one show a white male plaintiff told her, "that's your opinion and everybody has one." This bitch went OFF! Toler got to talking about her opinion being based on her having graduated from Harvard, having served on the bench for so many years, about her being "well-read" and so on. She took that shit personally! But remember: she's been diagnosed with depression before, and this might explain what appear to be her mood swings and certain "triggers," especially those that have to do with men who want to deal face to face with women, that prompt her to lose any cool that she might think she has.

For instance, during one show she got peeved at a female defendant, prompting her to asked, "How many different levels of foolishness can you engage in?" and then followed up, "Other than being young and cute, what do you bring to the table?" (a question that she should have been asked during her climb up the corporate ladder). She tells the same woman, "I have been married 23 years and my husband hasn't gone shopping with me yet!" This is probably a lie, but if it is not, the question is, did she ask him to go? Did she need him to go? And if she did in either case, then who is she to be giving out "life advice" on relationships when she's fucked up herself?

One sister comes on and introduces herself as a "professional woman." I took this to mean "ho."

At any rate, this young gold-digging sister came to court with the Muslim (named Muhammad) who was spoiling her rotten. Toler told the Muhammad, "If I had the power, I'd clone ya." She adds, "This man is Fan-tastic!" She dogs this sister who deserved it, but the materialistic orientation that this woman showed seems to be shared by Toler. She told this young woman, "You can't do any better. You can't. Brad Pitt's taken!" Then of course she "gives" them a copy of her book, *Making Marriage Work*. She pawns it off as a book that answers all questions, but if it is a reflection of her, it's just another piece of shit that answers questions that aren't asked and offers solutions to shit that doesn't exist.

She told one woman that before they got ready to shoot for one season she had gained ten pounds. She tells this white woman, who weighs well over 200 pounds, that she just replaced fried food with baked food and took off a pound here and a pound there – she tried to make it sound like it was easy. Bullshit! She only took that weight off because she had to be on television and the television camera already makes you look ten pounds heavier! She knew that! And the number one rule to losing weight is that you have to lose it for yourself, not for someone else. So Toler was giving out bullshit advice based on a selfish motive and then pawning it off on the ignorant plaintiff as if it was healthy to think that way when, in reality, it is not.

During one show she took a husband and wife into her chambers and started providing marriage counseling. This woman has no right to do that! She gets up from her desk, goes behind the man puts her hands on his shoulders and whispers in his ears things for him to tell his woman! "I hear ya, baby," she whispers. "I love you and I want us to be together, baby." That kind of shit. Like she's teaching this nigga how to rap to HIS bitch! She then tells the woman to tell him she loves him and that's supposed to be how things get fixed. The narrator comes on as the show concludes and says that after the show the two got together and things are good.

Bullshit!

She admitted, during one show, that she's been clinically depressed, "Been there, done that." And then added that "I'm seeing a therapist now!" For what? So she has issues that go beyond what she's doing on the air. Is she talking medication? Is she bipolar disorder? How far to her mood disorders go? Now think back a few paragraphs ago when I documented her stating that her husband has not gone shopping with her for 23 years. Is Judge Lynn Toler qualified to give out advice on depression and other psychologically related states of mind when her degree is in law? Not family law – not other areas of law. Not family therapy. She's not qualified to give out advice or information on *anything.*

Why did she conclude one show by saying, "I hope that you two stay together"? "Hope"? The ball is in her court: she is in a position to determine if the plaintiff and the defendant "stay together" or not. What is all this shit about "hope"? The name of the show is "Divorce Court." She's supposed to be granting divorces, not working toward reparations – that is what the separation period was for! In one case she told the woman to leave the guy because he was no account and added to him that he was "trifling" and "uneducatable." Even if these things were true, where does this woman get off insulting people ala Judge Judy? This is divorce court – she can just give them a divorce and stop all that bullshit "counseling;" if the marriage is done, it's done. This woman has a mean streak and, as we've already observed, she's had some psychological counseling herself.

If this is "Divorce Court," Toler is supposed to be considering the evidence and then confirming what has already been done. There are no attorneys present representing the plaintiff or the defendant. There is no legal intermediary or mediator other than Judge Toler. Judge Toler renders her decisions as if she is social worker, psychiatrist, counselor, attorney and mediator all in one. Why don't they call it Judge Toler's Court? I'll tell you why: because "Divorce Court" has a long and illustrious history, and therefore name recognition; Toler doesn't.

In fact, the other day (May 7, 2013), they bought up a couple that were there to seek a "dissolution of cohabitation." What in the fuck is that? Her name was Taiwanekiqua Mackey. That's right – Taiwanekiqua. His name was "Keith." They were two country muthafuckas and she was a walking stereotype: fat, stupid, fake ass hair (red wig) and embarrassing. She's going through his closet and finds two cell phones and she confronts him. He codes the names of the women he has with names like "Sleazy," "crackhead" and so on.

This is how country these niggas were. These two people are supposed to be getting married. They saw a marriage counselor and thought it was cool. Then, on the day of the marriage (at the courthouse), they arrive in separate cars. Waiting in front of the courthouse is Keith's ex-wife. So Taiwanekiqua and this woman get into a fight and the other woman gets her nose broken. Toler's conclusion is "you're a good looking man who takes advantage of women … Miss Mackey, he is who he is, and once he shows you, it's your bad if you stay with him … You can't fix it, you can't make him be what you want him to be. Those kind of men don't make good mates."

See? Toler is no better than some skank on the street who thinks that a man is there to be "repaired," "mended" or "fixed." Luckily, in this particular case, there was "no recovery in this matter," as Toler is prone to conclude at the end of most of her cases. Now it's degenerated to the point where at the end of the show, she stares into the camera and lectures to the audience. At one point she was talking about love but it was clear she was talking to women. "If you have to trace him, chase or follow him, then love ain't gonna cut it."

In other words, the show is supposed to make her, she ain't supposed to be trying to make the show. *And yet this is what takes place each week.* She's beautiful and she knows it and it comes across through the camera closeups, her tendency to pucker up when she pronounces certain words, her attempt at a "sister-girl" approach to addressing issues, and a know-it all summation when it comes to "sizing up" the men who come into the court, as if she is an expert.

During the show's commercial breaks viewers are asked, as they were on one show, "Do you think Anthony and Tamika should have ever gotten married?" And then they want you to call in and give your answer and ask you to hang on and listen for some "valuable offers." They're using these shows to peddle wares for various businesses! The point to be made here is who gives a shit what the public thinks? If that's the case, then why do we need her? Why do we need to air "Divorce Court"? People watch that show to get information, not to air their own!

Typical of her commentary are these: "First of all, he brings you no good, he brings you no light. He sucks the air out of the room. You are actively doing each other damage. You damage him and he damages you more, and its shredding up your kids and you can't live like that. It is darkness in your house, it is cold. Mr. Bolen you have no moral code, you really don't. You do what you want when you want. You are cruel. I want you to feel badly about what you've done."

Then why not grant the divorce right then? No, instead she keeps on talking, telling Bolen to "be a better person, don't be what your environment allows you to be." She tells Bolen's wife to make better decisions as well. I don't know what happened to the car, and I don't know whose fault it is. I cannot award you anything. Best of luck to you and your children. There will be no recovery in this matter. It is so ordered." She told one woman who she refused to grant a recovery to that, "you got to have some restraint in your game." Game? Who is this bitch, Iceberg Slim? Far too often she falls back in that ghetto star talk, trying to be hip and sounds like an idiot. At one point when a woman was leaving her man, Toler referred to it as "breaking camp." Who is this bitch, Sergeant Carter?

During one show she was pissed off at a male defendant (again) and said, "I'm so warm – I should go jump in a pool somewhere!" The only reason she said "warm" instead of "hot" is because the viewers might view it the wrong way, because there is no doubt that she thinks she's hot shit and many viewers can see right through her. She is an ego out of control and only deals with legal issues, at most, about 10% of the time.

So then, when all is said and done, what was the point of the show? Why even go to court? After this show the couple got back together and then separated. So of what use is Toler? Is the divorce granted or not?

No wonder the ratings have slipped. But now they have a new hustle. It's called "Divorce Court: Before the Vows Week." Because Toler is screwing up the ratings, they came up with a special week called "Before the Vows." It's a new take on "Divorce Court," which means bringing in couples who are about to marry but are having problems, and this includes using polygraph testing, if necessary. If they can fire Judge Joe Brown, then they should have let Lynn Toler go a long time ago. She thinks she's so fine (and she is), let her deal with the Hollywood casting couch and try to get a reality show or maybe a situation comedy.

Realizing that she had butchered the concept of the original "Divorce Court," in 2013 the name was changed to, "Divorce Court: Before the Vows." How in the fuck are you going to apply for or need a divorce if you're not married? Are they trying to give legitimacy to people who shack up, treating them as if they are "married sorta kinda"?

JUDGE KAREN MILLS-FRANCIS

Bullshit philosophy and hackneyed clichés permeate this woman's statements and this is just the tip of the iceberg. My question when I first saw her was, "who is this bitch?" She looked like a couple of skanks that I fucked back in the day. At any rate, check this out: she's got dyed reddish/blonde hair and she doesn't have on a wedding ring; maybe she's a dyke.

Wikipedia offers some background and insights to the rollercoaster road that appears to follow any mention of Judge Karen and her "shows." The source informs us that "Judge Karen" debuted on September 8, 2008 in 48 of the top 50 U.S. markets. You could have fooled me: I watch a lot of daytime television and I never saw this program listed. Anyway, she presides over small claims court cases, and is just the kind of Jemima that the doctor ordered. She is quoted as saying that, "justice isn't always black and white."

But here's what I noticed the three or four times I watched the show. Not only does she look like some ho off the corner with that blonde-dye job, but she doesn't even respect the court enough to wear the traditional black robe. What does she wear? She wears a burgundy one – burgundy! Her intro tells us that, "She's tough, she's fair, and she cares. Cares about what?

Let me interject a few points here before moving on. First of all, I did some research and found out that in an American court judges are free to select their own courtroom attire. The most common is a plain black robe that covers the torso and legs, with sleeves. Female judges will sometimes add to the robe a plain white collar or a lace jabot. But because America is so homoerotic (while claiming to hate homosexuality) a lot of people don't know that the lace jabot that can be worn by females today used to be worn by male judges back in the 18th century.

What makes this show especially fucked up is that she doesn't respect the traditional process. She allows the litigants to cross-examine witnesses, with a segment at the end where she answers videotaped questions from the viewers. Based on what I can find, this show lasted ONE season, and ended in 2009. I can see why. But wait: don't jack off quite yet.

It was announced later in 2009 that the show would come back under the name, "Judge Karen's Court." But then it was cancelled again. But wait, maybe she turned a successful trick because in November of 2012, it was announced that she'd be back and the title of the show would be Supreme Justice with Judge Karen, in fall 2013.

Typical of some of the crap I heard when checking out her early shows were statements like, "I've never heard of anybody having a quality relationship with somebody they met in a bar." The question is who gives a shit about what you heard. The people are in your court for you to apply what you KNOW. You're a lawyer; you ought to know that "hearsay evidence" it inadmissible in almost all cases. And in the few instances where it is admissible, being in a courtroom talking about meeting men is NOT one of those instances.

Bullshit advice, mixed with attempts at humor, are a part of this show. For instance, during an October 13, 2013 segment, she told a female plaintiff, "Life is too short to have bad pictures of yourself. If there's a bad picture out there you're supposed to get rid of it just like that." Say what? No wonder this bitch has her hair dyed blonde and wears a burgundy robe: she's self-centered, shallow and wants all the attention to on HER! That's why her show is on-again, off-again.

During a November 18, 2013 episode, a man was suing an older Latina, Ms. Melendez for some money he claimed he spent preparing a zoo for her kid. Check this out: this guy delivers goats, rabbits and ponies to homes, fences them in, and charges for the service. The charge is $5,000. The guy comes to the house and picks up the little 10 year old girl to put her on the pony. But when he picks her up he "feels" that she weighs too much. The weight limit, according to the contract, is 75 pounds, and she weighs 78 pounds.

The woman claims that the guy said, "She's too fat" and said it loud enough for the little girl and her friends to hear. The little girl had a fit, ran over to one of the picks, hit it, then ran into the house, slipped and fell, and supposedly broke her hip. The Latina is suing for the medical bills.

But any asshole knows that if she had gone into the emergency room, it would be more than the $198 that she presented. Judge Karen was acting country and confused. At one point when the man said that the little girl hit the pig, Karen said, "she hit a pig in the nose." She did it for laughs because when he initially said it, the audience cracked up. Then, when it was pointed out that she was wrong, she asked the bailiff. He didn't know. She said, "I wasn't listening."

Neither the plaintiff or the defendant bought any evidence: no paperwork, no photos of the little girl, no hospital information (except for a bill for $198). The man had no brochures, business papers, a business card – *nada*. Karen dismissed the case, not only for the lack of evidence, but also because, "I don't believe either one of you. I think y'all just wanted to be on "Supreme Justice With Judge Karen."

When the show was going off the air, the last words to flash on the screen were, "Entertainment Studios," and that said it all. As if I haven't proven it with the rest of these hucksters, that is what these shows were about: not about legal information, not about insight or decision making acumen. It's about entertainment, getting the audience to laugh and/or applaud, about judges screaming the way Judge Judy, Judge Milian and Lauren Lake (the men who are judges – Ferrer, Mathis – do not raise their voices) do.

Judge Mills-Francis: Her Out-of-Court "Advice"

She lasted for a few years, got cancelled and now reruns are picked up by BET. Prior to that, the announcement was made about Entertainment Studios picking up yet another court TV show. According to that website, "Entertainment Studios is adding another court show to our JusticeCentral.TV network with the launch of our newest HD television series "Supreme Justice with Judge Karen." (Entertainment Studios, 2018)

She had several more shows, "Judge Karen's Court", Supreme Justice with Judge Karen" and "Judge Karen" – all were names changes offering the same old bullshit, and all were pretty much cancelled with the quickness. According to Wikipedia,

> ***Judge Karen*** is an American arbitration-based reality court show that aired in first-run syndication and debuted on September 8, 2008 in 48 of the top 50 U.S. markets … As with other court shows, such as *The People's Court* and *Judge Judy*, a retired real-life judge presides over **small claims court cases.** On this show, the judge is Karen Mills-Francis, an African-American woman twice elected Miami-Dade County Court judge, who claims that **"justice isn't always black and white"**. (Wikipedia, 2018 – emphasis added).

First a little background on this little honey blonde-haired (dyed) black woman:

> Born and raised in Miami, Judge Karen practiced criminal defense law in Miami for 13 years in the Office of the **Public Defender**, as well as in **private practice**. After twice being elected as a county court judge, Judge Karen made it her mission to support those at risk of becoming lost in the legal system. Her mission has **always been to empower women** and provide direction and inspiration to children. She is as an ardent backer **of children's advocacy and domestic violence prevention programs**, regularly calling on lawyers to act on behalf of children in crisis. (Entertainment Studios, 2018 – emphasis added)

They skip over the formative years in the previous brief bio. They go from birth to the bench. She was born in Miami. Does that mean she was born in the ghetto or the barrio? Does that mean that she was a ho? What? I want to know what she did in high school and college to get to the level of becoming a judge. What were her parents like? Was she born wealthy or dirt poor? I notice there are no references to a "hard life" or being born or living in a low-income area. Maybe she was born with a silver spoon in her mouth like Judge Judy, Marilyn Milian or Judge Toler.

Notice that her work started off as a public defender. What does that mean? It means you get paid whether you win or lose the case. It means that poor people are coming to you for help and you may or may not give a shit. She claims that she's "made it her mission to support those at risk of becoming lost in the legal system," but where is the evidence? Where are the case studies and examples of what she's done in this regard?

Not only that, but the claim is made about "empowering women." What has she done in that regard? Who can she name who she as "empowered"? She sounds like these white groups that go around telling inner city residents that they are going to "empower" them through cooperation and the only people that end up with power and paychecks are those same peckerwoods. It's like the late Carter G. Woodson once wrote,

> Cooperation implies equality of the participants in the particular task at hand. On the contrary, however, the usual way now is for the whites to work out their plans behind closed doors, have them approved by a few Negroes serving nominally on a board, and then employ a white or mixed staff to carry out their program. This is not interracial cooperation. It is merely the ancient idea of calling upon the "inferior" to carry out the orders of the "superior." To express it in post-classic language, as did Jessie O. Thomas, "The Negroes do the 'coing' and the whites the 'operating'" (Woodson, 1933: p. 29).

And that is the way it continues on today, with white folks buying off Black leadership and using that to control the masses of people who, even to this day, are looking for the coming of a "messiah."

Judge Karen talks about her work in the area of domestic violence and children's issues. It sounds to me like she thinks she's all things to all people. The title of one of her numerous short-lived shows was "Supreme Justice With Judge Karen." Supreme justice? I thought these Christian soldiers believed that their god was the ultimate arbiter? I think this bitch has a God complex and I think her backers and sponsors are projecting her that way. After all, she has "blonde hair", doesn't she?

She says justice isn't always black and white. She's saying what these white folks like to hear because they know full well that it is. Both literally and figuratively speaking, justice is black and white. It is black and white because the white man's power of discretion has made it that way. He sees the world in black and white because when he sees his reality, he sees white as being superior to all other things and beings. How can it not be black and white? Figuratively, white is good and black is bad. Literally, blacks go to jail and do more time than whites even for the same crimes. The data makes this latter reality crystal clear. Judge Karen must be out of her damn mind to make such an asinine statement. Saying what the white man orders us to say (i.e., Pledge of Allegiance, wedding vows) and reading the scripts he hands us in order for us to gain "acceptability" is going to be the downfall of us yet.

Moreover,

> She did not wear the traditional black robe, but instead a **burgundy one**. The introductory sequence showed her presiding over cases, with the announcer saying **"She's tough, she's fair, and she cares"** … The show was produced and distributed by Sony Pictures Television .(Wikipedia, 2018 – emphasis added)

The issue is not the color of the robe you wear. You can wear a green polka-dot robe if you want, but the attire still represents the same thing: white supremacy as the final determinant in all things. But the burgundy flavor is just another example of how American society literally paints things, glosses them over and alters their hue and tint and then tells the public that there is "diversity" in the outcomes. It's called "camouflage" – and all of it ain't jungle green.

The promo claims that Judge Karen is "tough, fair and she cares." What are they supposed to say? "She's a wimp, she'll fuck over you and she don't give a shit"? Come on. In the white man's promotional scheme of things ALL the judges fit this criteria. They may be tough because a disproportionate number of the lititants are people of color. They may care because they make sure they don't allow too much money to be awarded or that the litigants don't sound too smart or sassy. But being "fair" when it comes to issues of race? If that was possible America wouldn't have a history of genocide against First Nation people, enslavement of African people, and a long-time tradition of anti-Latino images and impositions. And we won't even mention the racist Chinese Exclusion Act, the Indian Removal Act and the incarceration of over 110,000 Japanese-Americans.

Continuing with the overview:

> To distinguish itself from **other shows in the crowded field**, *Judge Karen* **permitted litigants to cross-examine witnesses**, with a segment at the end in which **Mills-Francis answers videotaped questions from viewers**.[1] This segment was entitled "Ask Judge Karen" It was announced on January 10, 2009 that *Judge Karen* would not be renewed for a second season … At present, reruns are being televised on the BET Network and TV One network.(Wikipedia, 2018 – emphasis added)

To begin with the reference to the "crowded field" of TV court shows. We have to ask ourselves why this is the case. What is the allure of these televised court TV shows? The public likes to see someone sitting in judgment of other people, and they like to learn how decisions are made and "law" is dispensed. But what the gullible public doesn't realize is that these court TV shows – from Judge Judy, Judge Mathis, the People's Court and Judge Karen – all have in common is that they are all "staged"! These people know about the litigants, they select the litigants, the select the audience, they know what is going to be said and so on. How "fair" can a venue be when it is scripted?

And a new twist for this show: litigants get to cross examine witnesses! Say what?! This isn't even done in the real-life court system! Why would a witness dare testify if he or she is going to be scolded, interrogated or questioned by someone who is on the stand trying to get paid … I mean, trying to get "justice"? This doesn't make any damn sense. Why don't the litigants just keep their asses in their home towns and argue the issue out in the local Wal-Mart or barber shop?

But wait, there's more in the way of "innovation." Judge Karen gets to answer videotaped questions from viewers at the end of the show! Well I'll be. How did they get those videotapes? Who are these "viewers"? What context were the questions framed and answered in? All this makes a difference because the process of questioning is as important as the answer to it: "To divide the process is to deform the product."

More evocative descriptions follow:

> Judge Karen Mills-Francis is known for her f**eisty, full-of-life personality and passionate advocacy for families and children.** Judge Karen Mills-Francis published a book "Stay in Your Lane: Judge

> Karen's Guide to Living Your Best Life." The book draws from **personal experience and her courtroom cases to deliver no-nonsense advice designed to push the reader in a positive direction** — socially, emotionally, physically, and spiritually. (Entertainment Studios, 2018 – emphasis added)

She sounds like a black version of Judge Milian. When the white man describes a woman as "feisty" that means that she's out of control. The definition of "feisty" is, "active, forceful and determined." What female has these attributes and expects to make it in a system that is misogynistic unless she has the "white man's stamp of approval" beforehand. That "feisty" bullshit is a façade that promoters and marketers use to dupe the public into thinking that these women are independent decision makers when they (the backers) know good and damn well that it's all a lie. These women kiss ass, take orders and kowtow just like the males in order to get a paycheck. The anticipated payday is the modern day version of the slave masters whip.

And the title of the book – "Stay in Your Lane" – that sounds to me like the white man's old demand for black folks to "stay in your place." What is "feisty" about complying to that? How is she giving no-nonsense advice when her presence on a bullshit court TV show is the personification of nonsense? And her "out of court advice" sounds to me like the rantings of a scatter-brained circus monkey!

JUDGE FAITH

Petite and super-cute, (a younger version of Marilyn Milian and Lynn Toler), Faith Jenkins is another one who the promotional ads claim has a "no nonsense approach" to meting out her version of "justice" is unique because she looks so damn young. In my view "no nonsense" simply means "no mercy" and that she's going by the white man's book. Any litigant who would appear before this baby-faced bitch has therefore got to be out of their mind

According to her website:

> Originally from Louisiana, Judge Faith graduated with a bachelor's degree in political science from Louisiana Tech University (where she was also the first African-American woman to win the title of Miss Louisiana Tech University) and a J.D. from Southern University law school in Baton Rouge, LA where she ranked #1 in her law class. (Judge Faith website, 2018)

More specifically, she graduated from a high school in Shreveport, and not only one Miss Louisiana Tech University, but "In 200, she won the Miss

Louisiana title and advanced to compete in the Miss America 2001 competition, where she was named first runner-up, winner of the Quality of Life award, and preliminary winner in swimsuit and talent" (Wikipedia, 2018).

So she is aware of her beauty and she took advantage of it – just like Judge Judy, Judge Milian, Judge Toler and Judge Perez. That seems to be a prerequisite for landing one of these shows. You have to look good in addition to having the judicial credentials.

The Faith Jenkins website reads, as follows:

> **Faith Jenkins** is the host of the new daytime court show Judge Faith premiering nationally **September 22, 2014**.Judge Faith's legal career has **spanned over a decade in New York** -- from working as a wall street litigator to a tough New York City prosecutor. **She's worked hard in the face of adversity to overcome obstacles and achieve her goals.** Now she takes the bench in her own courtroom on her own show to resolve disputes between real people with real cases. (Judge Faith website, 2018)

I don't believe much of what was just written. Look at this woman: she is the epitome of beauty. She's smart and obviously energetic. She's won beauty pageants and she cruised through school. My question is: did she do all this without screwing anybody? She has no children, no mention of a husband or boyfriend, and she's just rising up that ladder. So either she's performing behind the scenes with the white boys who have power or she's a dyke, one of the two.

What obstacles could Faith have possibly overcome? She had great parents, she was well-to do and she was physically attractive. And if she had any obstacles that were of merit, why not mention them? You know why? Because there weren't any. She had a silver spoon in her mouth at birth, was probably "daddy's little girl" and got whatever she went after. This in no way diminishes her intelligence or voracity, but the truth is total, not partial. There are people who face REAL adversity and they would resent the claim that this beauty had to face the kinds of trials and tribulations that so many black people, black students and black workers face on a daily basis.

And Faith Jenkins either has a super-agent (never mentioned) or is always at the right place at the right time. Check out the following:

> Judge Faith is also known for her legal and social commentary on television. Prior to signing as a legal analyst exclusively with MSNBC, she has appeared regularly on CNN, Fox News, and HLN to analyze the nation's most high profile cases and legal issues. (Judge Faith website, 2018)

She may be "known for her legal and social commentary", but she had to establish credibility first. Does she have any relevant publications? Did she serve on the Law Review when she was in law school? Does she have any major interviews in quality publications, and not just TV snippets? For a black person to get a position in the area of "commentary" is difficult because a commentary is based on your opinion. White folks usually don't allow that unless that black person is towing the company line. I have more than 2,000 newspaper articles in print and every single one of them were about issues important to the black community and to me. The newspapers were not national in circulation (except for two), but that's my point: for her to do what she's done requires someone standing up for her, someone behind the scenes. And perhaps under her skirt.

When you start appearing on networks as diverse as CNN and Fox News, MSNBC and HLN, then you are "connected." Either that or you are some kind of preeminent expert on some topic. What is Faith's area of expertise that a blond white women would not have been hired for? And that's my point because that's who she's competing against. Were it not for her beauty, all else is par for the course: but she's a looker (like Milian, Perez and like Mablean and Judy used to be), and that speaks volumes on TV, which is a visual medium.

For instance, let's check out the following scenario:

> During the George Zimmerman trial in Florida, **Faith analyzed the trial daily on all three major news networks.** She appeared nightly – from jury selection to verdict — on **MSNBC's PoliticsNation** to discuss witness testimony and opine on the trial's overall progress each day. (Judge Faith website, 2018)

What? The Trayvon Martin killer? She got that gig? Based on what? Is she an expert in homicide detection? What qualified her? When three major networks seek you out, something is going on behind closed doors. Now the fact is, all three major networks are owned by Jews, so those men may have collaborated through their interlocking directorates. But other than that, Faith Jenkins is no more qualified to "opine on" the trial's progress than the man in the moon. Her "opinion"? Based on what? Does she even date black men?

A second point is her appearance on PoliticsNation. Do you know who is the host of that program? None other than civil rights pimp and cockhound Al Sharpton. That's right, I said it. Sharpton hails from that Jesse Jackson mold: pimp the name of Dr. King, land some speaking gigs, scare peckerwoods into boycotting their corporations and then sell out for a show on MSNBC.

But the reason and basis for the "cockhounding" allegation is the way he acted in the Tawana Brawley case back in 1987. Judge Faith would not be the first cute young girl that Sharpton got "tight" with. I'm going to take some time to remind you of that case, using an article from the New York Post, and the role that Sharpton played because this will bring us back around to his "allowing" Judge Faith to appear on his show. So follow the logic.

The December 22, 2012 article about the Brawley-Sharpton incident is headlined, "25 Years After her Rape Claims Sparked a Firestorm, Tawana Brawley Avoids the Spotlight." Sharpton's presence helped make this case one of national prominence because of the lack of proof and some serious allegations lodged against a prosecuting attorney. But let me not get ahead of myself.

The article starts off:

> Twenty-five years after the spotlight first glared on Tawana Brawley — **a black woman who as a teen claimed she was raped by a gang of white men, smeared with feces and stuffed in a garbage bag** — she's desperately struggling to stay hidden from public view. "I don't want to talk to anyone about that," Brawley, 40, said recently after The Post found her in Hopewell, Va., where she lives in a neatly kept brick apartment complex with signs warning of video surveillance cameras. (Garland, 2012 – emphasis added)

The description of the incident was bad enough. But I was teaching at Milwaukee Area Technical College when the news broke and I opened the paper and read about the incident. My first response was the same as it is today: nobody raped this little girl. This is a lie. You will see how I came to my conclusion later in this analysis, and keep in mind the rape, the smearing with dog shit, and the use of the garbage bag.

Continuing:

> By all appearances, her life — so chaotic a quarter-century ago — now seems normal. Brawley, using aliases such as Thompson and Gutierrez, **now has a young daughter**, a neighbor says, and works as a licensed practical nurse at The Laurels of Bon Air in Richmond, **where co-workers were clueless about her past**. (Garland, 2012 – emphasis added)

So because of a fear of her father (I'll get to that in a minute), this girl made up a lie. To begin with, I think Tawana was a ho from the outset. She was worldly, cute and built like a brick shit house. Keep that in mind – she was no innocent virgin who was "defiled." That fear of her father now has her maintaining anonymity and living under various aliases to this very day. So anybody who thinks that child abuse is not important is out of their damn mind. It can traumatize a child long past adulthood. And now she's a single parent herself. What is she going to teach her daughter?

Moving on:

> On a recent Friday, Brawley, noticeably heavier and dressed in pink scrubs, emerged from her apartment at about 6:30 a.m. with a small child and a man wearing red hospital scrubs. The two left in separate cars — Brawley in a Chrysler Sebring and the man and child in a Ford Taurus. She arrived at work in Richmond about 30 minutes later, and the man pulled in minutes afterward. (Garland, 2012)

Of course she's noticeably heavier. She got paid from that "scam." Once Sharpton and the others teamed up, she became a national superstar. And money to someone whose never had it translates into: food, food, food. Not only that, but she got pregnant by some guy and that's not easy weight to lose. The man described above is probably a boyfriend who came in for a booty call and works at the same place she does. He talked her out of her panties and that's the way it goes in the big city.

Now pay close attention to the place where Tawana moved to and lives:

> Hopewell — where Brawley has lived for at least a year, according to a neighbor — has the highest rate of violent crime per capita of any city or town in Virginia, local cops say. Plagued by drugs and guns, it had five murders in the last three weeks. Jittery residents call police at even the slightest suspicion. (Garland, 2012)

In other words, it's a ghetto. This is what she was accustomed to. She was a ghetto star in her own right. And the fact of the matter is, it is probably an area that she was accustomed to from her days as a child because of its proximity to where she grew up. Check out the following:

> State records show "Tawana V. Gutierrez" and "Tawana V. Thompson" have held the same nursing license since 2006. The Virginia Board of Nursing confirmed issuing it to a "Tawana Vacenia Thompson Gutierrez." Brawley maintains a PO box in Claremont, Va., under the name Gutierrez, according to sources. **That town is a 45-minute drive from Hopewell and is the residence of her stepdad, Ralph King, who spent seven years in prison in the 1970s for killing his first wife**.
> (Garland, 2012 – emphasis added)

Reliable studies show that an abused child often gravitates toward the abuser. Could this be the case? Why live so close to her father? Now, you can see that he did time for killing his first wife. Tawana knew about that and he probably beat her ass when she came in late or did anything he didn't like. He may have sexually abused her, who knows? What I do know is that it takes a whole lot of fear to go so far as to run away for four days and then, as a cover or alibi, cut your body up and then tell a massive lie blaming it on a rape by four white boys. More on that in a minute.

The father was a brute and he was violent. According to the article, "Locals in the rural mill town described King, who lives in a ramshackle house near the end of a dead-end street where dogs run wild, as a nasty man and said they hadn't seen Tawana in years. "He's real mean," one man said. King declined to be interviewed." (Garland, 2012) So he lived in a slum akin to where Tawana had moved to. He was a poor man and was frustrated and violent. This is not the kind of person who should be raising any child, especially a young girl who is blossoming into womanhood. Tawana lived in fear more likely than not.

Here is the story she (and Sharpton and others) told the world:

> A quarter-century ago, Brawley, **then just 15**, told a story incredible for its sheer brutality. **After she went missing for four days from her home** in Wappingers Falls, Dutchess County, Brawley **was found in a trash bag on Nov. 28, 1987, dazed, covered in feces and with the words "n—-r" and "b—h" scrawled in charcoal on her body and "KKK" carved into her shoe.** Initially, Brawley said little, simply nodding or writing notes when investigators questioned her and revealing that **she had been abducted by two white men in a dark car who drove her to the woods, where four other white men were waiting.** Details were in short supply. Tawana **couldn't offer names or even a description of the attackers who ravaged her for four days.**
> (Garland, 2012 – emphasis added)

She couldn't provide names because the men didn't exist! But I'll tell you what: whoever was taxing that ass for four days probably made her feel like it was four men! I bet she had a ball: four days of screwing, probably drinking and getting high (they didn't perform a toxicology screen, did they?) and then having to come up with an excuse. Because the guy (or guys) she was screwing were typical teenage cowards, they weren't going to step up and tell a violent old man, "Hey bro. Uh… we was fuckin' your daughter for the past four days so here she is, unharmed. Bye!" No. They put it all on her. A little cutie pie out there to fend for herself – the polar opposite of Judge Faith other than the beauty aspect.

So now, almost two decades has passed since the assassination of Dr. Martin Luther King, Jr., when the poverty pimps like Jesse Jackson, Andrew Young, Ralph Abernathy and others crawled from under their rock and began trying to cash in on King's name. Sharpton, wearing a James Brown hairstyle (and dropping James' name whenever he could) was right out there "talking loud and saying nothing" (as Brown would put it). And since these pimps never met a cause célèbre that they couldn't resist, jumped at the Brawley situation:

> The case attracted attorneys Alton H. Maddox and C. Vernon Mason, and the then-**little-known Rev. Al Sharpton**, who used it to catapult to the national stage. Less than a week after Brawley was discovered, Fishkill Police Officer Harry Crist Jr., 28, was found dead in his apartment. Soon, Brawley's **advisers** would name Crist as a suspect in the rape. And when Dutchess County prosecutor Steven Pagones offered an alibi for Crist, **Pagones suddenly found himself also accused**. (Garland, 2012)

Pointing fingers without a scintilla of evidence. And Mason and Maddox should have known better. Maybe they got a shot at Tawana themselves, who knows? What I do know is that what they were doing was taking shots at powerful men with only little Tawana as a shield. After all, she would get the blame if push came to shove, right?

More specifically,

> Sharpton and Brawley's lawyers claimed — without proof — that Pagones kidnapped, abused and raped Brawley on **33 occasions**. They also **fingered state trooper** Scott Patterson, a friend of Crist and Pagones, who found Crist's body. (Garland, 2012)

Also involved in this, but never mentioned, is the media's fanning of all this bullshit. How can you blame men like this over thirty times for raping a child and not be seriously questioned or ignored? No evidence at all? That's the basis for a libel suit! But as we say in the journalism business, "If it bleeds, it leads," and if what Tawana was describing was accurate, there was a lot of blood during those four days. And every pedophile and pervert of any repute seemed to take a bizarre interest in the case. For instance,

> Brawley became a cause célèbre. **Bill Cosby posted a $25,000 reward** for information on the case; **Don King promised $100,000** for Brawley's education; and **boxer Mike Tyson** gave her a $30,000 watch to ease her pain. (Garland, 2012 – emphasis added)

And here we are three decades later and Cosby, who rarely does anything for black people (other than the ones who attend his homoerotic college, Morehouse College in Atlanta or his wife's alma mater, Spelman) and who toured the country castigating black families, comes up with 25,000. Knowing what we know about him now, he was never concerned about Tawana as a woman because we see what he ended up doing to women (with the help, I believe, of his psychiatrist friend Dr. Alvin Poussaint who could write prescriptions for the drugs that Cosby gave to the women he assaulted).

Don King? When was the last time you saw him with a black woman? In fact, his wife Henrietta died at the age of 87 (she was one year older than King) and she was white. So why would he get involved with the education of a young black woman when his history shows his only concerned for blacks were the exploitation of black boxers ("The Thrilla in Manilla," "The Rumble in the Jungle") and his financial abuse of former heavyweight champion Mike Tyson? And that money for education – all she got out of any education at all (if she ever received the money) was an LPN, a nursing degree. Yay!

And this brings us to Tyson himself. Just four years after the Tawana Brawley incident – July of 1991 to be exact – he was charged with raping a young woman during a beauty contest. And how is a $30,000 watch gong to ease the pain of this young girl? She probably pawned it and split the proceeds with Sharpton, Maddox and Mason.

But the case grows increasingly bizarre:

> **But a grand jury found in 1988 that Brawley was never raped and the whole incredible case was all a hoax**. The panel, which heard from 180 witnesses over its seven-month investigation, found evidence that Brawley **ran away from home and was hiding out in the vacant apartment from which her parents were just evicted** and that she spun her yarn to avoid being punished for staying out late and missing school. **Many believe Brawley feared her stepdad King's wrath and needed an alibi for her absence.** (Garland, 2012 – emphasis added)

There you have it. A young girl with her "own" apartment, missing for four days and probably fuckin' up a storm! Of course it was a hoax. Her father was such a loser that he couldn't do anything about an eviction and from the way the article outlines it, there was a "mother figure" at the house as well. Was it the father's wife? Was it Tawana's mother? The answer is that her mother helped her concoct the lie! While Tawana was on the run, her mother met with her at the old apartment and Tawana told her about the lie. Her mother covered her. But at any rate, it doesn't matter: in either case it is clear that Tawana did what she wanted to do, when she wanted to do it, and threw caution to the wind. And it is also clear that her father was so abusive that this 15-year old girl had to concoct this outlandish lie (probably with the help of the boys who were screwing her) and once it hit the media, the shit hit the fan.

The key lies in the statement that, "Many believe Brawley feared her stepdad King's wrath and needed an alibi for her absence." That's a helluva "wrath" to fear, let me tell ya: and I'm a male! When it was threatened that daddy was going to get in our ass once he got home, we kids were shaking like a Chihuahua trying to shit out a peach seed. Those old school father's didn't play that shit. When we called them "whippings," we weren't bullshittin': a belt, a razor strap, a switch from a tree outside – which you had to go and fetch and other forms of brutality in the name of "discipline." Perhaps her father went too far and then again, there is no mention of her having any brothers or sisters.

But she was young and stupid. She couldn't even get the shit right. Check out the following facts of the case:

> The hateful words scrawled on Brawley's body were upside down — likely written by Brawley herself, and traces of the charcoal-like material were found under her fingernails, the grand jury found. Brawley showed **no signs of genital trauma or exposure**. No semen was found. The feces on her body was traced to her neighbor's dog. One witness said Brawley was seen climbing into the garbage bag. (Garland, 2012 – emphasis added)

Obviously if the words were scrawled upside down, someone would have to be standing over her head and writing them. Perhaps she was giving someone some head while he etched out the evil words, right? No. she did it herself. She didn't even wash her hands – she just left the charcoal under her fingernails. No sign of anyone screwing her and no signs of getting head. The dog shit was traced to the neighbor's mutt. My question is, the neighbor who saw her climbing into the garbage bag: why didn't that muthafucka call the cops *at that time?*

If there was no sign of genitalia trauma or exposure, then why would Sharpton and company continue to promote the "rape" hoax? Where were the medical reports? And yet Sharpton – the man who has now wormed his way into his own television program on MSNBC and the one who invited Judge Faith onto the program – dug himself deeper and deeper. That may explain how he lost all what weight: he was suffering from fear! Check out how he made a bad situation even worse:

> These days, Pagones, still a lawyer but now a principal at a New York-based private-investigation firm, is trying to forget the name Tawana Brawley. But he can't."It'll come up randomly. It'll come up when something happens with Sharpton," he told The Post. In **1998, Pagones won a defamation lawsuit against Sharpton, Brawley and her lawyers. Maddox was found liable for $97,000, Mason for $188,000, and Sharpton was ordered to pony up $66,000, money that was paid by celebrity lawyer Johnnie Cochran and other benefactors.**Brawley was ordered to fork over $190,000 at 9 percent annual interest. None of that has been paid, which brings her total bill to $429,000. (Garland, 2012 – emphasis added)

Sharpton was such a leech that he had to get "financial assistance" from Johnny Cochran and "other benefactors." He talked all that shit and couldn't even pay his bills. Of course Mason and Maddox were probably insured. But because of the grandiosity of these three clowns, that young sister stuck with her lies and had to pay up $90,000 – which she has not done YET! Now the bill, because of the interest accrued, has risen to almost half a million dollars.

What has Sharpton done to allow this important story to slide under the radar? Whose ass has he kissed to get a TV program on a prominent news network called "PoliticsNation," which is really nothing more than his bloviating and babbling and asking loaded questions from guests who are so far to the left that they make Huey Newton look like a Mormon!

> Pagones, who served as Dutchess County assistant district attorney until 1990, continues to search for her."Through her silence, she's as guilty of libel as Maddox, Mason and Sharpton," he said. "The only way to hold her accountable — at least at this stage — is financially.**"Pagones contends that after all these years, Brawley still should publicly state he did not rape her**."I absolutely think she was manipulated by Mason, Maddox **and Sharpton**," he said. "But even if at the time she was being victimized by them, 25 years have gone by. At any time she could have told someone, 'I want to tell the truth.' To me, she's no longer a victim." (Garland, 2012 – emphasis added)

She's changed her name, but thanks to the article being quoted from, she was eventually located. Sharpton, in the meantime, has cut and run. And rightfully so:

> **Pagones blames Sharpton more than anyone else for his troubles**. "I don't ever expect him to say he's sorry, but he should at least come clean and admit that, after the trial, that now he knows Steven Pagones had nothing to do with Tawana Brawley," Pagones said. Pagones is correct: **To this day, Sharpton remains unapologetic**. (Garland, 2012 – emphasis added)

Of course he does. It was Brawley's lie, not his. He just rode that lie to national prominence by playing the role of super negro. Maddox was disbarred from practicing law in 1990 and Mason was disbarred in 1995 for, get this, "66 incidents of professional misconduct against 20 clients"! All three men were scam artists who got paid but in the end only two of them – Maddox and Mason – was actually punished for that national hoax. Sharpton got away scott free.

His refusal to apologize for his lie? Check out the "reverend's" explanation:

> "**Does Donald Trump** owe the Central Park Five an apology? He advocated in the Central Park case what he believed, **I advocated what I believe,**" he told The Post, referring to Trump's full-page ads demanding the death penalty for five teens accused — and eventually exonerated — of raping a jogger in Central Park. Pagones remains undaunted. (Garland, 2012 – emphasis added)

It is so appropriate that Sharpton would compare himself to Donald Trump. The article appeared four years before Trump would run for and win the Presidency, but if there is one thing that the American public has learned it is that Trump is a pathological liar. Want proof? On May 9, 2018 CNN reported the following:

> The Washington Post's Fact-Checker blog has been keeping a strict count of President Donald Trump's many misstatements, untruths and outright lies. And, over the weekend at a rally in Michigan, Trump hit a(nother) milestone: **He topped 3,000 untrue or misleading statements in 466 days in office. That means that, on average, Trump says 6.5 things that aren't true a day. Every. Single. Day.** (Trump is actually picking up the pace when it comes to not telling the truth; he has averaged nine untruths or misleading statements a day over the past two months, according to the Post's count – emphasis added)

That's a lot of lyin', folks. And there you have it – Sharpton earlier comparing his situation with the lies of Trump. And as the old saying teaches us, "Dress a liar as you will/A liar is a liar, still." And I'm willing to bet that since King was assassinated in 1968, Sharpton has told as many lies as Trump, hands down.

Why did I go through all that when this section of the book is supposed to be about Judge Faith? I do so to make comparisons: young pretty girls attract Sharpton's attention. Faith Jenkins didn't deserve to appear on a national program like Sharptons, regardless of how poorly it is done, and spew forth views on Trayvon Martin! But she was exploitable and isn't that what Sharpton did to Tawana Brawley?

Back to Judge Faith's background

> Judge Faith started her legal career in the New York office of Sidley Austin — one the nation's most prestigious law firms — where she represented high-profile clients in a diverse array of complex, commercial matters. Her practice included defending class action securities fraud lawsuits, white- collar/regulatory investigations, breach of contract disputes, and other types of high-stakes litigation. (Judge Faith website, 2018).

So far her life has been nothing but a protected, elitist and somewhat upper middle class existence. When she got out of law school she continued this tendency, although she had several choices. Her values are as Eurocentric as they come. But then came a change – a move to "the dark side," literally and figuratively speaking:

> **After five years as a wall street litigator**, Faith joined the Manhattan District Attorney's office as a criminal prosecutor. As a prosecutor, Faith handled hundreds of criminal cases and was the lead attorney in numerous jury trials. **Her work included indicting and prosecuting a multitude of violent crimes such as gang assaults, robberies, burglaries, kidnapping, drug sales, and firearms cases**. (Judge Faith website, 2018 – emphasis added)

So her real introduction to black people inside the system were as criminal defendants! She worked on Wall Street and met her own kind (bourgeois negroes) and worked in the D.A.'s office where she sashayed back and forth in front of white boys all day, but then she went into prosecution where she gave niggas time like it was lunch.

And this was where she got the "grit" that she then added to her otherwise elitist resume. For instance, check out the following excerpt from her website:

> **As Miss Louisiana 2000 Faith Jenkins became a distinguished young leader in America**. After placing **1st runner up at Miss America 2001**, Faith gained a national presence and began traveling extensively addressing **important issues facing her community and our nation**. She has addressed notable **academic institutions, business executives, state agencies, political groups, and student organizations**. Faith has served as a **positive role model for thousands of young people** by telling her personal story of perseverance and determination. (Judge Faith website, 2018 – emphasis added).

This is one of those "niggerlogist" resumes. Let's look at the bullshit that you have to win or be a part of in order to qualify. First, beauty contest competitions. You don't necessarily have to win because the people sponsoring them figure if you're a big enough egotist to sign up, and a big enough slut to prance around in a swimming suit with pumps, then you're just the kind of "desperado" that qualifies for the "brass ring" qualifications.

After that you tour and the claim is that you address "important issues facing her community and our nation." Notice it says HER community (which they assume is a black one) and OUR nation (meaning the white man's). So what can these presentations be about other than teaching kids how to kiss ass and kowtow and to "strive for success." In America when you hear the word success, you know that the white man is doing the defining and the criteria revolves around how well you serve or will be able to serve HIS system.

Then look at who she spoke to: areas that have a long history of denying and working to re-define the black cultural existence. You have academic institutions where kids go to learn how to think, act and promote whiteness and white values. You have business executives, a room full of drunk old white men who are looking at her legs and tits and wondering how much she'd charge to head up to the hotel room afterwards for a "quickie." You have state agencies where she tells those with some semblance of power to dole out as many food stamps as they can because if she sounds too confrontive, they'll kick her young-looking ass out of the building.

She claims to have spoken before political groups. Oh yeah? Which ones? Black Republicans? Black Women Who Hate Black Men? The United Dykes of America? Name them if you did it! Give it a name! And student organizations. She may look like one of them in terms of her baby face, but she's going to be giving that old "rah-rah-ree/kick 'em in the knee/rah-rah-rass/ Kick 'em in the – other knee" type presentations. She will lie to them and say "If I can do it, you can do it." But she won't finish the sentence. The means "you can do it" if you have what I have: incredible looks, a wealth background, contacts, a network, and the ability to get through law school.

She supposedly did all this "during her year of service." But that's not all. Pay close attention to the following:

> **During her year of service** she spoke to students in some of the most **economically depressed areas of the nation**, motivating them to **overcome life's obstacles and pursue their dreams**. In an effort to reach out to teens most in need of an encouraging word, Faith took her message one step further: **juvenile prisons and boot camps where hundreds of young people were confined.** (Judge Faith website, 2018)

They let this bitch go into the ghetto and into juvenile detention centers and spread that bullshit? She went in there looking like that and is going to try to convince those bruthas and sistahs to pick themselves up by their own bootstraps? Based on what – because she says so??? This is bullshit. She never went into any economically depressed area without a police escort and plenty of backup. I say this because if they did and she got her ass kicked, the Beauty Pageant people would be liable for it! Give it a name!

She has some talent it would seem. After all, the website claims the following:

> Faith not only placed first runner up to Miss America 2001 – she also made history. She remains the only contestant in the pageant's history to be awarded all three of the following awards: swimsuit, **talent (after singing Nancy Wilson's classic "If I Could"),** and the coveted "Quality of Life" national community service award for her volunteer work in literacy and education. (Judge Faith website, 2018 – emphasis added)

What?! She won a talent award for singing a song that came out before she was born? Well when I read that I had to check out the lyrics to find out why they appealed to the white judges. Following are those lyrics from Nancy Wilson's 1988 song, "If I Could:"

> If I could
> I'd protect you from the sadness in your eyes
> Give you courage in a world of compromise
> Yes, I would
>
> If I could
> I would teach you all the things I've never learned
> And I'd help you cross the bridges that I've burned
> Yes, I would
>
> If I could
> I would try to shield your innocence from time
> But the part of life I gave you isn't mine
> I've watched you grow, so I could let you go
>
> If I could
> I would help you make it through the hungry years
> And I know that I could never cry your tears
> But I would if I could
>
> If I live
> In a time and place where you don't want to be
> You don't have to walk along this road with me
> My yesterdays don't have to be your way
>
> If I knew
> I could try to change the world I brought you to
> Now there isn't that much more that I can do
> But I would if I could

A tear jerker, sung by a woman as lovely as the original singer of the song, singing about the fact that they CAN'T do what they claim to want to do. These women didn't want to change the world and the white boys who wrote the song knew that whoever sung it was singing about some kind of fantasy trip. After all, hope without a plan is a dream. And the "dreamy" Faith Jenkins chose a song that would make people want to open up their hearts to this beautiful young women, so the white man gave her a talent prize.

So what is she doing now? According to her website,

> Faith remains active in the Miss America Organization and judges state preliminaries every year. To date, her judging experience includes **Miss Texas, Miss Mississippi, Miss Washington, Miss Virginia, Miss Maryland, Miss Kentucky, Miss Louisiana, Miss Pennsylvania, Miss New York, and Miss Kansas, among others**. Faith has also judged the national Miss America Teen competition in Orlando, Florida. (Judge Faith website, 2018)

Well ain't that a bitch? This activist who's supposed to be so committed to low income areas and helping out locked up kids has the time to take an all expense paid trip all over the nation to judge other women who have fallen into the same egotistical and misogynistic trap that she fell into. What is the criteria for judging? Who has the biggest tits? The longest legs? The nicest extensions? What? Give it a name!

JUDGE GREG MATHIS

Having abused both alcohol and drugs during my incredible lifetime, I was able to kick the habit because of my ego. I realized that both of these substances were preventing me from becoming the superstar that I was destined to be. Unfortunately, not too many black people have that kind of self-esteem and therefore submit to the drug addictions that permeate our community.

Judge Mathis claims to have been in the streets, to have used drugs, to have gotten "locked up" and then he turned his life around and went to college and got his degrees and to law school where he became an attorney and, of course, a judge. But here's my point: sometimes you can say you "kicked the habit" but some of your statements and mannerisms clearly show that perhaps there are some residual effects of those habits.

This brings us to Mathis. In a number of his shows he does offer paid assistance to those who are on drugs, and he claims that he can tell if someone is "on drugs" or more clearly, a "Crackhead." But in doing so his show, like the other court TV shows, are providing an audio-visual record of the idiots who appear before them, people who either admit guilt or are found guilty and in doing so offers a posterity for all to see in the generations to come.

Mathis is not objective as the law claims to be. He is subjective and makes many of the people the butt of his jokes in the same way Judge Judy makes those who appear before her the target of her insults. Mathis calls out people who may be down on their luck and may be involved in drug problems by shaming them. He thinks that by calling them out like that, he hopes to shame them into getting help. But on other shows he begins to pry into those who are involved in drugs, asking them if they "bought a rock," or "did you buy a gram?" During one program he used his gavel to simulate a crack pipe and showed, right there on television, how said pipe is used. On another one while using the gavel and making the lighting of the crack in the pipe mannerisms, he added the commentary, "Beam me up, Scottie" and added, "Feel like you're on another planet!"

Mathis' involvement with these kinds of questions is more than just convincing the audience that he's from "the streets." But the intensity with which he poses these questions and makes statements gives me the impression that he may well still be taking an occasional "hit" or two.

You might ask, what was Mathis locked up for? According to his story, he was put away for seven years for possession of a firearm. He further claims that he got out of prison, went back to school and with the help of a number of programs, was able to get into college. He then got more help and somehow got into law school where he not only got his degree but is now a judge. In other words, he's a charity case and often looks down his nose at the losers in front of him, continually promoting that "Jesus saves" bullshit while also implying that college education is the key to success and so on.

But on his show he wants to sound like he's still in love with the streets. When people come before them he gives out tips on how they could have refined or improved their crimes; he defines and outlines the "dope game" and what they could have done better; he glorifies the "street game" and the "thugs" and lambastes those who make mistakes and come off more looking like suburban commandoes. And it goes on and on. I learned a long time ago that a crack head can never stop thinking or talking about crack, and will steer conversations into that subject area. That is exactly what Mathis does: he misses the streets and I conclude that he's still out there. He's just more careful this time around.

Moreover, he is like a number of Americans who don't see smoking weed as a big deal. He says it right there on television. And while I agree with him, I do think that this statement goes against his anti=drug theme. Furthermore, during one show he told a woman that her eyes turned hazel when she was smoking weed and then said that his own wife leaves the house and her eyes are brown but comes back with them hazel, suggesting that she may well be taking a hit off a joint herself.

And as for his relationship with his wife, it is clear that he is the bitch. I don't even think they sleep together. He talks about her as if she calls all the shots and runs his life.

BACKGROUND

Mathis is from Detroit, which he claims in the introduction of his show is a "city with a lot of love." Yeah – they love to rob yo' ass if you're stupid enough to be on the streets after 10:00pm! All kidding aside, this background information is from the internet and I'll use it to provide some insights on this weird man before moving on.

According to this particular site called Get Net Worth (2013) it claims,

> Judge Greg Mathis is a judge and writer with a net worth of $14 million. Judge Greg Mathis has earned his net worth through his career as a superior court Judge in the 36th district of Michigan, as an assistant to city council member, Clyde Cleveland, his running of the east side's city hall for Mayor Young, and with his reality courtroom show, "Judge Mathis." He is also the author of "Street Judge" and "Of Being a Judge to Criminals and Such," as well as having a video game in the works, entitled, "Mathis: Detroit Street Judge." He was born in Detroit, Michigan. Judge Greg Mathis Salary What is Judge Greg Mathis' salary per year? $5 million (GetNetWorth, 2013)

It seems to me that Mathis is trying to be all things to all people. He tried to be a baller on the streets. He went to prison for that. He got out and went to a community college and then, with references, somehow got into law school. Of his educational background I found out the following:

> Once out of jail, Mathis began working at McDonald's, a job he needed to keep in order to maintain his release on probation. A close family friend helped Mathis get admitted to Eastern Michigan University, and he discovered a new interest in politics and public administration. He became a campus activist and worked for the Democratic Party, organizing several demonstrations against South African Apartheid policies. He graduated with a B.S. in Public Administration from the Ypsilanti campus and began to seek employment in Detroit's City Hall. He also became a member of Alpha Phi Alpha fraternity. (Wikipedia, 2018).

Mathis undoubtedly put in work and gradually crawled his way up through the college ranks.

> Mathis was denied a license to practice law for several years after graduating from law school because of his criminal past. He received his J.D. from the University of Detroit Mercy in 1987. In 1995, he was elected a district court judge for Michigan's 36th District, making him the youngest person in the state to hold the post. During the five years he was on the bench, he was rated in the top five of all judges in the 36th District; there are about thirty judges each year (Wikipedia, 2018).

When you see him on television today, it is clear that he wants the world to know about his past. He wants everyone to know he dealt drugs and he gives out tips on how to be a gigolo. He talks about crack cocaine as if he is still craving it. But he did what he had to do to get his shot:

> Greg Mathis (born April 5, 1960) is a retired Michigan 36th District Court judge and syndicated television show judge. His show Judge Mathis is produced by Telepictures Productions, and distributed by Warner Brothers. It is seen five days a week in most television markets in North America. A spiritually inspired play, Been there, Done that, based on his life toured twenty-two cities in the U.S. in 2002, and Inner City Miracle, a memoir was published by Ballatine Books. (GetNetWorth, 2013)

And Fox News has some cities where only TV court shows are dominating. In Omaha, for instance, the lineup, starting at about noon, is "Court With The Cutlers," "Judge Greg Mathis," "The People's Court" and "Judge Judy." One after another, all making utter asses out of litigants.

Another site, radar online (2014) offer the following:

> TV judge Greg Mathis was once busted for carrying a pistol and faced a life of crime until his mom motivated the 17-year-old high school dropout to change. He says: **"I was sitting in jail when my mother begged me to turn my life around because she'd been diagnosed with cancer and had only 12 months to live. I'd been in college three months when my mother passed away."** (radaronline, 2014)
> (Order In The Court: 10 Secrets & Scandals Of TV's Judges EXPOSED! (Chloe Millar,
> Posted on Mar 31, 2014 @ 3:22AMhttp://radaronline.com/photos/order-in-the-court-10-secrets-scandals-of-tvs-judges-exposed/photo/638584/)
> (radaronline, 2014 – emphasis added)

Greg Mathis is definitely a mama's boy, and thanks to some of the deferential references he makes regarding his wife, he must be the kind of guy that fears and obeys females. He must be given credit: he turned his life around. But that in no way excuses what he does in that courtroom five days a week.

THE MATHIS WEBSITE

I add the Mathis website to what I have already shared because it is filled with the same type of syrupy bullshit that permeated the website of Judge Faith Evans. All these negroes talk about working their way up, but once they get there most of what they do is the kind of thing that PAYS. If you open a school you get reimbursed because it's nonprofit; if you start an organization you can get grant money because the donations are tax-deductible. These are the "tidbits" that you wouldn't know unless you were smart enough to pick up a book written by someone with my background and experience. And as you know "where much is given, much is expected."

So let's go through this website and see what it says about Judge Greg Mathis. It begins, thusly:

> About Judge Greg Mathis
> The real-life story of Judge Greg Mathis is heartwarming and inspirational. Greg dropped out of school and was in and out of jail and then overcame these adversities to become the youngest judge in the history of the state of Michigan (Mathis website, 2018)

Quite admirable, no doubt. In fact, his rise may be the most remarkable of all the other TV Court judges. But it's the end result, the outcome that must be dealt with because that is what the litigants are exposed to on national television five days a week. Continuing:

> The inspiration for his own TV court show, the Judge's personal story is also the subject of a book, "Inner City Miracle," released by Ballantine/One World Books in October 2002. Judge Greg Mathis, along with writer Blair Walker, co-wrote the autobiography to document his triumph over odds. The memoir takes a candied look at his triumph over odds. The memoir takes a candied look at the Judge's rise to success from the projects of Detroit. The success of the book earned Judge Greg Mathis the prestigious Blackboard Non-Fiction Book of the Year Award in May 2003. (Mathis website, 2018)

Like Judge Faith Jenkins, Mathis appears to be making the rounds as some kind of "celebrity. According to his website,

> Judge Greg Mathis has been called upon as a regular contributor to national television programs, including "Larry King Live," "Politically Incorrect," "CNN's 'Talk Back Live'," "Showbiz Tonight," and "Extra" to discuss his opinions on complex issues of the day, such as national

> security, unique sentencing, affirmative action and celebrity scandals. Judge Mathis also offers his take on high-profile legal cases (Mathis website, 2018).

He has been no "regular contributor" to any of these shows. He may appear sporadically – every couple of months, maybe four times a year. So the website is lying and embellishing. The fact is, Mathis is one of a long line of "negroes" who come in to talk about race issues. Like Al Sharpton, Michael Steele, Van Jones, Eugene Robinson, and several others, they are given questions, a time limit and then they're out of town by sundown.

Moving on:

> **Judge Greg Mathis has become a household name with a broad and loyal following.** He has enjoyed **major media exposure**, appearing on **numerous** television shows while being featured in **many** magazines, and other national and local press across the country. Mathis continues to **hit the streets in an effort to help others**, joining the fight for various causes and **drawing national attention and throngs of supporters** (Mathis website, 2018 – emphasis added).

Mathis must have written the previous snippet himself. There are no specifics. If he's appeared in so many magazines, why not mention if he made the cover or not? Why not name the magazines or be specific about the "national and local press" that he's been in? How many is "many" and "numerous"? What you just read was a public relations media release and it points out that Mathis' fame is the key. He's put in a lot of work but in my view it is overshadowed and neutralized by the dumb shit he says and does on his daily court show. I offer numerous examples later in this book.

Moreover,

> In October 2003, Judge Greg Mathis appeared in the stage play, "Tell It To The Judge," an inspirational piece about a young man whose future is undetermined because of his criminal past. The character played by Mathis, based loosely on his life, sees his own negative past in the young man and decides to mentor him. **This role, which paralleled his own life-story, gave Judge Mathis another opportunity to help change lives** (Mathis website, 2018 – emphasis added)

What? It sounds like one of those bullshit church plays that take place in every city of reasonable size. These church people get together because somebody in the congregation thinks they can be a playwright. The play is predictable and without real substance, on-going references to Jesus and God, but never any solutions. Everybody wants to be August Wilson but they don't want to put in the work and research that Bro. Wilson put into his great plays, all of which left a memory mark in the mind. These plays don't mean shit except to the locals who are usually charged a fee to get in.

Again, whatever that play projected is surely neutralized by the things that Mathis says on his television show. He calls junkies or former junkies "crackheads" and tells them that they're "acting crackish." That sounds funny but you know what he's really doing? He's snitching. He's identifying people with problems and even though he offers them help, if they decide to turn it down they've nevertheless been identified on national television. And don't think that the white man is not paying attention.

That is why the following statement really represents somewhat of a contradiction:

> **Judge Mathis is committed to helping troubled youth in and out of the courtroom**. In 1986, Judge Mathis and his wife co-founded a **non-profit youth agency** that serves thousands of young people. **The foundation** counsels youth from the ages of 17-25 about career and job opportunities, provides job training, and offers school and job placement services. **The foundation** has also opened **five pre-schools** in Detroit. In his various fundraising efforts, **Mathis has raised and donated over $2 million** for a variety of civil rights, political, church and youth causes (Mathis website, 2018 – emphasis added)

This is not to put Mathis down, but I call it like I see it and I have experiences and background that most black people will never have. And one of them is having written over $14 million in funded grants and grant proposals. Let me tell you something about the previous excerpt that is not explicitly mentioned.

To begin with, all of what is mentioned generates a revenue stream. It is not done for free. When you see the word "nonprofit," you have to also realize that the paperwork makes it "tax-deductible." If you donate, you get a tax write-off. In other words, free money. When you have a foundation, once again the source of free money, grant money from the feds, the state, the county or the city of Detroit. When you have a pre-school, that ain't free: you charge tuition and you get federal money and since its in Detroit, you probably qualify for the free food program. Again, this ain't out of Mathis' pocket.

So you see where he's "raised and donated" over two million, that ain't shit when you realize that he gets reimbursed on the back end and gets even more back in terms of national attention. These black folks talk all that "helping troubled youth" bullshit and then they point to job training and job opportunities which translates to mean assisting these kids in finding a white man to "adopt" them! Is Mathis creating a job other than for himself and his wife? Probably not. He has contacts and he funnels these kids into a job in a white corporation in exchange for some kind of tax credit or maybe an under the table payoff. Who knows? I do know that in America, social services and poverty are big business. And the white man can always find some "negro" to use as a "buffer zone."

I'm not saying Mathis is an Uncle Tom, because Uncle Tom chose death rather than snitch on his people. I'm saying that he's a conglomeration of his own contradictions – as the following passage bears out:

> Judge Greg Mathis is Chairman of the Rainbow/PUSH-Excel Board, a lifetime member of the NAACP and is a national board member of the Southern Christian Leadership Conference (S.C.L.C.). Judge Mathis is married and a father of four children (Mathis website, 2018).

When I hear the name Rainbow Coalition and PUSH-Excel, I immediately think of Rev. Jesse Jackson. Like Al Sharpton, who I dogged earlier in my assessment of Judge Faith Jenkins, Jackson has been a poverty pimp for a very long time. He was so desperate to "take over" the civil rights movement that no sooner did Martin Luther King Jr., get shot then he was on a plane, King's blood spatter still on his shirt, talking to the nation and basically ensuring the black community that things were under control – which they were NOT.

Jackson and Sharpton fought over who would be King's favorite and I'm going to tell you the truth: ain't neither one of them worth a shit. As for Mathis, if he's associated with any movement at all that has to do with so-called PUSH-Excel, then he's a poverty pimp, living off of grant money and getting paid for his time.

JUDGE GREG MATHIS: OVERVIEW AND ANALYSIS

The narrative to his daily program begins thusly:

> I grew up in Detroit and I'm proud of where I come from. It's a tough city but there's a lot of love there, and I carry that tough love with me as a judge, and I still keep it real. And I carry that tough love with me in my court room in Chicago. I'm Judge Mathis.

Of all the judges analyzed in this short book, I rate Judge Greg Mathis above them all, not only because of his knowledge of law, but because he does do what he says he does in the introduction: he "keeps it real." And by keeping it real, I am talking about his knowledge of the streets, of the "game," of the intricacies of drug abuse and his understanding of male-female relationships. And he shows an insightful and in-depth understanding of the law.

In my view, Greg Mathis could be the best judge of them all because he's articulate, he uses great stories before he makes his decisions, and those decisions are rational and sound. He has a great background of being in the streets and then rising above it and he's from the streets of Detroit, a city that is so fucked up that the movie "Robocop" poked fun at it. The reason why he's not doing better in the ratings (not that he's doing poorly) is probably because he allows plaintiffs and defendants alike to stroke his ego, compliment him on his books and so on.

But it appears to me that as the show gains in longevity and popularity, Mathis becomes more bitch-like, more prone toward comic delivery and most definitely more obsessed with discussions of drugs – or "dope," as he calls it. His on-going references to those who may have used or are using drugs or alcohol is a recurring feature and subject of each show. He also likes to talk under people's clothes, as the old folks call it; that is, if the issue of sexuality comes up, Mathis wants specifics or, in his words, he wants to hear about the "juicy stuff," as he put it during a program aired on November 15, 2017.

Mathis does not hesitate to call someone a "crack head" or a "weed head." He knows the streets and told one young brother one day, "You need to stay off the streets because you don't have what it takes," meaning that the youngblood was lacking in street game. Mathis has been there and done that, and credits his mother with hanging in there with him even when he was a self-admitted thug. The fact that he turned his life around, went to school, got a law degree and is now a television judge speaks volumes about him. Oftentimes I think he's full of shit with some of the things he does, but that could just be the influence of the Jews that are financing his network and his show. So for the most part I still rank him at the top of all the television judges.

"You got anything good you wanna say about me – am I handsome or anything?" he asked during an August 12, 2014 program. Someone appearing before him will tell him that they read his book and then, seeking out compliments he'll ask, "Well, did it help you?" Naturally they are going to say "yes," which translates into more book sales for Mathis. During one show, aired on May 2, 2017, some woman from Chicago presented him with a "pimp cup" and he said that he had "received many gifts on this show" and that this pimp cup was the best. Then the bitch went one step further: she asked for a picture with Mathis holding the pimp cup. He said he'd do it and would have his producer arrange it. A judge who accepts gifts? On the air in front of millions?

But back to that "pimp" stuff, during the July 6, 2017 show he showed his true colors. One brutha was running game on a woman and got some money, but Mathis complained that he was a "popcorn pimp" and that the money he was getting was not enough. At one point he shouts, "You just a popcorn pimp – if you gonna pimp, PIMP!" Later he said, "You ain't pimpin', you scrimpin'." See what I mean? Then, as the case ended and he ruled against the brutha, he told him that he ruled against him because "you got the game backwards!" And then he must have converted back to his other personality when he claimed to the audience that he "was just playing" even as the stupid bitches in the audience, despite having been insulted, applauded loudly.

Mathis is definitely open to flattery as plaintiffs and defendants alike shower him with hosannas or praise about how his book influenced their family, helped out their son, enabled them to stop getting high and so on. He usually falls for it.

A second reason is probably because of his continued references to his street knowledge. Phrases like "I know the game," "You can't run no game on me," "That's the game" and his classic line, "Do you think I'm naïve to the game?" These kinds of quips make him oftentimes sound more like Iceberg Slim than someone with a law degree. He tries so hard to relate that sometimes he sounds like some street corner or jailhouse philosopher than an award winning barrister.

Another thing is that he gives his bailiff, Doyle Devereaux, far more leeway that the other bailiffs get on the other courtroom shows. In fact, it sometimes appears as if they have a comedy act, with Doyle being the straight man and Mathis offering up some street-laced humor.

During the November 18, 2013 airing, some guy, claiming to be a good guy (dressed like a pimp) was suing this black woman for $3,500 that he "loaned" her. She was having a birthday for her son and expected him to keep his earlier promise and pay for the party. He didn't but he did loan her some money. Instead of paying she says she spent the money on her book that she was having published. Mathis accused her of deception. She was suing for breach of contract because he didn't pay for the child's party.

At one point Mathis said, "So you're having sex with him and then when he doesn't pay, you sue him" implying that she was a prostitute (based on the rags she wore to court, she couldn't have been a very successful one). Mathis says, "Independent women these days they don't rely on men to support them for sex." What planet is this nigga from? He said that she saw him as "a cookie jar." The "good Samaritan" helped her out, fucked her and basically had a relationship. But when he stopped coming she got pissed off.

During the show commercials (at least the ones shown in Texas) showing Mathis and a local lawyer named "Brian Longcar: the strong arm" are shown. Mathis is recommending him and introduces himself as "your favorite judge." Longcar then comes on, one hand on Mathis' shoulder, boasting about the excellent legal help he can offer. This commercial does not lend credibility to the image that Mathis conveys as he boasts about being "from the streets of Detroit" and "knowing the game." In fact, this commercial with Longcar, in my view, is another example of "the game."

During the August 27, 2104 program, Mathis' court was out of control as two gay young men were going back and forth at each other. Mathis sat back and watched as the gay defendant called the gay plaintiff, "You evil, pale-faced demon!"

During a November 18, 2013 episode a woman was suing a man for work at his small business she was never paid for. She kept all her receipts. She sent him an email that said, "as long as you owe me this money, I will hunt you down." Instead of viewing this as the possible stalking that it was, Mathis shouts out, "That's right! You're doing the right thing!" What? So what if the guy liked older women? So what if she gave him money and he didn't give her shit? Mathis is always talking about how hip and aware he is of "the game," isn't he. That bitch can't issue a threat about "hunting" somebody down for money. That could be a veiled death threat or at very least a stalking note.

During an August 12, 2014 episode, a Native American woman was suing a Latina and kept making references to a word that Mathis didn't recognize. He asked her if the term was derogatory toward Hispanics. She said no. He asked if it was derogatory toward Latinos – as if that's something different. Again, she said no and he asks her, "Are YOU Latino?" She said no, that she was Native American. Mathis was pissed and told her, "I don't allow any derogatory statements against another race or ethnicity in my court."

During an August 18, 2014 airing, a commercial break poses the question, "Can a paternity test help you collect child support?" So now Mathis is into the same business that Maury Povich, Steve Wilkos and the show "Paternity Court" are into. Everybody wants to be a "champion" for these women who come forth begging for child support. There should be show called "Child Support Monitors" where these bitches are followed when the check comes in the mail to see just what they are spending it on, or, when the welfare check comes, follow them and see if they're spending it on the child as they are supposed to be doing.

Ariel Whirley of Grand Rapids came in. She paid the defendant for a car that didn't work. Cory McGill says she has a split personality. He didn't believe he owed her shit. She starts off by thanking him for helping her cousin on an earlier show. She's a street bitch with a low cut blouse and extensions. She shakes her head to her hair can move – you know, that type. She says she feels intimidated. His argument is that she is crazy and has a split personality. He calls her "a straight gangster." He talked about her like a dog.

She's a drunk and a big mouth in real life, if we are to believe McGill. They're neighbors but he doesn't know why she acts this way. She has a split personality named Diamond. She says she owes him three thousand dollars for a car, a Chevy Malibu, 2004. He brought it to her house and she took it to a mechanic who said it was fine. She gave him the money, she says. She didn't get the title and he said he didn't have it. He had to get it out of his brother's name into her name. he brought her a title with a girl's name on it – his baby's mother's name. She has the car but has no title.

A few days later the woman says he wasn't supposed to sell the car. And she and Ariel argue. She goes out and sees two guys trying to break into her car late at night. She says it was God who woke her up. She turned on the lights and called Cory. Cory tells her not to call the police. She was going to move the car but he told her not to. Later that morning she moves it to her mother's house. Cory asks where the car is. He then asks her to give the car back and she wants him to return her money. He never did show up. She made him sign a promissory note and he signed it and she gave him the car. Early in July he still hasn't shown up.

He's shopping and she sees him. She confronts him and he pushes her. She's at his door banging and kicking, which is why they are in the court. The judge said that he and his brother conspired against her to run the scam after hearing both sides. There was too many coincides on Cory's side of the story. His brother sold his baby's mother's car and she reported it stolen. Hence, Judge Mathis' conclusion. At one time Mathis told him, "Your game is weak, sir … You're not a middle man, you're a con man."

Mathis' courtroom if often out of control because he gives both the plaintiff and the defendant far too much freedom to make their respective cases. They are on TV and trying to front and they make asses out of themselves (the goal of these types of shows) and Mathis stirs the pot with on-going references to his knowledge of dope sales, the pimp game and in his words, "do you think I'm naïve to the game"? He often falls back on his own personal life where he rehashes how his mother was understanding as he ran the streets and how he finally got himself together on the streets of Detroit and went to school, became a lawyer and then a judge. A truly incredible story.

But since he did all these things and even has several books to his credit, one has to wonder why he is so impressed or awed when a plaintiff or defendant prefaces their comments with how impressed they are with him, how they read his book or how they were inspired to change their lives and so on. He acts like an under aged bitch standing outside of the Greyhound station being sweet talked by a pimp. His wife often sits in the audience, obviously to keep him from cock hounding the bitches who are continually flirting with him. On the days she's not there, you can tell, because he's throwing double-entendres and veiled "raps" to cute bitches who stand before him.

Mathis seems to be the type of brutha who was raised by and around women. When he does his little skits and impersonates the female voice, he does too good of a job. During one episode aired in July of 2016 (probably a re-run), the subject was "in-laws" and he started out on one of his rants about his mother-in -law.

According to the story he shared, his mother in law comes into the room and starts pointing at things saying, "that is mine," and just takes it. He says he is sitting right there and doesn't say a thing. Then, after the laughs, he claims that she's a good person and they get along just fine. But you can tell that he didn't just make that shit up.

During an airing on June 23, 2017, he was in one of his "gut-spilling moods." He said that he met his wife when she was a freshman in college and he was a junior. They got married five years later and now, 35 years later they are still together. But on the internet You Tube, Mathis appeared on the Wendy Williams radio show and dogged her out about some things she alleged in her book. He told her that he never used or sold drugs, but was just "a thug." He also said that her claim that he didn't sleep with his wife was not true. Judging from how homoerotic this guy can get from time to time, including certain mannerisms, I wonder about that latter point.

During an episode aired on July 11, 2016 (perhaps a re-run), he shared some additional personal information. According to Mathis when he was attending a community college while in Detroit, he couldn't afford to live in a dorm on campus so he moved into some public housing. According to him, all he had was a fold-out couch and he admittedly had roaches. He says that when his girlfriend (now his wife) would come by, she was shocked because was middle class and wasn't used to that kind of squalor. His point was that people like the plaintiff and defendant who were standing in front of him, sometimes go through rough patches together and that if they can survive it, the relationship tends to get stronger.

Another time he was talking about how he courted his wife and "at the time I was a crook." He shared about how the mother of the woman "gave me a chance" and he changed his ways. Again, it is clear that although Mathis is street smart and charismatic, the "game" that he recognizes has all too often consisted of game that was run on him by females.

During an August 10, 2016, Mathis' wife was in the audience. She is nice looking but, if you want my opinion, appears somewhat slutty. Too much makeup, fake eyelashes and her hair dyed brownish-red (auburn). She looked nice, had on some expensive earrings, but I've been around enough bitches to be able to spot a potentially dangerous one when I see her. I then realized why she was in control of the money, doled out an allowance to him, and "allowed him" to go out on Friday and Saturday nights: it's because she is the one in control. When you see the two of them together, you'll see what I mean.

During the December 19, 2106 telecast, the issue was a white woman suing the son of a white man who she was "with" because she was in the will. In response Mathis made the statement that "separate accounts" between spouses is not unusual. He added, "my wife has a couple of accounts that my name ain't on."

Then, "and I got some that her name ain't on." He tried to cover it up by saying that with couples, the woman has a separate account to pay for clothes and the man has a separate account to spend at the strip club. My question is: what kind of perverted relationship does Mathis have with his "wife"?

During an August 10, 2016 "Throwback" segment, a kid is on and the man who raised him is there. The kid doesn't appreciate the fact that the man, according to Mathis, is a mentor. "He's raised you, he's been nice to you and he looks good," Mathis explains. Then he looks over at the rather tall brutha and says,"You killin' today, baby! Woooo. You killin' today." This is in reference to the man's white suit and the fact that he looked rather dapper. But Mathis' reaction was not like that of a black man giving another one a compliment; Mathis sounded very much like a fag with these comments and the actions he exhibited while making them.

He does "keep it real" as he says during the introduction of his show. His moral advice is a combination of that from big mama and a high school principal. There is no doubt that he has game and is intelligent. But for the most part his show is good because he sometimes gets out of control and he and his bailiff, a white boy named "Doyle," crack jokes and often insult the people standing before him. I've heard him refer to people as "crack head," "dope fiend" and "prostitute," claiming that he does it to embarrass them into seeking help and getting therapy which, by the way, he offers to them if they agree that they want or need it.

During a show aired on March 9, 2016, we found out some interesting things about Judge Mathis, which he had occasionally shared on other shows. It has to do with his wife who oftentimes sits in the seats and watches the show with the rest of the gallery. There is apparently a reason for that.

According to this man who "keeps it real," his wife takes all of his money and when he wants to go out somewhere she questions him and he has to tell her. Not only that, but she has his credit card and when he wants to buy something he has to ask for permission. What kind of bullshit is this? What kind of pussy does this bitch have to make a man this intelligent and this eligible for pussy cater to her needs? I'll tell ya: I saw her once when she was sitting in the audience and she ain't nothing to brag about, let me tell ya.

But the reason why she sits there on occasion – and on several occasions had a friend or relative sitting in her seat when she couldn't make it – is because she thinks (or probably knows) that a lot of the females who appear in Mathis' court are sluts or, at very least, are searching for a man. They compliment him, bat their extended eyelashes and flirt and his wife sees this shit. So she makes sure that Mathis doesn't creep up on any post-production pussy and plops her ass right there in the seats whenever she can. And as I discussed earlier, according to him, she's in charge of the family finances – meaning *his*.

Mathis may either have a problem with his sight or be an outright liar. During a show aired on September 25, 2017, there was a case in front of him but before he turned to the defendant he said he wanted to make an announcement. He asked an older gentleman who was seated in the back of the gallery, "Mr. Warren Powers," to stand up. The man on a green jacket, an orange shirt and a white t-shirt. Mathis said that Powers was someone that he'd known a long time and that they went way back together. Then suddenly, another man in the FRONT row raised his hand causing Mathis to immediately recant, "That's not Mr. Powers, HE'S Mr. Powers." The first guy that Mathis asked to stand up was the wrong man! The correct man was sitting right in front of Mathis and Mathis didn't recognize him. So either he was telling a damn lie about knowing Powers for a long time or he's as blind as a bat, even with those thick ass glasses on. You be the judge.

Another thing about Mathis that I disagree with is his tendency to promote religion. During one show aired on August 24, 2016, two women were before him and one charged the other one with being a drinker and a whore and then going to church on Sunday. Mathis responds by saying, "she's a member of a big club, there's a lot of people who do that." But then he added, "That's what she's supposed to do. If you break the law or do something bad, go to church the next day." What? Is this nigga daft?

And talk about a mama's boy! If someone says something negative about another person's mother, Mathis goes ballistic! He simply doesn't want people talking about other people's mother. Why not? If it's part of the case, people have the right to air their opinions when they want to. But see: he knows he's on national television and since he's a mama's boy, it is his natural inclination to defend the mothers of the world. I say fuck that: if somebody's mama fucks up, then she needs to get told! There's too many bitches walking around here and just because they gave birth to a kid – which, by the way, you had no choice in – they think they deserve a free pass. Not on my watch, bucko!

Judge Greg Mathis also gives away a lot of money in his decisions, too. In my view Judge Mathis settles more cases in terms of monetary amount requested than Judge Judy and Marilyn Milian *combined.* Judge Judy is, of course, the most chickenshit with the fines or monetary penalties because, after all, she is a Jew. Milian appears to be the second most stingy, but that is strange because she frequently makes references to the properties she owns and manages, so the bitch ain't broke. Mathis knows what people go through and a number of the people who appear before him are low-income and minority. He awards large sums and if a person has some kind of personal problem – a need for marriage counseling, personal counseling, alcohol or drug counseling – he makes arrangements for them to get it. In other words, he not only talks the talk, but it is clear that he also walks the walk.

During a show aired on February 22, 2016, the plaintiff is suing some bitch named Diamond Johnson. Both are from Chicago and the plaintiff says that Johnson "lives from couch to couch." When Mathis asked if that meant that she was homeless, the plaintiff said that Diamond was not stable and did not have a house. When Mathis was told that they were from Chicago, he quipped that, "They got a lot of empty houses on the west side," causing Doyle to add, "Yeah, you can get 'em for a dollar!" See what I mean?

Here's another one. On a show aired on November 18, 2016, these two fat black bitches are suing one another. They are about as country as you can get. The plaintiff (Dominqua Wright) is suing because the defendant, who used to live with her, used to drop her six kids off at her house, borrow her car and leave for days at a time. Once when she left she wrecked the plaintiff's car and guess what she did? She and another friend got a crow bar, went out and looked for another car, popped the headlight that needed repair from the plaintiff's ride, put it back on and brought it to her!

In court, the plaintiff produced a text where the same defendant vowed that "when we get out of court" she was going to 'get her.' Mathis read it and then put it to the side, vowing to save it as evidence in case something really did happen. Both of these women were admitting to crimes right there on national television, right in front of a judge, even as one was trying to sue the other for nonpayment of rent.

Dominqua brought a witness, another fat woman. They were talking all loud and acting like typical nigga bitches. It was getting out of control, fast and it was embarrassing. Both women received rewards and Mathis got the hell out of there. Even during the post-court interview they were screaming acting ranting.

One of Mathis' most outstanding qualities is that during the opening of the show when he tells the audience how much "love" there is for Detroit and how he administers "touch love," he is not lying. He has more street sense and "game" than any other television judge in the history of television. He truly knows the streets, and anyone who had been out there for any length of time will be able to detect that. At times he can appear somewhat effeminate, but he seems to catch himself doing it and straightens up real quick.

For instance, he will call out someone who he feels is a "crackhead," and he explains that the reason he does that is because he is hoping that the individual will get help. He will point someone out who he thinks is "cracked out" or is a "weed head" and tells them, to their face, that he can spot the symptoms. When he busts them out like that, I have yet to hear a single person deny it or tell him he is wrong. Game recognizes game.

Mathis' understanding of the streets and of the games that drug addicts play is most prominently displayed when these types of people try to "run game" or lie to him. He spots it right away and calls it like it is. He is frequently heard telling a plaintiff or defendant (depending on who is telling the lie), "Do you think I'm not hip to the game?" And once he does that, the person knows that they are wasting their time trying to dupe the judge and usually resorts to telling the truth.

In recent years he as began to crack a few too many jokes at the expense of the people who appear before him. He will crack on them, laugh along with Doyle, and then say, "I'm must playing." He acts as if he thinks he's still out there on the street corner. When you combine this happy-go-lucky attitude with the terms he uses, you have the kind of brutha that I think we need more of: not ashamed of where he came from, knowledgeable about what's going on in the streets, and yet smart enough to obtain the credentials necessary to not only make it into college, but to advance all the way to law school.

Mathis often mentions the amount of control that his wife has over his life and his money. He talks about how when they first met he had a night out with the boys but how that has changed in recent years. If we are to believe what he says, he has to get permission to charge things on his own credit card if that expense goes over a certain amount. It sounds to me like this former street thug turned lawyer is *pussywhipped*.

Not only is he pussywhipped, but he is rather effeminate. Under the guise of jokes, he can sound just like a woman during one of his skits. But every now and then when he gets excited, he responds with a bitch-like shriek. In most cases, he immediately realizes what he's doing and then reverts back to his usual high level of professionalism.

He has a tendency toward bitch-like gossip, storytelling and histrionics. He gets caught acting in an effeminate way and the calms it down. But if you watch, you can see that Judge Mathis has about four or five pints of sugar in his blood. I don't give a shit if he's married and has kids; the fact is, some of the biggest downlow niggas on record can make that claim. But if you got some "bitch" in you, it's going to come out, especially during highly emotional and exciting times.

Another part of "keeping it real" is where he continually has to share his life stories with the audience. He talks about his sons and how they think they're slick, he tells the audience about his "swag" and how "he's not new to the game." He uses gestures that show that he knows how to fire up a crack pipe, and he talks constantly about how things used to be when he was on the streets.

Older women seem to have a special place in his mind and heart. On several episodes he has threatened to call someone a name but opted out of doing it. He added, "Now if I was Judy, I'd call you a whole bunch of names." Of course he is talking about Judge Judy, the conservative curmudgeon who is the standard by which most of these television decision makers are judged.

Here's another part of "keeping it real": having gone to college and to law school and not being able to spell worth a shit. During one episode aired on July 21, 2016, a defendant alleged that the plaintiff was "excoriating" his character. I am a word smith and have won several spelling bees, most of them in lily-white Hastings, Nebraska where I attended grade school. I score high on various college entry tests, including the Graduate Record Exam, the Miller Analogies Test and even the Law School Admissions Test.

The word "excoriate" appears on these tests and I knew what it meant, even as a teenager. It is one of those words where, if you understand the English language, you should e able to spell with no problem. Mathis couldn't. He had to have Doyle go to the back and look the word up – which means that Doyle couldn't spell it either. So here you have a former law school graduate and judge, and police officer who can't spell this simple-ass word.

The defendant had already told him what it meant and then he spelled it. The defendant was a college student and was obviously intelligent. What Mathis' response showed is that you can get a law degree, become a judge, and not know how to spell worth a shit. The same more than likely also applies to Judge Judy Sheindlin, Marilyn Milian and most certainly to Judge Joe Brown. And it is also one of the reasons why I don't respect the intelligence of someone because they tell me that they're a lawyer or a judge. In law school you can work on teams and basically memorize the law precedents of previous scholars. Plus you have "spell check" for your papers. That doesn't mean that you're intelligent; it just means that you take advantage of the resources that are around you.

Major Lance was a brutha who had a few hits back in the day, the biggest one being the 1975 jam, "Love Won't Let Me Wait." During a February 9, 2017 airing of "Judge Mathis," a sistah was appearing before the judge for a "siblingship test." It seems that for 27 years she was raised by a man named Larry but when he died, her mother told him that her real father was Major Lance, the famous singer. She had searched and found nothing but eventually got in touch with Jacqueline Camp Harvey who was also a child of Lance's. Mathis read the test results and, sure enough, in addition to seven other children that Lance had (but never claimed), this woman was another one of them.

During the airing of a show on December 29, 2016, the defendant was being accused of using a racial slur, but then apologized for doing it. Right away Mathis "forgave" her and said that Paula Deen used a slur and apologized "and I'd eat her cooking." Then he added a comment about Dawg the Bounty Hunter and said that Dawg used one and apologized and "I watch his show. In fact, he had me on his show one time." What?

In the case of Paula Deen she called her employees "niggers" and cracked a bunch of nigga jokes around black people who should have kicked her ass. But Dawg went for the jugular. According to one source regarding the 2007 incident involving Dawg the Bounty Hunter:

> A&E has suspended filming of bounty hunter Duane "Dog" Chapman's reality show after a tape was released of him using the N-word in a racist rant. Chapman's bigoted remarks were directed at his son's African-American girlfriend, and were first revealed at a tabloid's website. On a tape, Chapman can be heard defending his use of the word "nigger," which he contends "doesn't [always] mean you scum nigger without a soul."(Edwards, 2007).

It really doesn't matter. In another essay I've penned, "Apologize For What?" I make the case for the day-late type apologies issued by white people who think that because they say "I'm sorry" that all is forgiven. My case is clear: I think NOT.

Mathis forgives them because now that he's a "FORMER" dope user (or so he claims), he has tasted some fame and, as in the case of far too many black men, it goes directly to his head. Look at Ice Cube, Ice-T and other so called "street bruthas" who make a few movies and now they're singing a different tune. Ice-T went out and married some big-titty prostitute looking bitch named Coco. Need I say more.

And finally, Judge Greg Mathis.

CONCLUSION: WHAT DOES HE ACCOMPLISH?

As if Mathis' show wasn't condescending enough, in around January of 2017 he started adding a new twist: a paternity test! They are promoting it hard and they've aired a few segments. That is not to say that Mathis is guilty: he's doing what his white master orders him to do. The sick bastards are the people who appear before him requesting a paternity test. Don't these niggas know that the tapes from the show are admissible in court and in front of the child support people?

Way to go Greg. From street pharmacist and smoker to henpecked homoerotic judge. Way to go. But there's more.

Of all the major court TV shows, Mathis accomplishes the least. "The People's Court" addresses legal concerns and gives people a chance to air their concerns in front of a judge who looks like a beauty contest finalist. She's bilingual and from time to time offers some translations for the audience. She appears to also be a landlord and knows a great deal about tenant-landlord law.

Judge Judy is a conservative curmudgeon who insults those who appear before her but she does offer up legal advice and knows how to explain the law to those who appear before her. Her area of expertise, Family Law, is not lost on viewers and she is especially hard on low-income people in the welfare system. But her elitist and pro-American racist views can serve as a learning lesson for viewers who are paying attention.

When compared to these two female judges, Mathis is a joke. He doesn't even offer up much legal advice but instead uses his place on the bench to hint around about "the streets," "back in the day" and his favorite, "the game." When it comes to his references about "the game," he frequently glorifies crack use while at the same time claiming to abhor it. He looks down on infidelity but uses these incidents as an opportunity to talk about how "the game" works and how much money you should make without "insulting the game". In these instances he sounds like a retired street pimp.

If he's not engaging in hyperbole about gangs, drug dealers or hustling, he's talking about "the streets" or the code of the streets. He then interjects himself into the equation as if he is some kind of recovering super hero who was once a villain but now fights for white justice. What does this solve? The time that he commits to paternity suits, drug abuse, alcoholism and the streets, all of which he has personal tales to tell, basically glamorizes these areas more than anything else. He's like the majority of ministers in America who shoot the shit on Sunday morning by religiously jacking off the congregation, and then get credit for being some kind of "change agent."

The best friend of this show are the people who do the "counseling" or "advising" for those who are hooked on drugs or alcohol. He doesn't call into account the doctors who prescribe this stuff that leads to addiction, nor does he call into account the media's glorifying drug abuse through movies like "Scarface," "Rush," "Narcos" and so on. He just picks on the people dumb enough to appear in his court and then works to funnel those who need help into a counseling setting where someone is going to get paid by the network to "help" these folks. The folks remain penniless but supposedly get the assistance they need. There is never any follow-up as to what happened to those who accepted these "freebies" from Judge Mathis or his producers.

Personally, I think Mathis is still doing drugs, marijuana at the very least. During one show, aired on Valentine's Day of 2018, two women appeared before him and were hurling names at each other angry because one messed up the other ones braids. One sent an email to the other that included a stamp with Mathis' picture on it under the heading, "I know a crack head when I see one." So he aired that picture and then played the victim game, "Why y'all wanna put me in it?" Just before that when one of the women talked about a quality of weed, Mathis interrupted and said he "knew all about weed" and asked the woman if what she was describing was "a form of home grown weed."

I mention this to answer Mathis' asinine question as to why these women "put him in it." Like any gossipy bitch, he is already in it when he claims to be an expert on drugs and the streets just because he did some jail time for possession of a firearm. He wants to get "street cred" and then when people take his embellished stories seriously, he wonders how he "got in it." He got in it because he put himself in it.

Mathis' bitch-like antics get the best of him and often force him to draw conclusions that are based on bullshit. In an airing that took place on May 14, 2018, two women were in front of him, one that specialized in making underwear for couples and the other the customer.

The customer, who was being sued, was saying that the things that were made had holes in them and were raggedy. The plaintiff, who was the owner of the company, kept talking about the woman complaining about the size of the boxer shorts that were being made for the defendants' "man." She said that the woman kept changing the sizes, prompting Mathis to make a comment about the brother's size as well. Then out of the blue Mathis asks the plaintiff if she's "obsessed" with the man because she keeps talking about his boxers. What the woman was doing was explaining what the defendant was saying. Mathis is asking, "Do you want him?" and queries along that line. His bitchiness says a lot about his character. I believe that "man from the streets" bullshit is just a façade for what he really is. Can you say "down-low"?

Also during the show the plaintiff stated she was from Dayton, Ohio (which he had to know already because of the pre-show interviews) and Mathis used this as a chance to say that the Executive Producer of the show was also from Dayton. And then he goes through this long spiel about how the brutha drove all the way to California and worked his way up and then created the "Judge Mathis Show." Then the brutha is brought out to be introduced, prompting Mathis to stay, "He looks fifty but he's seventy years old." Again, can you say "down-low"? Who fuckin' cares about this bullshit? This is TV and time is a premium!

By the way, this case between these two country bitches: the Plaintiff was suing for $45!

During a show aired on July 4th, 2017, Mathis told one defendant that he didn't know how to "gigolo" and lecture him. "If you're gonna gigolo, then gigolo! Thirty dollars is short money, man! I'm givin' you the game!" What's wrong with this nigga? Based on the things he says during one of his conniptions, it is clear he still craves crack smoking, still enjoys smoking a blunt every now and then, and still believes in "the game" and "the streets" and it shows. His kind of legal jurisprudence is the kind of decision making that low-income people do not need!

Another thing, somewhat related to his hen pecked relationship with his wife, is that he may well have some "mommy issues." During one episode aired on February 5, 2018, he was running his mouth about how lucky one of the young defendants was to have had a mother who sent him $100 a week when he was locked up, $50 for his phone use and $50 for his commissary. He went on to say that when he was locked up for eleven months his mother sent him "zero." Then he said that in the neighborhood when something went wrong, his mother would tell the cops to "check out my son. He's a thug." If this is true then it means that Mathis' mother had a low regard for him and secondly, that she was a snitch.

What does Judge Mathis' show accomplish? It brings in ratings because it features people of color, usually illiterate. Like other court TV shows, people appear and are flown in to appear and are supposedly screened. But you can tell by the way that many of these people dress that they have no business in a court of law, especially not one that is nationally televised. Their dress and their on-going butchering of the English language, make them targets for laughs throughout America.

Then, when Mathis adds his quips, back handed compliments, jokes and street-level anecdotes, it is clear why viewers, mostly African-American women, tune in to the show. Mathis tunes in to the lowest common denominator and the only things educational about his show is how he describes how to smoke crack cocaine, how to light a crack pipe, the effects of crystal meth and marijuana, what "the munchies" are and so on. In my view, many of his shows occupy the role of "the enabler."

JUDGE JOE BROWN

"I am all about the business or protecting womanhood and promoting manhood," he told one brutha during a show. This goes to show you how silly you can be even with a law degree and the kind of background that Joe Brown brings to the table.

Television judges all appear to need a hook of some kind: Judge Judy is a curmudgeon; Judge Milian is the hot-tempered Latina; Joe Wapner was a kindly old white soul; Lynn Toler is the cute and street wise "sistah girl;" Greg Mathis is the brother from the 'hood who made good; Mills Lane is a stuttering hick; So Brown's "hook" is that he's about this "protecting women and promoting manhood" which shows he doesn't know shit about either area. (The theme of one of the questions posed to viewers as, "Does your ex need to "man up" and "pay up"? Of course the question is directed at woman because females NEVER pay up). Another promo poses the following query: Have you ever been hurt by a man who needs to "man up" and pay you back?" Again, women win, man loses.

I'm surprised there hasn't been some kind of uproar over these statements. Most of the women today are so fucked up that they think they are not in need of protection – except when the end result is money. He can enrich them by ruling in their favor, but many women today view a man's "protection" as just another expenditure of their earnings, or an emotional investment that they may or may not want to make. Joe's job is not to protect women; it's to rule on points of law and make legal decisions. Who in the fuck does he think he is: Sir Galahad?

And based on what I've seen him doing on You Tube, he is in no position to talk about morality OR manhood. Pictures of him drunk as a skunk posing with young bitches who look like they were hookers; photos of him "partying down" as it were, behavior that you would think he would be more guarded about exhibiting to the white public. And after he got fired, he made an ass out of himself complaining, just like Mablean Ephraim did, about how he was treated and how he felt he deserved more money.

But it's not just black manhood; it's manhood in general. Brown seems to think that it is the number one priority to help, support and/or take care of women. Why? Because that seems to be, in Brown's mind, what a man is supposed to do. Why? Because women need to be supported by men. What kind of sick shit is this? Where are these feminist bitches who are always claiming that they want to be treated the same was men? Why aren't these black lesbians up in arms about Joe buying into sex role stereotyping and acting as if he's living back in the days of Ecclesiastes? As he told one Defendant, "you are going to learn the lessons of a man"? And Joe: specifically, what are those lessons?

Then there's the issue of promoting black manhood, in particular. What men? If he was about doing that, he wouldn't have a show. After all, Farrakhan promotes black manhood – where is his show? Malcolm X and Martin Luther King promoted black manhood – what happened to them? Joe Brown is a judge and is in no position to be promoting anything unless the white man says he can promote it. And white boys with power don't want to see black manhood promoted because they've spent countless quadrillions of dollars creating institutional arrangements that work toward sabotaging and destroying black manhood. So on both counts, Joe's words and his approach are dead wrong.

During the opening credits, Brown is credited with standing for, "experience, knowledge and a passion for the truth." He may have experience because of his age, and he may have knowledge based on those experiences and law school, but when it comes for the "passion for the truth," that statement is biased: far too often, Joe's version of "the truth" is based on his hillbilly-like conclusions that are all too often rooted in and rested upon gender-biased beliefs and hackneyed clichés.

Earlier I talked about Judge Judy and how much she got paid; her reported $45 million annual salary, which made her the highest paid person on television. Now compare this with Judge Joe Brown who was rumored to be making $20 million a year, but Brown said that was not the case, claiming that he quit the show because CBS "only" paid him $5 million a year. Now remember back earlier when I shared that the going rate for these judges was $2 million a year and Mablean Ephraim wanted more and didn't get it and Judge Glenda Hatchett was treated the same way.

So did Judge Joe Brown quit? On March 30, 2013 it was reported that he quit because he was making $20 million and they wanted to reduce his salary to $18 million because of low ratings. This brutha was on the air for fifteen years, having premiered in 1998, second rated behind "Judge Judy" that whole time. But all the court shows, the ones in this book, were losing audiences, but Joe's ratings were slipping so CBS decided to offer him a salary cut. He refused.

I don't give a shit how he left – he left. And they took him off the air in Dallas, Texas where he was appearing in back to back 30-minute segments from 3:00pm to 4:00pm with "Judge Judy" following. Now, instead of Brown preceding "Judge Judy," we have none other than "Kris," which features that no talent slag, Kris Kardashian. You know her: the woman whose daughter are on an never-ending search for black dick – with money. Imagine: training your daughters to suck dick so that they can get paid. None of those bitches has a lick of talent, but black athletes and entertainers can't resist them. Kris herself is talentless, so how did she get a show? Let's just say, "like mother, like daughters." The show has since been cancelled.

Just as "they" did with Judge Marilyn Milian, those in decision making positions have made a total ass out of Joe Brown over the years – only in reverse. Judge Milian started off low key, was transformed into this "hot Latina," and was then returned to her previous state only with a louder mouth. Judge Joe Brown was promoted as a tough Judge and then became a clown with a monotone voice. Every now and then they'll start the intro to the show showing him with his arms crossed, facing away from the camera, looking over his shoulder like some wannabe pimp and he'll even try to cut a few steps like he's trying to dance.

Brown's slogan, "Promoting Manhood, Protecting Womanhood" has led to several theme shows such as "bad girls" and "bad girls gone bad." The narrator is some boney-necked blonde white woman whose eyes are bugging out of her head and who wraps up Brown's decisions with puns and quips. The show begins with the bug-eyed narrator declaring, "Now, it's Joe time." Not now it's time for

JUDGE Joe Brown, but "Joe," a name that implies that which is average and uninteresting, as in "average joe."

First of all, this shit about "promoting manhood, protecting womanhood." That court bench ain't no fuckin' soap box! He ain't supposed to be doing anything except deciding on points of law and rendering decisions on these bullshit civil cases and small claims cases. This "promoting manhood, protecting womanhood" shit sounds good, but it's the same subjective and "discretion-gone-wild" type shit that the white man used when he (Chief Justice Roger Taney) ruled in 1857 that "black man has no rights a white man is bound to respect." It's the same kind of shit that this country's decision makers agreed on when they said that black man was the equivalent of 3/5 of a man. It's the same shit that was handed down when women, time and time again, were denied the right to vote.

Secondly, let's call it like it is: Brown is slow-witted, possesses a cliché-laden vocabulary, and has a voice that is so monotonous he could put the road runner to sleep. When you combine these three facts and then add television and his laid back, on the border of appearing drunk or high in appearance,and it makes for hilarious viewing (even though its not trying to be), granted -- but it's not very informative on points of law.

How many times is this man going to say, "you can't squeeze blood out of a turnip," explain "caveat emptor" (let the buyer beware), define what a "bailment" is, and/or harp on the basis of American law, paying tribute to Britain and England as the formative bases for said Anglo-American law? Who gives a fuck? This is about arbitration, not a Introduction to AngloAmerican law course!

In my view, he comes across as either being on some kind of medication (barbituates), drunk as a skunk, or having smoked at least five blunts (marijuana). If you can find it in syndication, tune in and see for yourself.

The TV promo, before every show, claims that Brown is "Bringing no nonsense justice to Americans everywhere." Does he? Or is he a gimmick who used to represent much more than he does now? During one segment he told the plaintiff that it was in the man's "gene code" to take care of the family and support the woman. Another time he said, "The man's thing is to take care of the women even if it's not your own." Or how about, "If you see a woman, go help her carry the package even though today she might think you're trying to rob her." What's wrong with this muthafucka?

When these judges, including Judge Judy, start making these mega-bucks, their personalities undergo a profound transformation: they lose their damn minds. They want to crack jokes and say stupid shit that they think is cute, but it's not because while they may have forgotten about the protocols of being a judge, the viewing public has not. And then when you add the fact that the signed agreement makes them "insult proof" (they can crack on you but you can't respond), then that is why a lot of people don't take these shows in general, and Judge Joe Brown, in particular, seriously.

As part of the promo he is shown claiming, "If you listen, you might learn something." Yeah, you might. You might learn how a man who boasts about all this experience can nevertheless be manipulated into using a monotone voice and words most of his ignorant plaintiffs can't understand to make a complete ass out of himself five days a week on national television. And the more recent promos show him clad in judge's robe, spinning a circle as if he was a member of the Temptations and putting on a pair of dark shades. What the FUCK does that have to do with legal decisions and/or arbitration?

According to the research, Joe Brown was raised in a tough neighborhood in south central L.A. His family moved to the Crenshaw area in southwest L.A. where he graduated at the top of his class from Susan Miller Dorsey High School (as if that was difficult). He got his law degree in 1973 from UCLA and worked his way through college by substitute teaching.

Joe Brown's claim to fame is that he was a prosecuting attorney for the City of Memphis, the first black person to ever hold the position. Later on he opened up his own law practice and then went on to become a judge at the Shelby County Tennessee State Criminal Court.

More importantly, at least to me, is the fact that in 1997, Brown presided over James Earl Ray's final appeal of his conviction for murdering Martin Luther King Jr. Brown was later deemed biased and was removed from the investigation. Of course he was biased because one thing about Brown: he ain't no Uncle Tom! He probably dogged the shit out of James Earl Ray and, being in the city where King was murdered, he probably didn't say what he was expected to say.

At any rate, according to the research, notoriety from this case gave Brown national fame, and the white man discovered him. Just as they did with the other prosecutors who they "discovered," the white man then gives Joe a show and, beginning in 1998, Joe got his half hour reality show that comes on every day, sometimes in back to back segments, in cities all over the country, which lead to his reality court show "Judge Joe Brown," beginning in 1998.

The people who appear before Joe Brown are either low-income whites or black folks, neither group appearing barely have finished high school, let alone understanding terms like "restoration of property," "bailment" and some of the other terms he throws around to show that he has a mastery of the law (read: rehearsed).

Following is one what one on-line reviewer had to say about the program:

> On his show Judge Joe Brown is known for his strong opinions, his
> deep throaty chuckles, and his very v e r y s l o w - t a l k i n g

> deliberations which at times, ironically, accuse losing parties of being "fast talkers" or "smooth talkers" (a.k.a swindlers who use misleading or coercive language). Brown will typically allow litigants on his show to argue openly for several chaotic minutes before he stops them. This can result in some tense scenes in the courtroom, and all too often the baliff, "Madam" Sonia Montejano, must intervene to keep the peace. (Remember! Judge Judy doesn't even let her litigants speak to each other for ONE SECOND without threatening to have them tossed out!)

Most of what is written above is based on what the reviewer probably saw on one show. I have seen over 200 segments of "Judge Joe Brown" and as I say, he does talk slow and in a monotone. I don't know about the swindlers, but I have heard Joe tear more than a few people a new asshole.

The reviewer says that "Brown will typically allow litigants on his show to argue openly for several chaotic minutes before he stops them." I don't think Joe does this on purpose; his courtroom gets out of control because the plaintiffs are amped up and the defendants are allowed to respond, and then they go at it back and forth while Joe sits up there reading something. He doesn't even try to stop them. So when the reviewer talks about Judge Judy not letting the litigants speak to each other in her courtroom, that is because she is a control freak and wants to maintain order. Joe is more concerned about the verdict than he is courtroom demeanor.

Joe Brown doesn't have any control over his courtroom. When there's an argument, it's just like typical nigga arguments. Volume increases and the loudest voice wins. Joe has a lot of bass in his voice, so he usually ends up making his point. But you rarely hear him using his gavel to tell people to shut up – he lets them ramble on and on. These people, white and black, talk over him, interrupt him, crack jokes, plaintiffs shout at defendants and vice-versa – it's a zoo.

Joe acts as if he's an expert on "body language" (he's used his "explanation" on at least five shows that I've seen) about how eighty percent of what you say is nonverbal. I've read Julius Fast's work, *Body Language*, and I'm not sure if this is even accurate. At any rate, it has nothing to do with settling any cases when it comes to determining guilt or innocence. And yet Joe wants to babble and engage in his mind-numbing monotonic banter for what seems like weeks, when it's really only a few minutes.

I think that his hook is that he thinks he's an intellectual, not just a judge. He seems to take the long way around explaining things to the audience and the court. For instance, in one episode, he was talking to a young brother who drove cars for a living for a company. Instead of saying, "There were other times when you drove cars as a part of your job," Brown says, "There were several other expeditions that you went on at her behest." His use – and abuse – of quadra-syllabic words obviously confuses the plaintiffs and the defendants because these hicks often appear and sound as if they couldn't pour piss out of a boot if the instructions were written on the heel. Brown's intellectual flexing at the expense of these individuals is one more reason why his show is an insult to the judicial process.

Want proof? During a June 27, 2013 segment, Brown allows a plaintiff to sue an event coordinator (defendant) to appear along with a plaintiff who is accompanied by a "comedian/ventriloquist" to bring his wooden puppet to the podium with him. Brown says that if the plaintiff wanted the ventriloquist to speak, he'd have to swear in the dummy as well! Ain't that a bitch? Was the puppet a human being with its own mind and vocal chords? Hell no.

The show continued with Brown getting the man's status wrong, calling him a "promoter" when the man was nothing but a subcontracting event coordinator. Then he calls on Roscoe the Dummy! The ventriloquist comes up and the dummy starts talking: "That dude is fake," he says. Brown says, "He (the dummy) hasn't been sworn yet." Then he asks, "Is that a good tooth," referring to the tooth in the dummy's mouth. The dummy says, "Yeah, I got that in St. Louis." Clownishness! Buffoonery! Idiocy!

During one episode a Latino brother was riding his bike and got bitten by a Doberman on the back of his leg (behind his thigh). He showed the photos to Brown and he said, "You're a man. You're supposed to be able to handle something like that. I'm surprised you want four thousand dollars for what amounts to a little bruising … Permanent disfiguration? Hell no." This is another one of Brown's bad rulings. California law says that a dog is supposed to be on a leash in a park and the dog wasn't. But at the same time the Latino was rising his bike on a sidewalk – that's another violation of the law.

In another program, aired August 13, 2013 (a re-run), he faced females on both sides regarding a car accident. The theme of the show was "Bad Girls" and the Defendant had children in her car and her brakes went out. Brown went ballistic. At one point he scolded her about points of law and about her emotional state after having an argument with her boyfriend and then getting into a car with children. She got pissed, asked to say something and Brown shouted, "No. You can't say anything. You lost." She started mumbling and then walked out of the courtroom. Brown shouted, "That's probably why your boyfriend left ya, and if you walk out of here, I'm going to hold you in contempt. She kept walking and mumbling and Brown fined her, "One hundred dollars – no, make it two hundred." Then he turned to the Plaintiff and said, "I'm going to add it to your award." What?

In another episode, aired July 1, 2013, a young brother is suing two other young black men – one a rapper and the other the manager – for theft of his equipment. He also said he wasn't returning the video that was filmed until he got his money from these two wannabe thugs. It seems that he loaned it to them to use because he and his "crew" didn't want to go to that neighborhood. The two brothers never returned, hence they are being sued. Unfortunately, for them, they came to court looking like typical young niggas. The plaintiff was dressed alright, but the other two: one had on shorts and some Nikes and the other was sagging with some kind of jean shirt on. Brown DOGGED these niggas.

He went into his spiel about dressing for success and how they came to court. One of the assholes said that he was from Philadelphia "and this is California." Then Brown started screaming at them telling them that the reason that they dress this way is because they don't have a daddy present in the house and they're being raised by a 14-year old aunt and the mother is 17. Damn! He didn't let the plaintiff off, either. Although he awarded him $1,700 for the loss of his equipment he added, "I'm awarding you this because I don't think you're telling the whole truth because you've got one hand in your pocket the whole time." What? Who is this muthafucka – Julius Fast? (the author of a book called "Body Language").

During another case on the same as the prevous one, Brown told two black men who opposed each other, "Y'all from Detroit – y'all get thuggish up in that place!"

In one episode a man invites a woman on a cruise. She pays for his ticket and he's supposed to reimburse her. They go on the trip and he pays for the hotel room the night before the cruise and a bunch of incidentals. They get back and she wants to sue him for his part. They had broken up before the trip but she tells Joe Brown that they were "still friends."

Brown, relying on that old school bullshit bluff that women have financially benefited from for centuries says, "I should divide everything down the middle because this is the day and age of equality, but I look at both of your birth days and you should be old school." He then looks at the guy and says, "You should just do the right thing and pay for the entire trip for the lady," or some shit like that. Say what?

Brown tells the plaintiff (female), "I suggest you kiss and make up because it's hard to find a guy in southern California who's not in and out of jail. It looks like he has a good job, he's an inspector," then to him he adds, "You look like an old time real guy. She does look pretty good coming down this staircase on the cruise." What kind of shit is this? They used to have a court show called "Moral Court," and that shit flopped. But that sounds like this is what Joe Brown is doing in his quest to "protect womanhood." He's acting in a way that nevertheless degrades any woman with any dignity. These bitches don't need "protection;" they need INSPECTIN'!!!

If two people come on who are married, he takes time out to congratulate them. If a plaintiff or dependent is in college, he congratulates them. If a plaintiff or defendant as a college degree, he compliments them. My question is this: what in the FUCK does that personal career bullshit have to do with the case that he is supposed to be arbitrating? He's just promoting "traditionalism" and "old-school thinking" which, in this case, it usually outmoded because the people who come before him don't know SHIT about black history and probably not even their family history.

In a couple of episodes he's brought in "hair experts" to give testimony to power point photos a plaintiff was suing for getting "their her did" (as they say) and it turned out fucked up. I notice that these two experts have nice breasts and Brown wastes time asking bullshit questions about a subject that is not worthy of consideration. He uses country colloquialisms like, "fried, dyed and laid to the side," street shit that was popular in the 1940s. When these sexy "experts' get ready to leave, he'll say, as he did to one, "Thank you Miss Nora." I think Brown is either fuckin' these hos or they're his relatives.

Judge Joe Brown is old school, alright. And that is both positive and negative. It is positive in the sense that some of his values need to be imparted on some of the stupid youngsters that have the nerve to appear in front of him in a court of law. You know that the white people who run the show are going to pick the most ignorant, idiotic black people (and hillbilly type white folks) they can find. But that old school stuff also includes some rather parochial attitudes when it comes down to what Brown calls, "promoting manhood and protecting womanhood."

Following are some examples: On one show, two black women were going back and forth arguing their respective positions. Joe looks up from the papers he was reading and says, "Stop talking, ladies. This is not a hen house." Another time he asked a defendant, "Where you been, in a coal mine and you just now coming out of it?" When it came to bailment, he told one woman, "So what are you going to do to undo 2,300 years of law with your ignorance today?" He continued by asking them if they had ever been to a mall that had a gate that lowers and raises and has a machine with a ticket that you take. None of them had. He acted as if they were in another time or century.

He scoffed and then started laughing at them, implying they were country if they hadn't been to this type of mall. He then went on to tell them, "Then go on an adventure and try to find one. Try to go to civilization." If he wasn't such as asshole he'd know that there are more malls with outside parking than there are with inside, underground parking. There are many malls that are built without electronic gates that provide for entry and exiting.

An older white professional male was suing a younger guy for overdue rent and damages to the apartment. When the defendant was speaking, Brown asked him why he thought the old dude was suing him. The young guy said he made many attempt to pay the man but when it came time to leave the premises the man was "a little bit of discrimination against my fiancée Monica moving in." She had applied to move in before he did and the doctor turned her away. Brown asked her why he turned her down. The kid said, "maybe he doesn't like women." Brown said, "your young lady is a stripper and there's all kinds of scandal that can take place."

Brown reads the plaintiff's note and it's about the stripper and her three year old daughter. Brown says that the man's neighbors watch dressing "like that" because "you're walking in here like that." The scantily-clad defendant pissed him off, prompting him to tell her, "You come in here dressed like that with all that off the shoulder stuff – it's not appropriate." Brown kept digging: "You didn't write down that you had a child – that's ground for rejection right there. A 20 year old woman walking in there doesn't look right.

The older man was seeking "a professional man" to watch over his house while he was out of town. This kid came in with a red perm and got the place when he was alone. The guy said that from time to time, he could bring a girlfriend over. Instead, while the old guy is gone, the kids moves his girlfriend and her young daughter in. And didn't pay a dime the whole time. Brown dogged the kid and his woman, and ruled in favor of the business man.

Or how about the time he told a female defendant, "It's over, you lost – your ignorance is appalling!" "If you were in the South they'd say, 'you ignint'." The bitch he said it to was so stupid she replied, "Well I ain't from de Souf so I guess I ain't ignint." He responded, "you ignint and your ignorance will not suffice!"

During one of the "bad girls" specialty shows, he referred to one young sister as, "You devious little denizen of a loser region of hell." When she asked him why he was talking to her that way he said, "I don't like what you are."

On one episode this young asshole had the nerve to bring this guy to court over some expensive gym shoes that cost almost a thousand dollars. The plaintiff made his case and then Joe asks the Defendant, where's his money at? This street asshole says, "I gave him back five hunnud." Joe asks where's the paperwork and the brother starts talking about the streets and how he's the middle man. Joe got so pissed he tosses his gavel down and said, "Get out of here, both sides of this are crooked." Which they were – one guy bought shoes that he knew were stolen and paid cash and then when he found out they weren't what they were supposed to be, he comes to court to sue for a refund: seeking benefits from an illegal act. What an asshole.

During another episode a brother had ruined a woman's artwork because she was about to evict him and he also did something to her cat. Brown lost it and told him, "That's why the cat don't like you! then added, "And I can see why!" Later he told him, "Damn how you feel, you owe this woman some money!"

I have seen two episodes where the defendants have walked out of the courtroom, risking contempt citations. He gets angry and dogs them so badly that they just say, "fuck it" and leave. Defendants on no other court show behave in such a manner.

And as for Sonia Montejano, the bailiff, she might not have the nicest face in the world (although she's not ugly), but her body is *tight.* She wears a uniform that is tailored for her body and there's not an ounce of fat anywhere on it. Firm breasts, but a flat ass (you can't have it all). Unlike the other bailiffs, she rarely gets to comment or get involved or interact with the judge, although from time to time she has had to warn several of the plaintiffs about getting out of line or talking when the judge is talking. Sometimes they bring in "expert testimony" from some low-key losers and Montejano gets to swear them in. They raise their right hand and check out what they have to swear to: *"Do you promise to provide this courtroom with accurate testimony?"* What kind of bullshit is this? Accurate compared with what? Accurate based on what sources? Primary? Secondary?

The blonde court reporter, the woman who announces the cases and closes them on screen replaced another other woman, who was nice looking. This new one is blonde and has a face that reminds you of a Chihuahua trying to shit out a peach seed. Her blue eyes are huge and look as if they are about to pop out of her skull at any minute. To make matters worse, she tries to sum up the cases in the fifteen or so seconds she gets, with puns and quips.

The Black Power Movement and Joe Brown

On or about January of 2015 an internet radio station ran a long series of interviews about some personalities from the 1960s. The station was black and the name of the station is WeAllBeTV - News Free Dixie for the 21st Century. One of the guests was Joe Brown and the topic was why he (Brown) doesn't celebrate Kwanzaa, with the main reason being that Maulana Karenga, the founder and chairman of US, killed some of Brown's best friends. What Brown shares lines up with history and his life, so I'm taking him at his word. I'm transcribing what was said and offering my analysis as a Black Studies scholar, at the same time.

The show begins with Brown explaining that he knew both Alprentice "Bunchy" Carter and John Higgins, who he recruited when he was a counselor at UCLA. Bunchy had been a Slauson gang member but got out of the penitentiary, taught himself to read and write so he got into UCLA under a special program. Let me add that the program Brown is referring to is one that I also got into college on. It was called "The High Potential Program" and it was for black students who were intelligent but whose background in politics (or whatever) made them the bane of the administrations or the system. Bunchy, John and Angela Davis went the UCLA route, while I was from northern California and ended up at St. Mary's College of Moraga, California.

Huggins and Bunchy, as both history and Brown recall, "were gunned down in front of 43 witnesses in the school cafeteria in broad daylight by four people who were members of the US organization. According to Brown, the authorities only caught two of the assassins for accessories. Brown says he remembers running into one of them after he was prosecuted and claims that he served as one of the witnesses against him. He went to prison, but two years later Brown ran into him at the Paladium in Hollywood at a concert.

Brown says the both of them, the two accessories, were sitting at a table and he asked them, "What are you two doing out?" Brown says they told him that they had escaped and had an all-points-bulletin out for them, but after two days they cancelled it. He says that about five or six years later they showed up to surrender and they were told that nobody was interested. The two people who actually did the shooting, their names were known, and the home of the mother of one of the men was identified as the place where the two were staying, and the police didn't even go by there to get them.

Brown accurately remembers that Karenga got five years in the California State pen for torturing several women. He got paranoid thinking they were going to poison him, so (according to Brown) they let Karenga out after one year exactly, and then within "forty-something days" he became a tenured professor in the California State University system.

Brown talked about the FBI COINTELPRO that was set on to Black Power types to destroy the organizations. He called the US group "simpatico negroes who go along with it." Brown said the main people behind it were an LAPD special group known as the "SIS." Brown claims that he was actually told by several of the detectives who was investigating the murders that they thought I was right because the only people that knew the information were in the police department, but when they got there, the US organization had already been by.

Brown said that Elaine Brown was "a smart individual" who worked in the clerical area on the UCLA campus for some years and she took the test and wound up being recruited as an undergrad. Brown says, "I knew all of 'em. I was the BSU community liaison and at that point we had tripled the number of African-Americans in UCLA." He said that they got "good ones in" who couldn't be counted on. Brown says that when he got to UCLA in 1965, there was a grand total of 73 African-American full-time grad students, 72 full time undergrad students in a student body that totaled 64,000 students, full time.

He says that eight years ago (2007) the student body total was 95,000 and they admitted one African-American. Brown said, "But going back, we ended up getting more African-Americans in in 1966, in 1967 we got 250 in and in 1968 we got 250 in, and we got those who wanted to be Black Student Union members for the "appearance." Brown said that Kareem Abdul Jabbar, Big Lew then, the basketball player – Mike Warren, Lucius Allen, all the UCLA basketball team. There was a lot to lose, so they made a move on the Administration Building. Brown pointed to the team as people who didn't want to go and even Eddie Macks, the BSU president, didn't want to go.

Brown says that the primary group didn't get in through any back doors but were conscientious and willing to sacrifice our lives for that cause. Brown says a lot of people got killed around UCLA back in those days. Brown says that he felt the US organization had a lot to do with it.

Brown said that he doesn't celebrate Kwanzaa because he thinks that Karenga is a "sellout negro of the worst type." Brown says he met Ron Karenga on a field trip to L.A. City College. His name was Ron Everett and he had a Jamaican accent, green eyes and wavy hair. After mocking Karenga, Brown said, "He killed some very good friends of mine."

Joe Brown was relevant at one time. He grew up in the heart of the black power movement and made some contributions. He got some black kids, like myself, into college despite our high school backgrounds of militancy and radicalism. But the country was in a state of fear at that time because they were afraid niggas were going to take over. That is why Karenga and others were sent in to dissect the movement. Joe Brown's courage to expose what he knows and saw is important and in my book, despite his drunkenness and buffoonery on the bench, he has good intentions and at heart is the kind of "fatherly figure" that the movement spawned. And he should be remembered for that.

JUDGE LAUREN LAKE, PATERNITY COURT

This is, by far, the worst court show on television. I don't know where they got this woman, but the presentation of this show is on the level of a cable access program. The set is horrible: it's a courtroom, but the stands behind which the defendants and plaintiffs stand look like they were put together in a high school wood shop class. But then when I did some research, I found out why this bitch comes off as being insane: she's from Detroit.

Her name is Lauren Lake, and she's one mean bitch. Look at the photos of her: she looks like somebody just slapped her mama. She's very loud, all the time, and she acts as if she's got a wild hair up her ass. This show is a bit different because it is just what the white doctor ordered. Like Maury Povich, Steve Wilkos and those other assholes who give out paternity tests, the men who come on these shows are crazy. All these findings are admissible in court and will be presented in the 'real world" as evidence of their paternity.

Here's one problem: the women usually get away scot-free. The question that is always posed, according to the website, is, "Will the DNA result be the key to unlocking a freedom for those who stand before her?" Like Judge Toler, she also claims to be a relationship expert, but adds one more thing: she's a motivational speaker. How is a bitch like this going to motivate anybody other than to inspire these crazy black women out here that men ain't any good and to try to avoid them? This DNA shit (on this program an agency called DNA Diagnostics receives regular mention as the source of and just before the "verdict" is read) is not what people think it is, because the Jews over in Israel – according to reliable news reports – have been tampering with the genetic material and can now manipulate it so that one person's DNA can be a attributed to someone else.

According to the New York Times,

> Scientists in Israel have demonstrated that it is possible to fabricate DNA evidence, undermining the credibility of what has been considered the gold standard of proof in criminal cases. The scientists fabricated blood and saliva samples containing DNA from a person other than the donor of the blood and saliva. They also showed that they had access to a DNA profile in a database, they could construct a sample of DNA to match that profile without obtaining any tissue from that person (Pollack, 2009)

Continuing:

> The planting of fabricated DNA evidence at a crime scene is only one implication of the findings. A potential invasion of personal privacy is another. Using some of the same techniques it may be possible to scavenge anyone's DNA from a discarded drinking cup or cigarette butt and turn it into a saliva sample that could be submitted to a genetic testing company that measures ancestry or the risk of getting various diseases. Celebrities might have to fear "genetic paparazzi," said Gail H. Javitt of the Genetics and Public Policy Center at Johns Hopkins University. (Pollack, 2009).

Therefore, I predict that these TV shows that are so dependent on DNA results ("Maury Povich," "The Test," "Paternity Court," etc.) are going to be found to be fraudulent in future years. As long as "Israeli scientists" are continuing to manipulate the genetic codes the way they currently are, then who knows? Maybe the next battle front will be the genetic manipulation of human beings, combining them with animals so that they can have super powers. When it comes to the white man, who in the fuck knows what's next?

Shows like "Paternity Court" are, in my view, finding people to be guilty when they are not, to be parents when they are not, and there is going to be plenty of litigation as a result of the dependence on DNA, which is as prone to error as any other "scientific method."

Lake, with long black hair cascading down the sides of her face (real or not?), is a loud-talker in the mode of Latina judge Marilyn Milian. The louder they talk the more excited they seem to get based on audience reaction. The more excited they get, the louder they become. Lake allows her audience to applaud throughout the testimony.

Judge Lauren Lake and Paternity Court: Format

If more evidence of paternalism and racism on these court TV shows was needed, if the foolishness of the people who appear was ever in doubt, then the conception behind and the format of "Paternity Court" should be more than enough evidence.

> Unlike most present-day court shows which typically have two cases in each episode, **Paternity Court only focuses on one case per episode**, though a second case can make an uncommon appearance … Lake takes time before and after the results to speak with her litigants (Wikipedia, 2018 – emphasis added).

If you watch "Paternity Court," you can see that the reason for one case per show is that each case is dragged out and there are constant commercial breaks, How long can it take to check a DNA test that has already been conducted and read a verdict?

Once source offers the following regarding the "conception" of the show:

> An article in *Broadcasting & Cable* talking about the conception of the show **listed the paternity test-focused episodes of the daytime talk show *Maury* as a direct inspiration for Paternity Court**, as Bryan said in the article that the **high ratings for Maury among women 25-54** and the popularity of the court show genre made fusing the two concepts

> possible. Weigel Broadcasting president Neal Sabin, whose station group was among the first to take the program, thought it was a natural fit for the court show-heavy lineup on his stations, **saying it was 'a little bit Maury and a little bit court-y'** (Wikipedia, 2018 – emphasis added)

Maury Povich – another Jewish TV personality who likes to exploit poor and minority people, joining a long line consisting of Jerry Springer, Mike Wallace, Judy Sheindlin, Howard Stern, Bill Maher, Marv Albert, Rickie Lake, Howard Cosell, Mike Wallace, to name but a few. So they clone the attitude, place the star of the show on a court bench, paint her black and then use the same "exploit the poor" motif that the others have used over the years in the name of entertainment and news.

And don't forget: this shit is all on tape and distributed all over the world. Paternity is no joke – people get killed because of it. And when you are dealing with black people and other low income types, that free flight to the courtroom and to be on TV can have major repercussions once you get back to the 'hood and have to deal with what you just claimed or what you were just exposed for. But poor people seem yet to have learned that "short term pleasure yields long-term pain."

> Producers of the series have argued at the same time that Paternity Court and Maury do contrast, **as Paternity Court does not focus on the narrative of Maury in building tabloid drama solely from the "who's your daddy?" question** posed by paternity tests and the issues of multiple partners possibly being so with only bare follow-ups by that show's staff, but instead uses the tests on their show to build long-term relationships in a healthy manner once those results are revealed …. Bryan has stated the goal of Paternity Court is to reinvigorate the court show genre. (Wikipedia, 2018).

The previous statement contains a lie, which is why in these sections of various analyses I included some direct quotes and references from the shows. They very well DO focus on the narrative of each plaintiff and work like hell to eke out emotion and anger between plaintiff and defendant.

Next we come to the format's "approach" and format which lend even more credence to my earlier allegations.

According to Wikipedia (2018), they call it the "Lauren Lake approach." Don't ask me why because she relies on others to give out information that these same litigants could get from any nickel-and-dime legal aid worker in their respective communities. At any rate the snippet says that, "Paternity Court' provides guests with unspecified resources in or near their hometowns, regardless of the outcome of the DNA results. A psychiatrist, Carole Lieberman, is always on-site, and the show says Lauren Lake frequently follows up with guests. Lake utilizes her experience as a woman, a mother, a relationship expert, and an attorney to help the litigants through the problems they bring with them to court, and beyond."

For instance,

> *Paternity Court* is a half-hour hybrid of a talk show using the court show plaintiff/defendant format. Lake talks to the show's litigants and decides cases based upon the results of DNA tests. While the show's title is *Paternity Court*, it also looks into other situations using DNA verification, such as probate disputes over wills, which are litigated under a binding arbitration arrangement ...

These people love to act like their lie detector tests, their "truth serums" and their "DNA testing" are infallible. Well they're not. They can be tricked and neutralized and they simply don't apply to some people. I have already stated that Israeli scientists have found a way to manipulate DNA.

This DNA shit is not what people think it is, because the Jews over in Israel – according to reliable news reports – have been tampering with the genetic material and can now manipulate it so that one person's DNA can be a attributed to someone else.

According to the New York Times,

> Scientists in Israel have demonstrated that it is possible to fabricate DNA evidence, undermining the credibility of what has been considered the gold standard of proof in criminal cases. The scientists fabricated blood and saliva samples containing DNA from a person other than the donor of the blood and saliva. They also showed that they had access to a DNA profile in a database, they could construct a sample of DNA to match that profile without obtaining any tissue from that person (Pollack, 2009)

Continuing:

> The planting of fabricated DNA evidence at a crime scene is only one implication of the findings. A potential invasion of personal privacy is another. Using some of the same techniques it may be possible to scavenge anyone's DNA from a discarded drinking cup or cigarette butt and turn it into a saliva sample that could be submitted to a genetic testing company that measures ancestry or the risk of getting various diseases. Celebrities might have to fear "genetic paparazzi,"

>said Gail H. Javitt of the Genetics and Public Policy Center at
>Johns Hopkins University. (Pollack, 2009).

See what I mean?

Therefore, I predict that these TV shows that are so dependent on DNA results ("Maury Povich," "The Test," "Paternity Court," etc.) are going to be found to be fraudulent in future years. As long as "Israeli scientists" are continuing to manipulate the genetic codes the way they currently are, then who knows? Maybe the next battle front will be the genetic manipulation of human beings, combining them with animals so that they can have super powers. When it comes to the white man, who in the fuck knows what's next?

Paternity Court: Examples from 2018

The first example is the case of Hendricks v. Hendricks. These were two white people who had previously appeared on "Couples Court." Now what is that about? They were vetted twice and made two different shows and got paid and got free plane fare. With that out of the way, let's get down to the facts of the case.

They begin with a review of the show on "Couples Court" where Mr. Hendricks was found to be telling the truth when he said he didn't cheat. According to Judge Lake, this time around "the shoe is on the other foot and he accuses you of cheating and says he is not the father of the one-month old baby, Chris, Jr. Is that correct?" Mr. Hendricks says he confirmed that his wife was unfaithful and there is no way that the child could be his. He's also petitioning the court for a lie detector test to determine the extent of his wife's cheating. Ain't that a bitch? If the bitch cheated once, that's all you need. What do you mean "extent" of her cheating? "Did she suck his dick," "did he dick her in the booty," "did they hang upside down"? What does "extent" prove and of what relevance is it in a case of alleged infidelity?

When asked how she feels about her husband's views the woman just outright says, "I'm pissed off" and then adds, "he's his twin." She named the baby after him, circumsized him, just as her husband wanted her to do. He says he doesn't feel that bond the way he does with his other children. She has cancer but she is now in remission, but she found some messages on his phone from one of his co-workers that were very sexually explicit. He said they had tried for four years, including the use of fertility pills, before they had their four year old daughter. He says "Four years after we have our first daughter she comes up pregnant just out of the blue, after we've had all our issues."

Judge Lake calls in a Dr. Jameelah Gater, and you can tell by the name and the spelling that she's black. Gater reviewed the file and babbled her ass off. The finding was because of the woman's medical condition, they couldn't tell. He wants the boy to be his child "so we can be happy again." The paternity results were that he is the father. He was happy as hell and started crying. The woman says "I told you, you have no reason to doubt me." Lake tells her "He DID have reason to doubt you." Next came the lie detector results.

The bitch wouldn't give the lie detector results and said she'd read them in her chambers behind closed doors. Ain't that a bitch. He STILL wants to know.

In another segment, Hunter v. Holden, an auto mechanic suspects his live-in girlfriend had another man's baby and is only using him (Mr. Hunter) for the money. They're black. She was confused at first because she claims she was "given incorrect medical information," but now she's sure that Mr. Hunter is the baby's father. He says that he is taking care of her financially. "I buy milk, clothes, everything a father has to do to take care of a child, I do it." Lake says, "So you pretty much stepped up as a father?" He says "yes."

Okay, let's pause a minute. This shit about "stepping up," as if claiming a kid that may or may not be yours is some kind of act of valor whether it's yours or not. How is that "stepping up"? This bitch gapped her legs and then "informed" you that she was pregnant. You're in the fog as to what really went down. As the old saying teaches, "Mama's baby, daddy's maybe." He is emotionally attached to Josiah as well and has accepted him as a child although they are only "boyfriend and girlfriend."

There was another guy but she claims she stopped having sex with him. Hunter says she told him he COULD BE the father. Lake tells them that, "in this court COULD is an action word because it means that you or someone else could be the father." The pictures of the baby show a dark-skinned kid with a large Afro, she's brown-skinned and he's very dark. He's been in the situation before with paternity. She named her son after someone else, okay? He wasn't invited to the hospital for the birth. She slept with two different men (Hunter being one of them) three days apart. Lake explains that this is called "a window of conception."

She says she doesn't know where the other guy is. She told him he could be the father but that guy don't give a shit. "He don't care," Hunter says. It was determined by the court that Mr. Hunter was NOT the father. He began crying. She says, "Sorry." Hunter says, "I'm gonna still be in his life." Hunter says they don't want to have nothng to do with the man but Lake says "every child has a right to know who their biological father is and they also have the right to be supported by that man."

Check this episode out. It's the case of Chmielinski v. Brown/Long III where this woman says that a ghost is the father of the baby! This white woman had a five year relationship with the Defendant's son, Georgie who died in a motorcycle accident. The black grandparents initially accepted young Xavier as their grandson, but now they changed their mind.

Mrs. Brown and Mr. Long say that they don't believe that their son was ever in a relationship with the woman, that she made up a fairy tale love affair with Georgie and he is not Xavier's father. The white woman says that her son needs his family that he calls Mrs. Brown "nana" and she's been in his life. But Mrs. Brown says she didn't know anything about the New Jersey white girl. The white girl says she doesn't know either. "We were just friends. It was a sexual friendship we had for so many (five) years. No matter who we were with, we still had sexual relations."

Both of Xavier's "potential fathers" had passed away. Now check this out. There was a video when Ms. Chmielinski were sitting in a car." The mother interrupts and says, "The video was a spirit of Georgie." The video, which is in the court is of the woman's son Xavier "and in the video you can see Georgie's spirit." The white woman says, "It looks like a spirit – it looks like a cloud." There was smoke in the background and she sent it to Mrs. Brown who was told "This is Georgie's spirit."

The DNA of Georgie and of his surviving parents were all tested. When it comes to two year old Xavier CHmielinski. The relatedness is ZERO percent! Ain't that a bitch. Mrs. Brown started bawling like an abused child. The white woman just stood there, staring into space. "Sorry Mrs. Brown," the white woman says.

More laughs. In the case of Ramos v. Evans, a Latina who says that Evans fathered her one month old son, Xavier. Lake explains, "After sharing your news that you were having his baby, women who he was cheating with started coming out of the woodwork trying to convince him he's not the dad." Mr. Evans says that he's not the father and that the Plaintiff "changed up her due date" to cover up her own infidelities. He says he "brought a bombshell witness who will reveal the truth and seal your case."

Ms. Ramos says she's tired of his lies and manipulations and that he's done this to other people. They flash the infant child on the screen and she asks, 'How can you deny such a beautiful baby?" They knew each other for years before and then got together. She says she gave him the benefit of the doubt, but "that's when he started doing the cheating for the whole time." She said she had sex with an ex boyfriend "but me and him wasn't actually in a relationship."

He came to the hospital during the whole time. His witness is brought in. Her name is Miss Shacacia Vaughn. She begins by saying that when Ms. Ramos was saying she was pregnant, "There was already a rumor going around that she was already pregnant by somebody else." Ramos says, "Disagree." Vaughn says, "Everybody knows about it." Ramos said that it's because "everybody's always making up lies. Nobody likes me. Evans wants to know why the baby was born a month early to which Ms. Ramos says, "I can't help it because he was born a month early!"

Now for the results. The results, prepared by DNA Diagnostics, in the case of Ramos v. Evans, he IS the father. No sooner were the results read, Ms. Ramos began lambasting Evans: "I want you to apologize to our son because I told you since day one." When Lake asks Evans how he feels he has his head bowed, lifts it, and then says, "I'm afraid." He explains, "I just don't feel like she's going to allow me to be in his life, that's all." Ms. Ramos blamed it on his lifestyle and as Lake is explaining it, a picture of him holding Xavier in the hospital, baseball cap still on, is shown to the entire court on a huge screen.

A final point. Judge Milian has a black bailiff named Douglas McIntosh. Judge Judy has a black bailiff named Petrie Hawkins Byrd. Judge Faith Jenkins has a bailiff, a former boxer, who is simply known as "Juan." Judge Mathis' bailiff is Doyle Devereaux, a white man with New Orleans roots. Now get this: Judge Lake has a white bailiff as well and he has a stereotypical black name. His name is "Jerome."

JUDGE JUDY SHEINDLIN

She is the most well known of them all and she is the biggest bitch on the TV bench. Before sharing my analysis of her long-running television show with you, let me provide an analysis of her background based upon her own words. Since she boasts constantly about being "the star" of her show and about how wonderful she is, let her own statements be the determinant.

Background

The following interview took place with the (British) Daily Mail, and appeared in publication on September 14, 2017. My analyses will filter in and out with the final production being a prelude to my "review" of her television program. The title of the piece, very lengthy, was "Judge Judy reveals she left her first husband when he belittled her legal career and divorced her second when she got sick of catering to his demands (but remarried him a year later)."

The article, inclusive of my analyses of course, begins, thusly:

> Judge Judy Sheindlin's rulings are not always final it seems, especially when it comes to her love life. The 74-year-old jurist-turned-television star is speaking out about her personal life in a rare interview, revealing

> that she divorced her first husband over his disregard for her career and got rid of her second husband when she grew tired of catering to his demands. (Spargo, 2017)

These actions make her sound like some kind of feminist iconoclast. But what do both marriages have in common? She said "I do" to someone she obviously didn't know that well. So she fell for the okey-doke and then had to correct the mistakes with divorces. What makes her think she's better than anyone else? Her occasional references to how "gorgeous" she is evidently did not make a difference and her knowledge of law and constant boasting of how long she's served in "family court" evidently didn't mean anything. In other words, it seems that if it ain't in a book, Judy can't chew gum and walk at the same time.

Continuing, "That second divorce was a brief one however, with Shiendlin making the decision to remarry husband number two after just one year apart. Twenty-seven years later, she and second husband Jerry are still going strong."(Spargo, 2017) They might be going strong but they've had issues. Jerry was screwing around with some young babe in their home while Judy was out of town. She made him go live in the cottage in the back and then they made up. She has no control; her whole life is ego-centered and she lives for the television limelight. That's why it's so easy for her to get played.

Check out her philosophy and explanation:

> 'I missed him, I missed him and I really found out - this is not to denigrate your species - actually, most men are alike,' says Sheindlin of her split from Jerry on the premiere of the Fox News show **OBJECTified**,' which airs at 8pm this Sunday. She then jokes that while all men may be alike, Jerry was a bit different than other males his age, saying: 'Mine had hair! ' (Spargo, 2017 – emphasis original)

"Most men are alike," she says. This is a stereotype and it's dangerous. Maybe the type of men she attracts are all alike. After all, she only dates and marries Jews and we know what they're about. The only difference is that Jerry had hair, she says in jest. But one more thing Jerry had: his own money and a financial future. And Jews take that into consideration when they decide to make a commitment. Notice that there is no mention of brothers or sisters that she can use as a support group. The fact is she's one of those "know-it-alls" and that's how she comes off on television. And that's the reason for her personal and intimate mistakes in her marital life.

So Jerry and Judy (ain't that sweet?) continued down the road. The article says that, "Over the next 13 years the couple rose up the ranks in the legal system, with Jerry taking a post on the New York Supreme Court and Sheindlin being appointed as a family court judge by Mayor Ed Koch". (Spargo, 2017) Koch, also a Jew, did what Jews do: they take care of their own.

Moving right along:

> Things took a turn though in 1990, leading to the couple's divorce after 14 years. It was a brief separation however, which came soon after Sheindlin lost her father, but in the end she says she learned some valuable lessons. 'I just had to come to terms with the fact that men of that generation are different,' explains Sheindlin. **'They expect, even if they have no right, they expect to be taken care of or catered to.'** (Spargo, 2017 – emphasis added)

I think she's got it ass backwards. Women tend to view men that they allow into their lives as being in need of "repair," "mending" or "fixing." That is why women like Judy spend so much time working to "change" the men in their lives. First come the premarital "tests" to see if the financial and emotional commitment is where it should be. Then comes the sex test and if he passes that, then they pretend that they are so much in love with this guy and can't do with him. In other words, women become territorial. So what she's saying about men being in need of care and catering is actually what women are all about, which is why they insist on paying the bills and handling the household duties. In that way they can make sure that they maintain control

The first marriage was to another Jew:

> Things were even more difficult for Sheindlin after her first marriage back in 1964 to attorney Ronald Levy. She had just graduated and was soon to pass the bar exam, but her life as an attorney on hold to be a housewife. 'It was time for me to get married. I was 20, almost 21. So I became a mom,' says Sheindlin of her thinking at the time, going on to say that she soon grew bored. She also began having trouble with how her husband treated her desire to work. (Spargo, 2017)

She set him up. The was young and she put her life on hold because SHE decided it was time to have kids. She had them and with that done, it was time to continue on with her career. As a Jewish male, he didn't want his wife to work – that's what these men are known for. But they ain't gonna win any awards in the sack – their sexuality or lack thereof may be one reason that of all white women who marry black men, a disproportionately high percentage of them are Jewish women. And black men sho' ain't got no money. But we know one thing they've got – and so do those Jewish women!

To cover up her selfishment and ego-centric goals, here is how Judy explains her career decisions:

> 'My first husband is a lovely, lovely man but he always viewed my job as a hobby and there came a time where I resented that,' explains Sheindlin. **The two were divorced after 12 years in 1976**, and the **following year she married Jerry.** She brought two children into the relationship - daughter Jamie and son Adam - while **Jerry had three children from his first marriage:** Gregory, Jonathan and Nicole. (Spargo, 2017 – emphasis added)

What this means is that she was fucking around with Jerry while she was still married to her first husband. How else to explain being married to a new man within a year? It was pre-planned! She took the kids she made and Jerry brought his three along and they were like a Jewish version of "the Brady Bunch."

She was shrewd and she was slick. So they paint her resume with a brush of "service" and then sell it to a gullible American public like so:

> Sheindlin's success made her one of the first women in the country to become a judge, and yet when asked about this or if she considers herself a feminist, Sheindlin is surprisingly dismissive. **'I don't feel as if anything that has happened to me in my life was sidetracked because I was a woman,' she reveals, downplaying her success.** (Spargo, 2017 – emphasis added)

The interpretation of what Sheindlin just said is no act of humility. This evil bitch is trying to say that she got everything she got because of merit and hard work! That is bullshit. First of all, she was gorgeous. Secondly, she was a Jew. If her looks didn't count, then why is she pouring pounds of henna into her hair to keep it looking blood red? Nothing was sidetracked because she was connected, had a network, was on the east coast and was short in stature but high in sexual allure. Plain and simple. She's smart, but she would have never had a chance to exercise that intelligence in law school without that network.

Further,

> And as for the feminist label, Sheindlin says: 'I don't think so. I don't think so. I don't know what that means. I actually don't know what that means. Do I want equal pay with men? Absolutely not!' That may be because Sheindlin earns far, far more than the 'man.' (Spargo, 2017)

If she didn't know what it means, why answer the question? Is that not what she advises litigants to do? She knows what a feminist is. And she doesn't want equal pay with men because she not only believes she deserves more, but she also doesn't want to be required to put in a whole lot of work. Judy has always had assistants, interns, aides and the like to do the grunt work in her offices. She never really "worked" other than as a housewife and mother and admittedly that is difficult. But I'm willing to bet that she had some kind of nanny assisting her with those kids. She's lived the life of Reilly and she knows it. A person with an ego like that would not be doing all that boasting if she had come up the hard way and faced some serious trials and tribulations.

Check out how she supposedly "negotiates" her salary:

> In testimony given back in July 2016 that was recently released and obtained by The Hollywood Reporter, Sheindlin described the unorthodox way that she negotiates her salary with CBS. 'We go to the Grill on the Alley **with the president of the company**. We sit across the table, and I hand him the envelope and I say, "Don't read it now, let's have a nice dinner. **Call me tomorrow. You want it, fine. Otherwise, I'll produce it myself."** That's the negotiation,' explained Sheindlin. (Spargo, 2017 – emphasis added)

This is not a negotiation: this is an ultimatum! She's imposing her will from a position of power! There is no middle man, no attorney or mediator – she's talking to the president of the company, who is also Jewish! This is a family affair at worst. The people in power try to avoid the behind the scenes dirt they do to get what they have. But I've studied them and I know how they got it. It's about connections, networking and interlocking directorates. Judy and those other TV court judges have the benefit of all three because if they didn't they wouldn't be on television broadcasting their bullshit decisions all over the world.

> One year, a CBS executive did try to present Sheindlin with a counter offer, at which point she informed the man**: 'This isn't a negotiation.'** In that same testimony Sheindlin also said that **she could produce the show herself if she wanted, earning another $20 million a year on top of her current $47 million salary.** Sheindlin's testimony came in a deposition in response to a complaint filed by Richard Lawrence of Rebel Entertainment. (Spargo, 2017 – emphasis added)

Just like I figured: negotiating from a position of power. She knows she can produce her own show because of the interlocking directorate I just mentioned. She won't do any grunt work and barely any paperwork. She'll make a phone call to make sure her name appears prominently in the credits and the rest of the work will be done by staff who will be paid by someone else. All she has to do is appear, take her short ass up to that bench, pontificate before millions and collect her paycheck. She may have been a judge in family court for decades, but she doesn't have one scintilla of grass roots knowledge or street cred. During one episode this bitch didn't even know what "holla" meant; she had to reach over and ask Byrd the bailiff!

Skipping ahead past her ego trips to more pertinent information, note the following:

> 'And in 2013, when Scheindlin [sic] was reportedly receiving $47 million annually, no one else came close, as the next highest salaries in non-scripted television were **Jon Stewart ($30 million), Matt Lauer ($25 million), and Jay Leno ($20 million),**' claims the court filing.'In making this deal with Scheindlin [sic], Defendants blithely ignored their contractual obligations to Rebel. As a result, almost immediately after Scheindlin's [sic] pay raise, Rebel's backend compensation nosedived (Spargo, 2017 – emphasis added).

Look at who appears above: Jon Stewart and Matt Lauer – both of them Jewish. Leno is Italian, but the point is clear: the people making the money are white and that's the way it's going to stay. Judy is a TV court judge and gets paid far more than Milian, Joe Brown, the Cutlers, Christina Perez, Laura Lake or any other the others – combined. That's right, I said it: combined. I'm counting he salary and those other perks that aren't being mentioned.

Occasionally on a show she'll go into one of her rants when she comes across a welfare cheat or someone running a scam on the government and she'll declare, "not in my America!" Yeah, because your America exists in a gated community and an ultra-sheltered lifestyle. She appears every now and then on TV talk shows but other than that she's living a lifestyle that is totally insulated.

Review of "Judge Judy"

Considering this bitch is a Jew, you would think that she was one of Adolph Hitler's lieutenants or a Nazi of some rank. I say this because one of the Judge's favorite sayings when dealing with one of the plaintiffs or defendants that she doesn't like (which is most of them) is, "not in my America!" *Her* America? If this bitch had her way anybody on welfare or a fixed income would be lynched! This bitch is always talking about "get a job" or "are you working" and if you're not, she's going to lambaste you in front of millions of viewers.

Here is evidence that this woman is also stupid or has some kind of psychological impairment. On more than one occasion she's "boasted," in passing that, "My parents didn't put me through seven years of post-graduate work for me to listen to this nonsense." Seven years? Even if she has a master's degree, which usually takes two years, three years max, law school only takes a couple of years as well. All told, both should have been acquired in around FIVE years, not seven. So she's an idiot, a name she's called more than a few of the people who appear before her in court. It's called "transference" – referring to other people by labeling them to be those things that YOU actually are.

A second bit of evidence is where she admitted, on August 28, 2015, that her father used to tell her, "KISS – Keep It Simple, Stupid." This means her father either referred to her as "stupid" or used the word "stupid" in her presence on numerous occasions. I think this bitch was traumatized and this explains why, to this day, she is so caustic and callous and why almost everything out of her mouth amounts to nothing short of a cacophony of emotive labeling. And it also explains why she wrote a book with that title: "Keep It Simple Stupid."

Her husband is former "People's Court" judge Jerry Sheindlin. A kindly old man, I don't see how he and this crazy bit stayed together for more than 40 years. During a September 7, 2015 segment on "The Wendy Williams Show," Jerry was in the front row of the audience as Judy was a guest. She said that she stayed in good shape and that Jerry, who was 81, is fit and tight as is she. She explained if you get together with someone because of how they look, why would you allow those looks to change? She added that if he ever slipped up and got flabby, she would leave him in a heartbeat.

Moving on, during a March 3, 2015 airing, Sheindlin told a Defendant, "There are no coincidences in life." Say what?? In another segment aired the same day, this pompous bitch told the Plaintiff that the last time she was late was when she was born!! What happened - did it take longer than usual for the goony bird egg to crack?

Speaking of money, of all the judges on television, it only figures that the highest paid would be a Jew, and its Judge Judy Sheindlin. Do you know how much this bitch makes? To begin with, keep in mind that she only works 56 days out of the year. That's right: that's about one day a week. Now, let's talk salary.

On April 4, 2013, the Associated Press reported that Judge Judy and CBS Television Distribution announced that she would be singing on for two more years of the show, a show that is supposedly viewed by 10 million people each episode. It was also reported: "Her current contract runs through 2015,and the new deal extends her through 2017. That would give her 21 years o the air, which she compared to a winning hand in blackjack. Sheindlin, who is 70, gave no indication that she plans to retire."

Now get this; "a spokesman had no comment on whether Sheindlin will be getting a raise from her reported $45 million annual salary, which made her the highest paid person on television." Now compare this with Judge Joe Brown who was rumored to be making $20 million a year, but Brown said that was not the case, claiming that he quit the show because CBS "only" paid him $5 million a year. (If he was sincere and serious about his promo and claim that he was there to "support black manhood and protect black womanhood," then it seems that five million dollars on top of that proclaimed "mission" would have been enough).

One more thing about Judy's salary. During a show aired on April 3, 2015, this bitch made the comment that, "If there wasn't a check in my box every Monday, the lights would be off." I don't know what that means, but is it possible that this bitch gets paid every week? On the one hand the bitch says that they don't keep her around because she's beautiful, they keep her around because she's smart. Yet during the airing of an April 6, 2015 show, she tells a plaintiff, "I don't know math, I don't know science, and I don't know how to spell, but I know diamonds." Don't most Jews? And don't I say elsewhere in this book that based on her own comments, Judy is a stupid bitch that got through law school with the help of others? Well, she admitted it!

Back to Sheindlin and her money: that means this bitch makes almost a million dollars an episode. And to do what? To dole out her opinion, insults and remarks and every now and then a few points of law. In other words, she gets paid to insult people for laughs. Want some evidence. Check out the following.

"They don't keep me here because I'm beautiful. They keep me here because I'm smart," "What's the matter with you?" "You're a big zero." "Maybe you're mentally challenged so maybe I shouldn't yell at you." "You're an idiot." "You, sir, are a moron." "You see how nice I was to you before? I can turn on you like a viper." "Keep it simple, stupid." "This can either be hard, or very hard," "I know I'm going to get a lot of letters from used car dealers. They can join a long list of people who I offend on a regular basis." "I don't care what you think. I think you're an idiot." "You have an attitude. The only person who's allowed to have an attitude here is me," or how about, "Your counter-claim for your lasik surgery is denied. Go find a lady who likes you without glasses."

But there's more.

Consider these statements from this mean woman: "People are idiots." Or one of her favorites, "there's something wrong with you." How about, "Women don't usually fight over anything but a man. That's how dumb they are." She said to one female defendant, "You're mentally challenged so maybe I shouldn't yell at you. Maybe …"

Now this bitch is over 70 years old and she knows it. That means that somewhere behind the scenes, this bitch is on meds. She works long hours and sometimes it shows. Another one of her quips is if a plaintiff or defendant makes the mistake of saying, "I wish ..." she comes back with her rapid fire response that, "I wish I was five-eight." During a November 17, 2014 segment she told the Defendant, "I could be was five-ten and forty – but I'm not." During another shoe, Judge Judy was dealing with two people who weren't married and were fighting over ownership/possession of a car. During the January 7, 2015 program JUDY SAYS, "Pox on both of your houses in regard to this car."

This last statement is borderline evil. "a pox on your house is a term that hails back to Medieval England, and it is basically a phrase wishing bad things on a person and their family. This woman is a judge!

Let's face facts: in real life this bitch stands about five-two. Were she a man her attitudes and actions would be dubbed "the Napoleon complex": cracking on, insulting and using power to downgrade other people to compensate for the lack of height. She's a runt and would never qualify for any beauty competition. She was probably mocked and dogged throughout her school years for being "short." Now that she's got fame and a little power, she takes her deep-seated feelings of inadequacy out on a gullible and foolish public viewing audience.

And she's also a stupid bitch. Other than schooling and a law degree (being cute, she could have worked in groups or had someone like me write her papers for her; or since she was dating another Jewish attorney who would become her husband - she could have gotten help from him or any of her hymie relatives. During a segment aired on March 30, 2015, Judy said to one plaintiff, "I don't know about tools. The only tools I know are a screw driver and a hammer."

More evidence of her occasional conniptions is her statements of near omnipotence. During an October 31, 2014 segment, this young brother was a caretaker for a brother in a wheel chair who had obviously ripped him off. What happened was that the handicapped brother was paying his nephew, who wasn't even certified, the money that he owed the caretaker, So they were running a scam on the state. At any rate, Judy got pissed off at the old brother in the wheelchair and snapped. She started shouting, "I've been in this business forever! I know it up and down! And I know all about scams!" All of this on tape and performed unedited, in front of millions. This is what the producers want to see and hear. And as I've alleged, there is a reason for it.

While claiming near omnipotence, this Yentl (her words, not mine) is nevertheless a technological idiot by her own admission. So either the bitch is a liar and trying to be funny about the toilet paper, or she's telling the truth and like a lot of people who go to law school and rely on classmates, cheat cheats and other ways to skim through to get the degree, they can be dumb as doorknobs in those things that are social, political or cultural. Judy, in her quest to be cute and funny in front of millions, admitted it on this day.

Another time, she was really on a roll. During one segment, aired on October 15, 2014, she told one plaintiff, "I'm not good at changing a tire or much else. I can't even change a roll of toilet paper. But I can do this." During a November 5, 2014 segment she told both the plaintiff and the defendant that, "These eyes see everything."

During another episode, while staring into the camera, she used a stolen cliché as a preface to her insult: "If it walks like a duck, quacks like a duck and walks like a duck, it's a duck – not a pig. The silver costs $9 an ounce, not $6 an ounce. Any idiot should know that." What? Why would someone know how much silver costs? Of course, she's a Jew and as a group they are obsessed with valuable gems. Haven't you noticed that many of them have surnames that denote jewelry? SILVERstein, GOLDberg, RUBInstein, Rapaport, SILVERberg, PEARLstein, GOLDstein, DIAMOND, SILVERman, WOLF, FOX, and so on. Do you think that's a coincidence?

It gets worse. At least once during every other show, this bitch tells someone, "Look right here," pointing at her eyes - as if she is some kind of mindreader. This kind of behavior has an historical precedent. During slavery white folks, especially men, would convince the enslaved that they (the whites) could read their minds or had eyes in the back of their heads. Judge Judy makes statements, on a regular basis, implying that she can read minds. She acts like she shows the plaintiffs and defendants before the show even begins. "I don't believe you." "That's not what happened." "That's not how it happened." How can you mediate or arbitrate a case when you think you have made a decision before the case even begins?

But it's on fairly regular basis that her most insulting attitudes come forth. At any time during a plaintiff's testimony or a defendants statements, this bitch will stop them and tap on her watch: "It's almost time for lunch," "Can you hurry up? I heard they were having sushi today" or some rude shit like that. What message do these antics convey to those in the court and her ten million viewers (she claims)? It tells them that no matter what situation they are in, one that is going to cost them money in some form or fashion, their situations don't mean shit to her because she's hungry. And when she's hungry, she doesn't give a FUCK what these litigants have to say. Remember: she's getting paid to do this shit, and she's getting paid by other Jews, the ones in charge of the show and the ones in charge of distribution.

Moving on.

On November 5, 2013 she tells one kid, "I want you to speak really slowly, as if you were talking to an elderly, deaf person, because in actuality I am an elderly deaf person. I don't understand all that new teenaged talk where you mix all these words together as if it's a veal stew. Am I making myself clear?" Veal stew – a Jewish delicacy that everybody is supposed to relate to. Later a Defendant who stands up to her (appears to have an alcohol problem) tells Judy, straight up, that she doesn't know what she's talking about. She responds, "He's got a hot temper. He doesn't like me, I like him less, but it's MY show, and I can throw him out!" He tells her, "You don't even know what you're talking about!" and Judy immediately tells him that his case is dismissed. As he storms out of the chamber (going the wrong way) he says, "I know, I know."

In addition to her admittedly being hard of hearing, during a November 18, 2013 segment she said, "I'm really bad with math and numbers." Say what? When a person who fronts as if they are all-knowing, tells people she doesn't know, "I'm smarter than you" and challenges them with queries like, "Do you think you're smarter than me? I'll tell you: you're NOT!" and then turns around and talks about mathematical weaknesses, this does one thing: makes that person irrelevant and insignificant. The fall from claims of omnipotence to "duh, I can't add very good, duh …" is a long fall. And if she's bad at math, who knows what other simple exercises this cranky bitch is incapable of?

During the September 8, 2015 show, she finally admitted what I already knew and again, another contradiction to her previous statements of near infallibility. She said, "I'm not a stupid person. I may *look* stupid, but I'm not stupid." And three months earlier, during the May 7, 2015 show, she tells both the plaintiff and defendant, "I don't have a lot of time, so let's make this easy. I'm getting very old." She finally admitted it!

Maybe she explained her conniptions, contradictions and hypocrisy best during a November 14, 2014 segment of the show. She told a defendant that she didn't know much about bourbon or Jack Daniels but, "I don't know one from another, I just know my vodkas."

During a program aired on May 1, two black women stand before Judy with one suing the other because of an assault. I t seems that they were fighting over this black man -- who was in prison at the time. Judy immediately flatters them for being nice looking and smart and sums up the case by charging them "fighting over a piece of trash." It gets worse.

One of these women is 61 and the other, the plaintiff, is 54. These women find out about one another and begin feuding. The man had been living with one of the women (the Defendant) The Plaintiff says he defendant said, 'I'm here to beat your ass." And then fired on her, hitting her so hard the Plaintiff said she saw stars. Ms. Canti, the sister who blazed on the Plaintiff, had come to the plaintiff's apartment complex for the sole reason of kicking that ass. All this took place on December 26 – the day after Christmas.

Ms. Canti said she was there to fetch some things from the man's apartment as he was in jail. She looked through the window and saw that the apartment was vacant. She claims the Plaintiff, Ms. Pashon called her a "stupid stalker." She asked her, "do you still want to whip my ass?" But here's the interesting part. Judy said, "Instead of the two of you assaulting each other, why don't you both assault HIM?

Here we have a judge telling two black women to commit the crime of assault on live television. Only a Jew could get away with that without being censored or canned!

During an October 28, 2014 segment this conservative curmudgeon admitted something else. The issue was if this black woman had been bilked by these Asians who rented her a studio. She moved in and smelled gas. They said it was the pilot light on the stove and said they fixed it. She came back and the next day, she smelled gas again. She moved out and wanted her rent and security back. Judy sided with the sister stating that "I've had gas smells before because of a pilot light. You know, sometimes the flame can blow out. But that was a long time ago –I haven't used my stove in 27 years." Twenty-seven years? And this bitch has the nerve to act as if she can relate to the common man?!

She more insults to go along with her negative and vitriolic tone: "When you came here, did you think it was going to be easy?" she'll ask on a regular basis. "Where did you think you were coming to today, to the beach?" On the November 5, 2013 episode, she says in reference to a Defendant, "Not only is he an idiot, but he's an idiot and a liar," and on the same show follows up with, "You're an irresponsible idiot"

Her "Jewishness" comes out on a regular basis. She throws in these Yiddish words like schmutz, schtooping (which could mean fucking), kerfuffle (fight), chutzpah (pronounced "hutzpah"), kosher, schmuck, geshikhte (which means "history or long story" in Yiddish. During one episode aired on July 27, 2015, this guy stared describing the background and model of his car as Judy says, "I didn't ask you for a geshikhte ..."), glitch, and others – including "goy," which is a term that they use to describe anyone who is not Jewish.

In an August 3, 2015 segment she asks a defendant, "Did you think we *shlepped* you all the way from Minnesota …? Interestingly, schlepped means, "to haul or carry (something heavy or awkward) as in "she schlepped her groceries home." But it can also mean, when it comes to a person, to "go or move reluctantly or with effort," as in, "I would have preferred not to schlep all the way over there to run an errand. " In either case Judy's choice of words proves that the solicitation or invitation of this person to appear on "Judge Judy" is anything but pleasant.

In fact, this "Yiddishization" of American language is being done on the big screen as well as television. Jews are slick: they want to incorporate their words into the English language so that their small numbers can be negated and so that their hidden agenda of "Israel first" and Zionism can be better disguised. (I cover this in another book that addresses the American Israeli Public Affairs Committee).

Television shows like "The Goldbergs" (ABC), "Seinfeld" (NBC) and others that have members of the family who have Jewish backgrounds are increasing on a regular basis. Prominent display of names of producers, directors and executive types are flashed on television and movie screens: Spielberg, Goldberg, Silverman, Kraft, Rubinstein, Sterling, Bernstein, Diamond, Berg, Jewison, Tisch, Gould, Wolf, and so on. It's subtle, but then again, so are many of their tactics. The women of Jewish persuasion are more aggressive, overt with their actions, and short-tempered. Witness Joan Rivers and now, Judge Judy.

As she was castigating a defendant who had been fired by his mother during the October 17, 2104 episode, she used an example of how someone who owns a business can fire anyone they want. "If you don't like your beard, or the way you wear your pants, they can fire you – in MY America!" She belted out an example of how she "happens to adore Leslie Moonves" who is her boss, and how she would wave at him at a stop sign but if he wanted to fire her any time he could. By the way, Leslie Moonves is the Jew that owns CBS and he's married to Judy Chen, the Asian chick that hosts "The Talk" and "Big Brother."

And one more thing about Moonves: in July of 2018 he got busted for sexual harassment. This powerful Jew, married to this foxy Asian chick, simply let power go to his head. On July 30, 2018, Variety reported the incident as follows:

> Moonves was accused of sexual misconduct by **six women** on Friday in a report by Ronan Farrow in the New Yorker. Among the accusers are actress Illeana Douglas, who claimed Moonves had her fired from a CBS pilot **after she turned down his advances**; writer Janet Jones, who alleges he assaulted her **during a pitch meeting** while Moonves worked at 20th Century Fox; and producer Christine Peters, who accused Moonves of making an advance to her **when she was up for a job at CBS** Films.(Rubin, 2018 – emphasis added)

"During a pitch meeting." "Fired from a pilot." "Up for a job." This is the casting couch and it has existed for centuries and these white women full well know it. People come to these powerful men trying to sell a script and the next thing you know they are told to drop their draws. This is going on all over Hollywood, and I documented in my book The Casting Couch. But my emphasis was on the pedohilia and homosexual behavior of these men. But it all comes from the same source. As we learned from Machiavelli, "Power corrupts, and absolute power corrupts absolutely.

To add an important "sidebar" to this before moving on, note that the self-proclaimed moralist and host of "The Talk" on CBS defended her husband. Of course she would: he got her the job and not only that, but she is host of TWO shows – "The Talk" and "Big Brother"! At any rate, check out the following:

> CBS Corp.'s board of directors is meeting on Monday to consider the fate of the chief executive. After allegations were leveled, Chen posted a statement on Twitter on Friday night. "I have known my husband, Leslie

> Moonves, since the late '90s, and I have been married to him for almost 14 years. Leslie is a good man and a loving father, devoted husband and inspiring corporate leader," she said. "He has always been a kind, decent and moral human being. I fully support my husband.(Rubin, 2018)

Chen claims that Moonves was kind and decent. But she cannot speak for his morality because they are apart for long periods of time. And as the saying goes, "When the cat is gone, the mouse will play." He just got busted by six women; he probably engaged and provided opportunities for scores more, who knows.

Just remember that Moonves is a man that Judge Judy says she "adores." And he did the same thing to Julie Chen that Judy's husband, Jerry, did to her. At any rate, I hope you see Judge Judy's value: the popular show is used to promote "yiddishization" on a number of levels, and she has it down to a work of art.

These Jews take care of their own – as all groups should be. But they control the media, the movie industry (even the old fashioned celluloid that the movies were made on), the casting and so on. These "stars" you see (most of whom are lacking in real talent) include pretty girls who have had nose surgery and who are willing to suck dick to get a break (guys as well, gay or not). Here's a few names: Shia LeBeouf ("Transformers," "Disturbia"), Mila Kunis (with her fine brown ass, just got impregnated by Ashton Kutcher), Kate Hudson, Cole Hauser, Seth Green, Pink, Gwyneth Paltrow, Jack Black, Robert Downey, Jr., Sarah Jessica Parker, and so many more. These people are "famous" and get television exposure because they are Jews and because Jews are determining what gets on TV and on the movie screen.

And there's a bunch of them who you didn't even know were Jewish. But guess what? The Jews know, and that's why the marketing and distribution of movies can make a show a hit in certain sections of the country and that's why even TV shows that ain't about shit can last and last and then make even more money in syndication and residual payments for the actors. Here ya go: Zac Efron, Janes Franco, Jake and Maggie Gyllenhaal, Scarlett Johansson, Joaquin Phoenix, Winona Ryder, and many more.

My point is to show that Jewish nationalism is alive and well. It's as if Hollywood was in old Harlem and all the casting directors, executives, producers and other decision makers were black nationalists (if they were typical negroes they'd be hiring white girls too), But if they were '60s militants and had all the power. A few whites would be hired just as they were during the 1970s "Blaxploitation" movies, but it would be for token and degrading roles – just like the Jews do to black people to this very day.

Judy is not only a part of this trend but is a beneficiary and a leader. She constantly hurls statements like, "This is America!" after making an insulting comment about some law or rule that this country promotes that she doesn't like.

Judy sometimes attributes Yiddish sayings to her husband Jerry and offers such pearls of wisdom as the ones she offered during a November 5, 2013 segment where she told a Plaintiff: "Never lend your friends money because you lose the money and you lose the friend." The ultimate piece of evidence of her ego came during a November 12, 2013 segment when she referred to herself as "a truth machine."

During the airing of a July 20, 2018 show, two neighbors opposed one another. The plaintiff was claiming that as an animal lover, he and the defendant fell out after thirteen years because the defendant took some cats and instead of turning them over to take to a shelter, took them up to the nearby mountains where they could be food for wolves. The defendant was then questioned by Judy. His story was that the plaintiff was placing "no parking" signs in front of the house so that visitors could not park. This was done after years of people parking wherever they wanted to. This was the story of these two men. At one point she called the plaintiff's marking up of a paper he gave her as "stupid." Later she described this same plaintiff as "a bad neighbor and stupid." Seconds later she said he was "a fool."

You know what this bitch said after listening to these long explanations from these two curmudgeons? She told them that she "didn't care" and that she "wasn't interested." The question is why in the hell did she put them through all this? I'll tell you why: These shows give people a chance to air dirty laundry in front of millions of viewers as Judge Judy, for one, asks personal questions and gets all that information on tape to be preserved for all eternity. Who knows what these Jews are going to do with that information? I'll tell you one thing they're going to do: they're going to distribute copies of that show all over the world and paint a picture of how depressed, neurotic, vindictive, petty and silly the American public is. Judy does to all races what shows like "Judge Mathis" does to black people and what "The People's Court" does to Latinos: *degrades and publicly humiliates them.*

During an August 27, 2014 airing, she was on a roll. This asshole had wrecked three of his girlfriend's cars over the three years they were together. The woman was suing him for wrecking her car. The plaintiff looked fat and she looked serious. As Judy was grilling this idiot, he kept answering "yeah," like the thug that he probably was. He left a six year old and a ten year at home alone. Judy says, "You're more pathetic than I thought you were." Terrea Hardin was pissed when she found out that Younger allowed a woman, who was supposed to be buying the car, to total it.

Terrea got the police report, found out a woman was driving, and decided to sue Alan Younger. His excuse is that he pays bills at the house and does a lot of "dad work" around the house and "believes that that's my car, too." To "satisfy my hordes of fans" as she put it, she explained that Younger should sue the woman he let to drive the car because "I'm awarding Miss Hardin the $4,500." That took care of that.

During the September 2, 2014 segment, we find this 40 year old woman Barbara Borsodi, is pregnant by a 20 year old, and she's trying to sue him. They lived "Wherever they could go." She's suing this kid, Harley Howard for back rent and her washer and dryer. They're from South Bend, Indiana. She says she's on leave because she hurt her shoulder. She is now pregnant. She has a 19 year old son and another one 22 and 24. The father of the child is the same age as her son! She sold her 1998 Firebird, got the money, and moved in with her son, his son's pal. The other two are over 21 living in Hammond, Indiana. They lived together from March 2013 to December. She says he owes her for the washer and dryer and rent and "we entered into this agreement together."

He told her he could be a man and wanted to date her. "His mom said she was good for us being together," she said. Then she breaks out crying. A 41 year old woman with three kids, all of whom are older than the 19 year old that she's pregnant by. "He begged me to date him," she said. Judy dogged this bitch. He signed documents that the woman wants him to be responsible for. He was 18 when he signed the lease. "He can't enter into a binding contract, he can't pour wine in a restaurant," Judy says.

She admits that the pregnancy was "a mistake." Judy says, "He has no judgment – he's a teenager. You treat him like an adult, but he's not an adult." She has a lot of disabilities "and he's going to be responsible for that baby for twenty one years," Judy says. Judy warns her that 10 million people in the audience know who the father is so she can't hide it. "You can't obligate a teenager to honor a contract," Judy says. "Case is dismissed."

During a September 1, 2014airing, this sister (Frances Howard) called the cops on her baby's daddy (Otis Mays, Jr.) and said he kidnapped her. They had been living together for five years; he had a job and she didn't. He supported the household and she had occasion to call the cops on him two times – in July of 2013 and September of 2013, she claimed. She says he got a little physical (as did she) and she called the cops. "Mr. Mays was talking to other women …" And she got physical first and then called the cops.

Kevin Williams Jr. is suing Rufus and Michelle Dixon for a car that the Hixon's totaled. Judy starts off by saying that it is a police fraud case that they want her to be a part of. "Start off with your bologna, just tell me what you're suing him for." She suspects them "I'm going to listen to the fairy tales on both sides," she says. Kevin said his car was stolen and he saw it pull off. He immediately called the cops. He had gone to get charcoal and was dropping off mail and that's when somebody jacked his car.

He called Lucas and his phone was going straight to voice mail. He called Michelle and she came to get him. Cops were already there, they made a report and then went to Michelle's house. Rufus is pulling up behind her car and he's crying. Kevin got in her car, he was upset and Rufus followed him in his car. Michelle was loaning him her car. The next day she texts and asks if he's okay. A week later they found the car and it has been in an accident. Rufus said he did it and he would make it right. "Did you call the police because they have an open case against a car jacker?" Judy asks.

Kevin says he didn't call the cops and explains why. Rufus tries to explain it, but Judy cuts him off. "Your case is dismissed. I hope the police and the insurance company are watching this. I think it's a scam," Judy said. And during the September 26, 2014 segment she told one black man who had been paying another brutha "off the books" that, ""Don't you know I have IRS agents who sit around and do nothing but watch my show?

That makes sense and that's why she gets paid so much. The program gets these dumb ass people to sign forms before the show, and part of that contract is that the show will pay part of the lawsuit money that Judy charges them. Then, there HAS to be another section that swears them not to dog out Judy or rebuke her - so she gets to insult them at random but they can't respond. And then there's the screening that she admits takes place: IRS agents watching her show and watching these idiots tell on themselves. And if Judy's doing it, so are Mathis, Milian, and the rest of them. America is full of idiots and the people who appear on television and before these TV judges are classic examples of this fact.

During an October 27, 2014 segment, a Latino was suing a black man and his wife for the fact that his dogs (the brothers) ate 73 of his chickens. The Latino could barely speak English, and the black couple came off as brash. He was about 6'5" and she was light skinned with blonde hair. Both the plaintiff and the defendant lived in a rural section of California, outside of slum-as Moreno Valley (my opinion). So the brother got pissed or appeared to be so when Judy asked him a few questions. The Latino was away from home and when his friend found the dogs eating the chickens, he ushered the dogs into their house and left a note telling the couple that "we've got your dog."

All perfectly legit and the Latino won $2,000 for the loss of his chickens. But during the decision, Judy cracked on the black man by stating, "Either you got up on the wrong side of the bed or your underwear is too tight." The brother, under his breath, denied that his underwear was too tight but then, after rending a decision against him and his wife, Judy walked off the bench and said it again:

"You're underwear is too tight." What would make this bitch make such a statement. Was it because the brother was tall, did she think he had an eight foot dick?

During an October 2th show, a white woman was suing her ex-husband, Benny Morales. Judy asks him why the woman shelled out all the money she was suing for. He said he "tracks light," which was never explained. He said the money she gave him was a gift, not a loan. He said he told her that his financial status was not stable. She nevertheless allowed him to move him in. Then Judy turns to the white woman: "That makes you like a lot of lady suckers around. You were supporting the live-in sponge." The white girl found out he was cheating, and kicked him out. The white woman had red hair and blue eyes. Judy's conclusion: "You look like a very intelligent girl. Your eyes and nose knew he was a loser. Follow your instincts: he's a loser." Her case was nevertheless dismissed.

In September of 2013 (which Judy found out later was a lie) she says she had access to his computers and she found some x-rated pictures "of naked women which were not myself." So she confronted him when he got home. She said it was over "and you can just be here for your daughter and that's it." She never said one time that SHE was leaving, but she told HIM to leave. She admitted that she knows that she can get physical, so she gathered some things to leave. Judy said "He didn't care if you left, but you weren't going to leave with his daughter."

The next morning she told him to leave and get his belongings. His name is on the lease because she claims she's the head of the household. This bitch gets welfare and is therefore considered "head of the house." The brother was packing and what she says is "taking his time." The brother took his kid and left and she called the cops, they came and told them it was kidnapping. He wouldn't pick up his cell phone. Judy read both complaints and claims she can "just fill in the blanks."

As a result of her lie, he was arrested and booked – the day after Christmas. Not only that, but he lost his job. The charge was for "aggravated domestic assault." Judy said she didn't a single word about aggravated domestic assault. The cops told her that the man was her biological father. So she came up with the assault charge. Judy ratted her out saying that the State "might" come forward and make her payback all those welfare payments they extended to her. She said that Mays was a "co-conspirator" against the welfare system, since he had a job, had lived there five years and knew she was on welfare.

He lost his job as a security guard. Judy awarded him $5,000 because he lost his job because of the woman's lies.

During an October 27, 2014 segment, these people who live in a commune are dealing with a wrecked car. Two women who appear to be hippies, were suing a man named "Mateo," another one of the commune members. He was teaching one of the women how to drive and she went to turn a corner and ran into a tree. She didn't feel she should have to pay because "I shouldn't have been in the car in the first place," although she was 25 years old and held a driver's permit. Judy goes on one of her "American decadence" spiels and says, "We used to be a great country. We have become a country of avoidance, a country of 'somebody else did it,' 'somebody else's fault.'"

During an October 10, 2104 segment, a black woman was suing a black man for $3,500 that she gave him to pay a deposit on a house they were buying together. Both of them were in the military. They also had a child together.

Judy treated them both like shit. At one point she told the black man, "If it doesn't make sense if can't be true." That's bullshit. A lot of things that don't make sense are nevertheless true. Take white racism, for instance. It's not logical and it doesn't make sense, but is surely exists and is therefore true. Later she told the brother, Antonio Jackson, "I'm 71 years old, and I'm smart, you fool!" Jackson ended up kicking her out of the house because they fought when she had another man in the house and he claims she "cheated on me." He says she broke a lot of stuff on her way out. "As long as she pays bills in the home, you can't throw her out," Judy explained. Then she gave the woman the $3,500 back. "As soon as he puts that first hand on you, get out of there," she warns viewers.

During an early morning airing of the show on Monday, November 18, 2013, Judy was hearing a case where a woman told her what another judge had ruled on. Judy responds by claiming, "I've known a lot of dumb judges in my life." Really, now? By making that statement, if she's telling the truth, Judy is admitting that judges can be assholes. Even though it is just her opinion, she is making that opinion as a member of the court – her words mean something. So if she knows 'a lot of dumb judges,' then we have to assume that such a statement means more than one. If she knows a lot of dumb judges, she has a moral and ethical obligation to not only state the names of those judges but the work toward exposing them. In the case of judges, like cops, one bad apple CAN spoil the whole bunch.

Now when you take that caustic statement and add to another one that she makes on a regular basis – that being that, "They don't keep me around here because I'm beautiful, they keep me around here because I'm smart" – then that means that whoever makes the decisions agrees with the egotistical Judy that she is smart. If she's smart and she knows "a lot of dumb judges," then by not reporting them to the proper authorities she is aiding these judges in their on-going stupidity. And those judges are hurting the people who stand in front of them with Judy being aware of it. That means that Judy is aiding and abetting these judges in the commission of their poor decisions against the people. That makes Judy a "co-conspirator."

But that's not all. Judy's got these bullshit beliefs like this one (which she claims she learned from her grandmother): "If you tell the truth, you don't have to have a good memory." Not only is this bullshit, but she repeated it time and time again. Then, on November 15, 2013 she said it and claimed that lying was something that men and women do, but men do it more. She added, "When you get caught in a lie once, the person who is listening to you is not about to believe anything else you say."

A black woman and her son were being sued by this Latina for hitting her car with his niece's go-cart. Why this old ass nigga was riding around in a go-cart designed for a 5 year old is beyond me, but that's the way it goes: the stupider the case the more fodder Judge Judy has to work with and the more people she has to insult and poke fun at.

Judy told the Defendants, "Your mother may buy that, but this truth machine doesn't buy it." What? Who does this bitch think she is? Of all the mistakes I've caught this bitch making, many of them documented in this book, how can she consider her statements or decisions as consistent or irreversible as a "machine"? This is the same woman who says, "If it doesn't make sense it can't be true." I believe she has since modified this bullshit statement, but my point here is that she is, in no way, like a machine.

During the September 1, 2014 show, we find Shannandoah Baker (actual spelling), a white woman who gets disability for a bipolar disorder – she gets $1200 per month. Judy doesn't like anyone who gets "free money." Her "this is America" comments usually follows, as if people have it easy no matter how hard life is – something Judy wouldn't know a damn thing about. When Baker told her that she was in jail for two months for possession of stolen property, the first question out of Judy's distended mouth was, "and you continued to get your disability while in jail? ? When Baker said yes, that is when the "this is America" comment came forward.

During a September 24, 2014 segment, she listened to a Latino kid describing the meaning of words that kids use on the internet. In this case it was "hmu", which means "hit me up." Judy replies, "America is going down the toilet." Then she repeated it and added, "That's why I'm glad I'm old."

Baker was suing Cynthia Wagner because she says that Wagner took money off of her debit card (stole money from her bank account). Wagner was counter-suing for money owed and pet sitting.

The disability check is automatically deposited onto her debit card, and Baker only gave Wagner permission to take off the money for the rent ($300) and money to care for her pet pit bull. Baker says when she got released, the pit bull was skinny and hadn't been cared for. Therefore she (Baker) was suing Wagner for $920 for stealing money that she didn't have permission to take.

Wagner showed Judy a contract that she and Baker had made out. Baker said she never signed a contract so Judy showed it to her. "I don't know how she got my signature on here, I swear that I did not sign this." Baker's mother came up to testify and reminded that her daughter had brain surgery. The mother than sat down. The defendant said that Baker "wouldn't know the truth if it slapped her in the face." Judy dismissed Wagner's counter-claim.

During an August 21, 2015 show a woman was suing her brother Kenneth Vincent and his woman, Heather Blackmon for $800 that she loaned them for a boat. Vincent said "she didn't loan us the money, her boyfriend and they're no longer together." Judy, about to feel defeat, said, "That's okay. You're going to pay HER and she can pay him." Then, out of nowhere, she explained her decision by calling the man and his wife "ungrateful pigs."

On August 19, 2014 Judge Judy told another lie. A landlord was being sued for not making repairs. Amy Hansen, who admitted doing damage and who was the defendant, was suing because the landlord didn't want to return her security deposit, and was complaining about this middle eastern man's lack of due diligence as the basis for her nonpayment of rent. Judy spent most of her time scolding this landlord and at one time told him, "Most landlords paint the apartments every three years." *That's a damn lie and she knows it.* She's a "truth machine," but she has her own version of the truth. If landlords painted every three years, they'd be charging more rent and tenants would be a lot more satisfied with their domiciles.

During an August 29, 2014 segment, a woman was suing a man. He purchased the cars but put them in her name. Judy knew this was a scam right away. But again, she attributed her decision to her experience and how "when somebody starts to grin and move from side to side," she knows something is wrong. She's full of shit. This guy was black and when it's white folks it's a smile, when its black men it's a GRIN – there's a history to such a designation. She added, "Your mouth is getting dry, do you know what that says to me? It says I'm getting a whole lot of bologna." More Jewish bullshit – it's derived from that old racist psychology white folks used to run on us when we were enslaved by them – they wanted us to think that they had eyes in the back of their heads or could read our minds. And again when the black woman started with the statement, "I don't feel …" Judy again came up with the reliable, "I don't care how you feel. How you feel is not important to me."

When the brother asked, "What about her trashing my house?" Judy whispered across the courtroom, "I don't care." After the case, the two were airing their opinions back and forth and this woman said her solution was "get me another man and keep on moving." See how they think? Black men think the same way, but in many cases believe women are above such thoughts and actions. Bullshit if they are.

During an August 29, 2014 segment, a 37-year old woman is suing a man she bought a car from and another man, who is her ex husband who did the work on the car. She didn't get a bill of sale and she paid them in cash. At one point Judy says, "You know that you have no case, and I know you have no case." I have a question: if this bitch knew that the woman didn't have a case, then why did she bring it forth on national television? She did it so that she could make fun of the man who she paid – a Mr. Sprague. She asked Sprague his age and he told her he was 58.

She asked him if he knew what she was, and then answered, "Still working." So she allowed all this to take place so that she could make fun of a man who works on cars for a living, who is barely getting by, his pal who helps him and a woman who is so stupid that she allowed herself to get bilked by these guys who, for the most part, buy cars from auto auctions, fix them up and sell them. All this while she brings in $45 million a year for working less than six months. Judge Judy is into humiliation regardless of gender, but since she probably hasn't been fucked in years, her frustration enables many of her arguments to be substanceless and she'll launch insults even if they come back to bite her in the ass.

Again on August 29, 2014 Judy handled a case where a man was suing his young niece after she let him move in with her. She was charging this older man five hundred per month and he only got seven hundred from disability. Judy called her charging him that much "unconscionable" and the court wasn't going to enforce an "unconscionable contract." That's bullshit: courts do it all the time, especially when it comes to marital situations. They garnishee men's paychecks for huge amounts, they put men in jail for not paying child support for kids that are found out not to be theirs. What's more "unconscionable" than that?

Judy denied the woman the rent even though he slipped and admitted that he made money on the side by working on cars (in addition to his disability payment). She was holding on to all of his stuff because he didn't pay her. The girl kept arguing with Judy saying that it was fair for "a room all to yourself." She said she was storing stuff for him until he paid her. Then she turned on the plaintiff, a "Mr. Granado." He didn't pay her and said he didn't. He's 53 years old.

Judy tells him to "pay something" implying that he's a leech. She awarded him nothing but told him to "box up all this stuff" and she gave him five days to do it. When the show was over the girl snitched him off and said he was fabricating information on his disability. Do you think they won't check on that? She fucked over him and got revenge on him not paying her.

During the November 4, 2013 segment, this bitch must have been in one of her "playing the dozens" moods. The only difference is that she is the only one who can hurl insults and the plaintiff/defendant has to stand there and take it up the ass. For instance, on this show she told one young Latino plaintiff, "I've been doing this for twenty-five years. You know what that means? When I was becoming a star, you were still pooping in your pants." Then, with his mother standing right next to him, Judy said the following: "I wouldn't believe your mother if she stood up there on a stack of bibles. You know why? Because she believes YOU. If your mother believes you were in your room sleeping by yourself, then she's a fool. I, on the other hand, am not a fool."

She told one smart-ass defendant, "I don't need to be validated by you." Then the asshole winked at her in a way that nobody would have noticed, but Judy had to make a big deal out of, telling him, "Don't wink at me. Wink at Byrd. You'll get the same reaction." At first Byrd quickly turned to her as if he was going to say, "Whatchu talkin' about bitch?" but quickly came to his senses that this woman was his boss and immediately turned back around and adopted his stoic, robotic stance.

Once, this guy named Barrows got busted for a Driving Under the Influence and had to go to court some place else. But he went to court drunk and this incident came up on "Judge Judy." The narrator even mentioned it. That should have been embarrassing enough, but not for Judy.

When Judy talked about it in her court she described the man as an "idiot, moron, and fool" who went to court drunk. Granted, it was something stupid to do. Maybe that man had an alcohol problem or perhaps he was, indeed, an idiot. But that ain't for this bitch to say on national television! She's supposed to be above the fray, she's supposed to be setting moral standards with her decisions. Instead, since Jews control television and she's a Jew, she gets away with murder and, for the sake of ratings points and her number one rating among TV judges, she spends her time calling names, throwing lugs and insults and ratcheting up her reputation as a true bitch on wheels.

This gay guy sponsored a competition and vowed that the first prize would be three thousand dollars. He didn't pay up, to the plaintiff, also gay, took him to court. Judy lambasted the defendant and then the plaintiff provided a video that showed the trophy that was promised. Judy aired it and sure enough, the brothas name was announced and the defendant, dressed like a female, said, "And the winner of the three thousand dollar prize is …" and then said his name.

Judy had Byrd turn off the tape and started at the defendant, who had been lying about promising three thousand dollars. Then she said, "Your goose is cooked!" She said that he had committed a fraud. The defendant claimed that the rules were that there had to be a minimum of eight contestants in order for the money to be handed out. July pointed out that on the tape he announced, in front of an audience, that the winner was supposed to get that money. She then told him that she doubts if he'll ever be able to sponsor another contest again. The defendant won his case.

One case was about some teenage boys who messed up some jet skies. The Plaintiff wanted one of the boys to pay for the damage to his boat, as they had rammed it. One of the white boys was sitting on the bench as the Plaintiff spoke. Judy called him to the stand and said, "I saw him over there with a wise-guy look on his face. I just wanted to call him a jerk." What's wrong with this bitch? How can she do this and continue to keep getting paid millions? I'll tell you why: she's Jewish, and so are the producers, the distributors and the people that own the major television stations. And Jews appear to be the only ones on television that can call people names (whether it be through cartoon characters, on situation comedies or even during news commentaries).

"I know you're scared to death of me," she told two young plaintiffs (who were gay, no less), and added, "It gets worse." Before even hearing their case, she explained the pre-appearance process, where she reads over statements that they have signed, highlights certain parts of it and writes notes to herself. She then refers to their claims as "convoluted" and tells the defendant (who was also gay) that his is "equally convoluted." She begins grilling the plaintiffs and told the defendant, "I don't care about your feelings. Your feelings are totally irrelevant to me."

She's made similar comments before in other shows, but this one was particularly insulting because the truck that was being sued for was a1986 and the man wanted to sell it for $500. Judy says, "That's about right." One of the plaintiffs explained that it had new suspension and some other new parts but Judy, acting as if she is an expert on truck value, continued to claim, sight unseen, that $500 was a fair price. Throughout she was fixated on the fact that they (she and the staff) were going to have Chinese food for lunch and made references to looking forward to having "fried rice;' in a word, not giving much credence or paying much attention to the case in front of her. Not to be outdone, during a November 17, 2104 segment she told a Defendant, "Your feelings, legally untrained, don't mean anything to me."

But her own feelings appear to sometimes get out of control, as if her meds kicked it and she got a case of the "hot-to-trots." Take for example the show of August 21, 2015. It was the case of Linda Morrow, and her boyfriend George Wilson, two young people who were suing. Judy starts of the case in error stating, "This is your son ..." and Morrow immediately corrects her replying, "He's not my son, he's my boyfriend." Judy looked at him lustfully and then looked back at her: "My goodness! You have good taste! Nice!" The point is, there is no objectivity when this Jewish bitch is on the stand.

Chomocco Ferrell was being sued by his brother by not paying his younger brother, Jamerson Ferrell for helping to bail him out. His younger brother in South Dakota) so he (the older brother from Portland) was in jail for domestic assault. He needed $2500 and the young brother sent it. After he got out the older brother said it wasn't a loan. He wired it to his girlfriend to go down to the jail (a white woman) and pay the bail. He has five children paying child support for all three of his other kids and two live with him. The older brother was lying his ass off. Judy whispers to the elder to say "thank you" to his brother. She turns to the white woman and says, "Don't have any children with him." It cost $176 interest to wire the money, on line via Western Union. The older brother, still shirking his responsibility, says, "We didn't have a contract or anything. Don't we have to have a contract." Pissed, Judy says, "I know I'm dealing with somebody whose challenged, but try to listen to me. In other words, she was calling him retarded.

This was a set up case that didn't deserve to be on television because it was a slam dunk. This chickenshit muthafucka gets bailed out for domestic violence – probably against another white woman – by his younger brother who lives more than 1500 miles away. Later we find out that it was not domestic violence, but it was failure to pay past child support. At any rate the younger brother brings his older brother before Judge Judy because he wouldn't pay back the money and then has the gall to bring ANOTHER white bitch with him when he shows up in court. The brother who filed came in a blazer and looking appropriate for court; the slouchy muthafucka from South Dakota, white bitch in tow, had on a powder blue shirt with a white t-shirt on under it, looking like he just got off work at Kinko's. He had a shaved head and buck teeth.

So when Judy said he looked "challenged" and when the suggested to the white woman not to have babies with him, she was probably right on both counts. My point is that anyone could see that this case was going to lead to a lot of embarrassment and Judy doesn't appear to be a fan of interracial couples, especially when they involve white women and black men.

The plaintiff had him a white girl as well. These niggas deserved each other. After all, as I always say, you are what you sleep with.

On another show involving this Italian dude being sued by this little old lady, the plaintiff said he owed her the money because she (the plaintiff) had paid for his mother's divorce many years prior and the mother promised to repay that money and, in fact stipulated it on a document that the woman produced. The defendant resisted, claiming that HE had paid for the divorce, but his claims were found to be a lie. Judy dogged his ass and the decision was the full five thousand dollars.

He made a smart remark about the money being no big deal and Judy said, "You're a barber. I doubt if you've seen five thousand dollars in a month in your life." He said something like, "I make good money," and Judy, not paying attention (as usual) must have thought he said he made more money than she did – something he did not say. She got up and before walking away from the bench, remarked over her shoulder, "You think you make more than me? I doubt it." And then walked off. Everybody knows that this Jew, sponsored and supported by the Jews that own CBS Distributing, earns a whopping $45 million a year – and doesn't even work a full year.

On another show, these middle easterners, Maatsura-Smith, were suing this brother named Gerren Gray, who used to date this guy's sister, and when they broke up, he smashed Mastsura-Smith's car window with a rock. Gray was lying his ass off, claiming that a stranger he met in a bar at 4am in the morning was with him and he was giving him a ride home so this guy threw the rock. He should have just come into court and slapped the shit out of Judy, because that's how she reacted. She humiliated him, told him she didn't like him, and then proceeded to intellectually and legally cut his black ass to shreds.

One show featured a plaintiff named Caradad Cabrerra who was suing her brother-in-law. She had moved from Florida, Mississippi to Alabama. When Judy asked her about it she explained that it's all on the state line. Judy looked like an ass. The woman came on talking funny, but I believe it was because she might have been deaf, but at any rate she was animated and was acting like she was loaded. Judy asked her if she took prescribed medicine. When the woman tried to respond, Judy hit the top of the table and said, "It's my playpen!" Just before that she explained to the woman that she (Judy) "knew everything." The woman told her that she had PTSD and Judy kept telling her that she took prescribed medicine and the woman kept telling her that she did not.

Judy was pissed because when she tried to pry into the legal record of the woman's son, the woman said "that has nothing to do with this case." tells the woman, still pressing that the woman took drugs, said "I have a nose," as if this metaphorical reference had any relevance; unless that woman was musty or her pussy was stinking (which it most likely was not) Judy's crooked ass nose is not an extra sensory organ of any kind. The problem is that Judy thinks she has super powers and, as she put it, "knows everything." Nothing could be further from the truth.

The woman was talking shit to Judy telling her she was NOT going to "come back here." She kept talking and confronted Judy and they talked over each other. "My nose tells me that you have a problem," she said. "I have a problem – my stuff is missing, Cabrerra shot back. So in Judy's book, if you talk back to her or give her "two for one," and she gets offended, you've got to be high or out of your mind. This is one arrogant bitch, let me tell you.

On Halloween, October 31st, 2013, this human witch made an ass out of herself. The plaintiff was a man who impregnated this woman and then bought her a $4,000 car. She was supposed to pay it back but didn't. It must have been a full moon because Judy was hyped up on something. At one point, siding with the man and castigating the woman, she said that the man was a "stranger" who paid for food, rent and the car. She didn't attempt to clean up that asinine statement and continued to refer to the niceness of this man that the woman wasn't married to as a "stranger."

You see, Judy is one of those bitches who believes that marriage is somehow sanctimonious and the way it should be. If you come in her court as boyfriend and girlfriend, she might make a correct ruling, but she'll always throw in her little insults about "living together" and "playing house." Well, this bitch made the statement that this man, who this bitch had (in my view) trapped with a pregnancy and who had cared for her, given her shelter, fed her and bought her a 4,000 car – and even paid her child support WHILE she lived with him (how?), was a "stranger."

Really, Judy? The Merriam-Webster dictionary defined a "stranger" as "someone who you have not met before or do not know." The Cambridge Dictionary defines a stranger as, "someone not known or not familiar." The Longman Dictionary says that a stranger is "someone that you do not know." Now, Judge Judy has 25 million viewers – or so she claims. If that is the case, my question is this: why would this hook-nosed bitch tell a god damn lie and claim that two people who had a relationship and a baby, where the man was giving this woman money and fucking her regularly, were somehow "strangers"? In her world if you're not a brother, a mother or some blood relative, then you're a stranger. Jews like Sheindlin aren't married to the people in Tel Aviv, but mighty funny they keep sending them money, and they're loyal to them. Judy, in simple terms, is full of shit. She thinks that reality is whatever she says it is.

After the case was over the woman said, "I don't believe you. This is ridiculous" and continued talking shit. Judy says, "turn off her mike and then turned to the woman's son and says, "Try to see to it that your mother gets help. That's all." And walks off. So not is the a bully but like all bullies, she also appears to be a coward.

Smith showed Judge Judy an email from Gray that showed that Gray tried to cut a deal before coming to court. Judy reads it and then tells the brutha, "Oh by the way, you spelled "their" wrong; it's t-h-e-r-e." Gray tried to explain that he talked into a machine and the machine spits out the words, which is hi-tech at its finest. Judy, a technological dinosaur by her own admission, says, "then your machine is an idiot." First of all those machines spit out words based on how they sound, so misspellings are frequent. But how can a machine be an idiot? She's a mean old woman who's menopausal and not getting fucked and has nowhere to spend all those millions. So she takes it out on low-income defendants (and sometimes plaintiffs).

In one segment before the case began, Judy was going over the generalities with the plaintiff and defendant. The defendant told Judy that she moved out of the apartment and Judy replied, "That's a good thing. In that way we don't' have to worry about any problems when the case is over." So then she ADMITS that there is the potential, as I've stated elsewhere, that these cases can have repercussions and that the way she handles them can lead to problems between the antagonists once they have appeared and return to their respective towns.

Freaks galore. Take the August 15, 2014 airing of the case of Ticia Tinder, a plaintiff who claimed that the defendant hit her car repeatedly with a hammer. Tinder, a white woman with large lips, had as her witness a "Mr. Charles," a large black man who saw the incident. He put his phone number on her car because he lived in the same building and the next morning, Ms. Tinder found it, contacted him and asked him to be a witness. In addition to car damage, the computer was open and on and she had it on the patio. The same defendant sprayed water on it. She also said the woman poisoned her cats. One survived and the other didn't.

The defendant, Ms. Cynthia Hill, denied the charges but Judy told her she didn't believe her. "I believe Mr. Charles," she said. She said all she's done is "stand up to this woman." She said the woman was on the HOA Board and no one would come forward. She said she was the one who was being harassed. Both of these bitches were crazy, but I knew that Judy would side with the plaintiff because she looked Jewish. Judy awarded her the full $5,000 and added, "All these things happened as a result of being YOUR neighbor!"

During one segment she wanted to take a look at the diamond ring that two people were arguing over "because I'm a bit of a yenta," she says. More Jewish terminology and more Jewish tendencies: obsession with gems of various kinds, hence "JEWelry stores."

Two nasty looking bitches from Texas (claiming to be "family friends"), Jackquelyne (this is the original spelling!) Hall and Nicole Horton, appeared before Judy during an August 15, 2014 taping. Hall, the plaintiff, was paying for a car through MoneyGram. She paid $3200 in total and then she wanted Horton to sign the title over to her. Horton refused because of the agreement: she wanted payment at one time but got installments instead. Horton tried to repossess the car when Jackie failed to make payments – she refused. Everything was verbal. She tells Horton, "Take your hand off your hip. Only one attitude here and that's mine."

So associating the hands on the hip with "attitude" is part and parcel of Judy's belief system. That is a racist belief, stereotypically assigned to black women and girls. Horton was forced to sign the title, playing with he fake ass hair all the while. Judy ruled in Jackie's favor and Jackie didn't have to pay any more money. Say what???

But not only does Judge Judy have "attitude," which she has readily admitted. But during the broadcast of a show on November 20, 2014, she was dogging out a plaintiff and made it clear about her mental state. She told one woman, "Say what you want to say Miss Passive-Aggressive. The only one who can be passive-aggressive around here is me." Do you know what she's admitting to? *******

One woman, obviously a Latina (last name Rosales), was suing a couple (well-to-do Black male and white female) she had already evicted, then still had the nerve to want past rent. Judy told the woman, "I'll give you three minutes to sum up your ridiculous counter-claim, " Judy says. The woman began by saying, "I feel that …." Judy cut her off and said, "I don't care about your feelings. Your feelings are irrelevant to me. You evicted them." On the same show, but in a different case, Judy tells a Defendant named Schmidt, "Actually, for the first time in the history of this show, I'm concerned about how you FEEL." And on an August 20, 2014 segment, the jive-ass judge told a plaintiff who started off his statement with , "I feel …" that, "I don't care what you feel – feelings go to Phil" (referring to psychiatrist Dr. Phil McGraw who has another show and a different set of personality issues).

So there you have it. This high-paid woman can say or do whatever in the FUCK she wants to do, when she wants to do it, and because she's making so much money for the network, they let her get away with it. This is what scholar Christine Sleeter would refer to as "white privilege." But in my lexicon, I consider it as 'Jewish privilege' because that's who controls the decision making in television just as they do in the music and newspaper industries.

In another case a young lady was suing because she loaned a female defendant some money ($4000) and didn't get paid back. Judy asked the plaintiff about her college life and she said she got money for tuition and a thousand for books, which is not much. The woman kept saying that the college girl was well off and "gave" her the money and that it wasn't a loan. Judy looked at the college girl and said, "I can tell she's lying," speaking about the defendant. "She's sweating on her top lip." What kind of fucked up Judge Joe Brown body language bullshit is this?

Another time, these two fat bitches were "friends with benefits" of this rather smallish white man. He was suing them because he said they trashed his house. At one point Judy, obviously finding what was being said hilarious, said, "I don't know what to make of this. Here you have this nerdy little guy, and these two reasonably good looking women." First of all, both of those bitches were sidewalk crunchers and secondly, such judgments are not hers to make: she's supposed to be objective in her assessments of both plaintiffs and defendants.

This cranky bitch is the best there is at being a judge and the reason is clear: she doesn't give a shit about what anybody has to say. They got her from the family court and therefore she doesn't think very highly about young people shacking up, women loaning men money, interracial relationships or anybody who doesn't have a job. She pontificates endlessly on all her "experience," but nevertheless makes some of the most asinine statements of all the judges analyzed in this book.

Another thing about this cratchety curmudgeon is this: she's a major supporter of the red, white and blue. This bitch thinks she's a cop. She uses her shows, I believe, as evidence in a court of law when somebody foolishly comes on the show and admits that he or she doesn't pay child support. "In my state they'd take your driver's license or put you in jail if you didn't pay child support." She really hates California when the laws don't do things the way that New York does them. She's very hateful, testimony to the fact that she hasn't been fucked in a number of decades. Her sexual frustration, in my view, is the basis for all that vitriol that you see her spewing forth on her show.

Judge Judy is a stupid bitch, and here's two examlpes of it. For instance, she used to say, "If it doesn't make sense, then it can't be true." When I first heard it I knew that was a damn lie. If it doesn't make sense, then it's not true. She must have gotten dogged about that by her handlers because now she says, "If it doesn't make sense, it's USUALLY not true." Yeah, she was corrected because she knew that her initial view was out of whack with reality.

A second example: during one episode she argued with a young white man whose wife was black regarding his earlier marriage that he must have made a mistake or else he would still be married to his first wife. What? Once again she sets women as the moral standard. Occasionally she makes cracks about men and about how "stupid" or "ignorant" we are. The audience giggles because the bitches sitting in that audience agree with her. If men were so controllable, why was Jerry screwing around behind her back and she didn't even find out until many months later?

During yet another case (June 24, 2013) I heard her say, "There's no such thing as a coincidence." What's wrong with this bitch? Because she says it makes it so? This is the kind of attitude and ego you have when you make so much money for doing so little. And she brags about that fact. She talks about being a star, about "this is my show," about "no need for you to interview, I already got the job" and so on.

And once again, Judge Judy doesn't have a lick of street sense although she tries to use axioms from back in the day that she probably hears from some of the black women who frequent her social circles. It sounds new, hip and profound to white viewers because they don't know anything about black people (just like they're too culturally inept to see that "American Idol" is nothing more than a rip-off of Harlem's "Night at the Apollo"). In one episode a woman said she worked in a restaurant and a man ordered a drink. Judge Judy says, "You can't serve alcohol, you're only 19." The defendant explained that she can take the order but someone else has to bring it to the customer. Judge Judy laughed to cover up the fact that she didn't know what the fuck she was talking about.

But here is one thing she knows about: she knows about how television works and its impact, which is why she acts the way she does, says the things she says, and knows that she's protected by the Jews whose networks she is making money for. For instance, during a November 16, 2015 segment, a young woman was being sued by a young man for some money he said he loaned her. Judge Judy caught the sistah in a lie and then said something like, "I don't know why you would come on this show and lie to me to my face." Then she asked the sistah how old her son was. The woman said the kid was three. Realizing that the child was too young to see that the mother was a liar, Judy said, "Oh well, these shows are made to last for a long time."

She knows the history of Jews and how her people hold a grudge for a long time. That "never again" shit doesn't only apply to the Nazis; they hold a grudge against anyone who sees them for the charlatans, scam artists, liars and thieves that many of them are. Judy is surely no exception: *she is the rule.*

WHERE"S THE LOGIC IN THESE PROGRAMS?

What's the point? Where's the logic? What is the goal? Let's try to answer some of these questions using logic, not emotive labeling (although I will include it because in my view American law, in general, is totally fucked up).

To begin with the premise that mediation can solve problems. Two people who have legal issues sign paperwork to "work it out" in front of these TV judges. How is that logical? Somebody is going to lose the case, but BOTH will lose when they get butchered by one of these asshole judges, especially if it's Sheindlin, or Brown and in some cases if you piss him off, Mathis. You're going to be seen by millions of people, and that's a risk in itself. What if somebody sees you who wants vengeance or otherwise hates you? What about the impact that the humiliation has on your family? What about if you win and somebody you owe finds out you won a legal case? There's more than can go wrong on these shows, once these people get back to their respective townships, than can go right. It just doesn't seem to make much sense.

Secondly are references to local laws that may not even apply in other jurisdictions. This is especially an issue with Judge Judy because she has people coming to her from all over the nation (as does Judge Marilyn Milian). The decisions are made based on laws that exist, say, in California but may not be the same in New York. Judge Judy, who kisses the ass of any jurisdiction, is always siding with the police reports or any legal statement that appears in a report, but won't read affidavits from private citizens. To appear before a consistently ornery bitch like this, knowing that no matter what happens, she is going to force out a laugh at your expense, is just not logical.

The fact is, this bitch loves cops. To her, a police report is like a page from the Bible. For instance, during the September 9, 2014 episode this stupid young girl was drunk and got pulled over for it. Judy makes the statement, after the girl said the police report was wrong, that, "This was written by no stranger, it was written by a cop." In most cases, cops ARE strangers! The girl was white, but she didn't know that cop. What the fuck is wrong with Judy.

A few minutes later she says in reference to the police, "They're not in the business of making up false info on police reports." On what planet is this bitch living? The fact of the matter is that cops lie all the time, they pull people over for no reason, they pull women over and try to get dates, they lie to defendants and get them to confess to crimes that they didn't commit, and they lie on tickets given to people of color. This was just proven, once again, in the case of Ferguson, Missouri. Judge Judy lives in a dream world.

Third, somewhat related to the previous concern, these court shows provide the judge (and some angry plaintiffs and defendants) a free shot at insulting the people who come forward and sign away their rights to rebuttal. It is clear that Judge Judy looks for something, anything, to attack. Brown claims he's about promoting manhood and defending womanhood, but since he has the right to do neither, this oftentimes leads to conclusions based on sex role stereotypes ("men are supposed to be nice to women," "you're not supposed to hit women," "you're supposed to have job," etc.) It doesn't make sense to appear in front of people who are paid to not only make decisions of law, but who are also supposed to make jokes, wise cracks and insults, often at your expense.

Related to point three, the stupidity of people who agree to have their cases "heard" before an American public. Recorders readied, these people can't wait for the show to be aired. And even in that, they still degrade themselves, many of them are functional illiterates who don't understand the law, and most of them are on the air to "look cute" or to preserve a record for future lawsuits or civil action. This brings me to a fifth point.

What happens when the show is over? These people are pissed off in most cases. Who likes to "lose" in front of millions of viewers, have people walk up to them on the street having seen the show? This kind of public humiliation can only lead to a negative result. As is the case with "Maury," "Jerry Springer," "Steve Wilkos" and those shows where people argue, curse and in some cases fight each other all over the stage, the impact of the show is going to follow them back to the community they came from. There is going to be a lust for vengeance, payback for "embarrassing me," for "tearing out my extensions" or "pulling off my wig," for "telling the world you was fucking my friend" and so on. Doesn't make sense to set the stage for millions of potential witnesses, both local and national.

Sixth, the people behind these shows – usually Jews – make sure that the buffoonery, the insults and the people on the bench are from different races and ethnicities lest they (the producers and writers) be charged with being racist. So you've got Latinos (Ferrer, Perez and Milian), Blacks (Lake, Mills-Francis, Elder, Brown, Ross, Hatchett, Mathis, Toler) and of course, Jews (Sheindlin).

Seventh, and related to the previous point, why would black judges, men and women, be in the majority when it comes to these programs? We're not "allowed" or "written in" to the majority in anything else. So why in the legal arena where arbitration and mediation are the primary purposes (allegedly) of these TV shows?

There could be several logical answers.

This much we know: whoever appears on these shows has a great deal of influence with the Jews. That's who makes the decision by asking, "Hey, you wanna a TV show?" and that's who has the juice to make it happen. Then, that person who is picked has to have a gimmick and a large audience because those in power are going to put the entire public relations machine behind them. So for some reason, these blacks have curried favor with the powers that be and for whatever reason, those decision makers believe that they can make money (sell advertisements) off of these "black personalities."

So what is the slant of each one of these people? Joe Brown Larry Joe Doherty are both hicks – the former an African-American who speaks so slowly and has a voice so monotonous it sounds as if he's guzzled a fifth of Bacardi 151 before he takes the bench, and the latter, a loud-talking Texas boy who has the aura of being a former Klansman. You know: Yee-hah! That's why his show is called "Texas Justice" because that state dispenses a particular kind of justice: the kind that means long sentences for blacks, and used to mean lynchings. In other words, RACIST justice.

What is the gimmick for the Latinas? Loud and "hot-tempered" ala Gloria on "Modern Family" (although she's Colombian). Marilyn Milian leads the way in screaming with Pirro, who left the air to become a Latina conservative, coming in a close second. The latter couples her with bitterness and insults. A third Latina, Cristina Perez, has a gimmick: soft spoken and BLONDE.

Then come the 'sisters' – modern day "mammies" for the most part. You've got Mills-Francis, Hatchett (probably the most sane of them all), Lake, and Toler. The white man told former "Divorce Court" judge Mablean Ephraim that she had to change her hair. She said no and wanted a race. They said, "There's the door" and bought in this self-absorbed black woman with mental problems (by her own admission) named Lynn Toler. Can there be any doubt that a black woman who dyes her hair blonde has some kind of issues with her looks? That's what Mills-Francis brings to the table.

Mathis brings "the streets" to the bench and reminds us of that every day. Elder is a real-life conservative 'super-tom' who makes it clear that he's not really black but indeed, an "American." Two black men on the opposite sides of the spectrum. Although Elder has been cancelled he's still out there promoting conservative politics and trying to hide the fact that he's a black man. Ross brings the black, clean-cut look and Joe Brown is the old school hillbilly.

So then, what is the purpose of this menagerie and why are black judges in the majority? It's like having majority of blacks on the slave plantations: sure, there were more blacks, but they didn't have any juice, they followed the white man's orders and although many of them despised the system, they did what they were told. And that is the answer to this particular query: these "judges" do it because the bullwhip has been replaced with the paycheck. And most blacks in this country will do ANYTHING for a paycheck; these brothers and sisters on the bench are no different.

Eighth and finally, what is the REAL impact of courtroom shows like these? When you add it all up and watch the promos, there is a call for these shows to pretend to be problem solvers. This is especially true of "The People's Court," "America's Court," "Paternity Court" and "Texas Justice." If you can get people to buy into this belief, they will come forward and dupe even more people into believing that "the system is the solution." And in the final analysis, that is the purpose of these shows: to suck people into believing that when you have a problem, look to one of these nitwit judges to "solve it.'

I am of the belief that when these shows conclude, the problems for those who come forward are just beginning.

WHO'S THE BEST? WHO'S THE WORST?

I've shared with you a lot first-hand research and content analysis on the judges that I am most familiar with through my own observations. They have different approaches for the most part, but in this section I am going to address who I believe are the best, and who are the worst, and why. But first let me tell you who is the "cutest."

This woman, Faith Jenkins, has a show called, "Judge Faith." She has a baby face, a soft voice and a razor-sharp mind. She is one of the most beautiful women I have seen on television in a long time (outside of Viola Davis). Her show, as of October 2015, was airing on Omaha's WB Channel, so who knows how long it will be on. I only mention her here because of her appearance and general intelligence and, if she chose to, she could go a long way in movies and television.

With that having been said, let me present my nominations. In the best category I am going to declare a tie between Judge Alex Ferrer and Judge Greg Mathis, and here is why.

I like judges who walk the walk and then talk the talk. Mathis was a judge in hard-core ass Detroit and was active in the community. He helped bring down crooked ass mayor Kwame Kilpatrick and in the courtroom he displays a combination of legal sense and street sense. Ferrer is of a similar stripe. If you saw the movie "Pain and Gain," then you should know it was Ferrer who handled that case. Ferrer was a cop and a prosecuting attorney and, like Mathis, has a sense of humor and a sense of the streets.

But as I say Mathis may well be bipolar. He was raised by a single mother and he may have been in the streets, but his responses and reactions to some of his litigants are those of a confused, scatter-brained bitch! His voice gets high and any minute you expect him to flip his wrist and say, "You lyin', girl!" The more I watch him the more I see him as someone who is getting caught up in that television aura the way Marilyn Milian is.

Judge Jeff Ross is a clean-cut black kid who really seems to give a damn about his decisions. He doesn't have to insult you, talk about your mother or engage in a lot of hyperbole or gooniness. He simply gets to the point. In fact, if you want to see what a television courtroom show should be run like, perhaps Ross' "America's Court" should be held up as a prototype.
(on the other hand, how can you let a black man host a show called "America's Court" when, after all is said and done, he's not considered an American. As Malcolm X said, he's the victim of Americanism, the victim of American democracy - nothing but disguised hypocrisy).

True, like the men, some of the females also have impressive credentials. But it seems that they get carried away with some of the cases and are more concerned about being "cute" and "controversial" than they are about receiving kudos for their legal acumen and decisions. Among these are, of course, the crass curmudgeon Judge Judy; the loud-talking and tempestuous Latina stereotype, Judge Milian; the conservative and hard core Judge Pirro; and the "look at my pouty lips cutie, Judge Toler. All four are typical of what happens when a woman, in a man's world, is given a television show and adopts a "gimmick" of some kind.

For the worst, there can be but one. And that one is Judge Judy Sheindlin the self-proclaimed, "truth machine." Judge Judy is the worst by far. She will lie and pawn it off as the truth. When she gets caught in a lie she falls back on her "thirty-plus years on the bench" and her work in family court. In addition, she makes statements like, "if it doesn't' make sense it can't be true." That is a lie. Racism, for instance, doesn't make sense but it's true. Another statement she makes, out of sheer meanness, is that when one of slow thinking plaintiffs or defendants begins a statement with, "Uh," she'll jump on it like a pit bull in heat and fire back, "Uh is not an answer!"

Therefore it is probably not a coincidence that Judy is the meanest, most vociferous of the judge and is also, far and away, the highest paid. America likes meanness, especially cratchity old white bitches. It's funny when Betty White curses up a storm; it's hilarious if some old broad on television is show resisting arrest; it's a million laughs when an old sister stereotypically beats the shit out of her teenaged son or husband. The old white woman is today's old white man. She's mean, she has power, she's outlived her husband and she hates black people just as much as he did. She's just better at hiding it.

But there are others who are just as obnoxious as the red-headed septuagenarian, several who I alluded to earlier, and I want to take time to list and describe them here in more subjective and specific terms than I did earlier in this book.

Let's start with Judge Jeanine Pirro. When I first saw her she was hosting a court TV show. A few months later I was cruising through the channels and saw her as some part of a news program, lambasting the Obama Administration and appearing as nasty as any other conservative commentator. As an accomplished, real-life judge and attorney, she's top notch; as a political thinker, she's an idiot. As is the case with most of them, her hatred overrides her logic. As a TV judge she was mediocre because she had to watch what she said. In her current job as some kind of conservative legal expert, she can wail away at any opposition and make big money for doing so.

By September of 2015 she has her own show with her name, and somehow got a prime time interview with none other than Donald Trump. Trump was a Republican candidate for president and she asked him every "fluff question" in the book; it was as if she was his personal advisor, oftentimes making remarks like, "I've known you a long time" or "we go back a long way." She's a part of the system for sure and is most definitely ultra-conservative.

Judge Larry Elder is another accomplished conservative. As the former host of "Moral Court," he often made idiotic statements and arrived at conclusions that were jejune, at best. He's one of those negro types, along the lines of Supreme Court Justice Clarence Thomas, radio talk show host Armstrong Williams, and black conservative Republican Michael Steele. I thought that the concept of a "moral court" in a nation as corrupt as America, was a dumb idea to begin with.

Judge Marilyn Milian is a beautiful Latina who has lost her damn mind. In the early days of the show the introduction to the program referred to her as "the hottest judge on TV" and showed her dancing with some guy (presumably her husband) and waving her long red hair around like some beauty queen on crack. Now they've gone back to their original orientation, emphasizing "The People's Court" with Milian simply as the judge. But the preview of the show still shows her standing with her hands on her hips and wind blowing through her hair. Why? Why did she agree to this shit? Did she ask, "What in the FUCK are you doing with that fan blowing on me and why do I have to stand with my hands on my hips like some two dollar ho?"

Promises and fame and television exposure will make most people do ANYTHING. Just watch an episode of "Jerry Springer," "Steve Wilkos," "Maury Povich" or "Bill Cunningham" and you'll see what I mean.

At any rate, Milian's screaming rivals that of Laura Lake of "Paternity Court." She screams at Plaintiffs, which makes one think that somewhere down the line the people who wrote the show told her to do all in her power to affirm the stereotype of the "hot blooded Latina" and also the stereotype of "the emotional redhead." Every now and then she'll throw in a Spanish quip or quote to show that she hasn't been *totally* assimilated, but it is her screaming will grate on your nerves even as she tries to cover up her quips and screams with a beautiful smile. I don't see how this program stays on television other than for the fact that Milian is a beautiful woman who is also bilingual.

Judge Lynn Toler. The concept of "Divorce Court" was just that when Mablean Ephraim had the show. But it went to her head, she got greedy, wouldn't take a pay cut and now her claim to fame is limited to her appearances in Tyler Perry movies. As for Toler, I don't like her "relationship expert" demeanor and how she shamelessly peddles her books and makes frequent references to her family. The woman used to be a manic depressive and now, just because she has pouty lips, she gets to have a television program. They've altered it to become a "pre-marriage" type show, and like Springer, Maury Povich and Steve Wilkos, does more to divide men and women and families than repairing them.

Judge Lauren Lake, as stated earlier, is loud – very loud. The premise of her show, "Paternity Court" seems to revolve around DNA testing and finding out "who's the baby daddy." Like "Maury Povich" who first capitalized on this bullshit on a full-time basis, she concludes that, "It has been determined by this court …" and then she reads the verdict after extending the show with a number of poorly-timed commercial breaks. But she's wrong. Paternity is determined by two people; the mother and the father – in that order. These bitches know when they want to have a baby and they know who they want that father to be. If this wasn't the case, there would be no sex in the first place.

So they have sex, get pregnant, knowing that this society is going to come down on their side and assume that the man has to pay and pay and pay. They put men in jail in some states if they don't pay. They will deny some men their income tax refunds and driver's licenses. And all she has to do is lay on her back and dupe the man into thinking that it was "his looks," "his rap," "his style" or some other excuse that led her to make her decision when in reality, she made the decision long before she decided to give up that ass. And even if she just met him and gave him some booty, she was still in on it.

Once she's pregnant here comes society to kick in welfare stipends, food stamps, section 8 housing, jobs for intake workers, jobs for social workers and so on. She's insulted. What about him? A piece of stray pussy commits him 18 years to a kid he may or may not have wanted. The "liberated" women of today goes so far, in many cases, to get pregnant and then go off to have a kid "on her own." But the state, if they find out – and they will – will put a virtual bounty on his head, search him out and FORCE him to pay, even to the point of garnisheeing his wages.

This is what "Paternity Court" is about and why I don't like it. On the air, reading about this shit, is admissible in court. A company, "DNA Diagnostics," prepares the results. The decision is read aloud and then it's supposedly final. No second opinion because the DNA results are supposed to be infallible – even though the tests are administered by and analyzed by human beings, who are as capable of mistakes and error as anyone else.

More profoundly, some scientists in Israel have been tampering with DNA for a long period of time and I recall reading somewhere where they came up with a away to manipulate strands of the DNA so they could make a DNA sample appear to come from somewhere other than the original source. Expect this kind of manipulation to start being used by the same American legal system that consistently falsifies information and sets up black defendants so they can lock them up. In short, DNA is not infallible, although shows like "Forensic Files" continue to claim that it is.

Judge Lauren Lake is the ringleader of the paternity announcements just as Jerry Springer, Maury Povich, Bill Cunningham, Steve Wilkos and all the rest of these "stupidity pimps" are. Their collective purpose: to embarrass America, ship tapes of these shows overseas making fun of people and in doing so, setting the stage for this country's eventual undermining and destruction.

These then, are my rankings of the "best" and the "worst" of the television courtroom judges.

THE MINSTREL PRODUCTION MACHINE

What is a "minstrel production machine" you may ask. It is a term I've coined to describe how silly, backward, stupid - and yet entertaining – some of the people who appear on these court shows can be. They actually sign a statement to go on the show and plead their case on television, in front of millions of people. To name their home town, their families, to make threats, to display their illiteracy and lack of common sense, just to have their case "handled on television."

Now, the definition of the term generally says that a minstrel is "A musical entertainer in the Middle Ages." We're not in the Middle Ages any more, but there is a second that is far closer and more germane to what I am alleging on these pages. A minstrel is defined as, and read closely: "any of a troupe of performers typically giving a program of black American melodies, jokes, and impersonations and usually wearing blackface." The similarities are startling. "Blackface" refers to white people who used to wear black burned cork in an attempt to insult and imitate black people on stage. Today's version is actual black skin because the people are black: but the individuals are nevertheless clowns in their actions and statements. And further, they are there for entertainment because they are screened first; each case is selected and I am sure that these peckerwoods doing the selecting have, at the base of their thoughts, selecting a person who is going to make an ass out of him/herself.

Furthermore, these clowns do come in a "troupe," because they have so much in common. Whether they are black, brown or white, this "troupe" of people echo a melody of stupidity, they are the embodiment of "jokes" when it comes to their lack of intelligence, and they are "impersonating" people who know that they are talking about when, in reality, most of them, ranging from plaintiffs to defendants, couldn't pour piss out of a boot if the instructions were written on the heel.

Finally, they need not wear blackface. Judy Sheindlin is the personification of whiteness (Judaism) and Americanism, which means that even low-income whites who come before her will be "niggerized" before it's all said and done. She can't relate to very much, but as I said, she imposes her Jewish slogans and terms on the public, and she talks about what she views as the decline of America on a regular basis. In vintage white fashion, if one of her theories goes awry, she will quickly adapt her allegation so that her incorrect premise is somehow the fault of the other person.

CONCLUSION

The people who appear are "entertainers" and "performers." She then, becomes the foil – someone who prevents something from being accomplished. She rules on law but in the process, appears committed to stripping someone of their human dignity.

The more the world views these "court TV" programs, the bigger a laughing stock this nation becomes. If you can't take a legal system seriously, then the other institutions that purport to support America are assumed to be equally weak. Everybody's watching and America's enemies increase by the day. These TV Court shows, in my view, represent "the enemy within."

America has pompously sat in judgment of the rest of the world for centuries. From Manifest Destiny and White Man's Burden to the tri-lateral alliance and the use and manipulation of the United Nations, this country has always believed that it has the right to impose its rules and regulations –and punishments – upon others.

Court TV shows are big business. As Wikipedia (2018) explains,

> In November 2012, Entertainment Studios announced that they would be launching their fourth court show, *Supreme Justice with Judge Karen*, in Fall 2013. Entertainment Studios also produces the court shows *America's Court with Judge Ross*, *We the People With Gloria Allred*, *Justice for All with Judge Cristina Pérez* and *Justice with Judge Mablean*, all of which use a nontraditional/dramatized court show format …

Madness in front of millions, arbitration and mediation being pawned off as law. The mundane routinization reminds one of some of the lyrics from the old Sonny and Cher song, "The Beat Goes On":

> The beat goes on, the beat goes on
> Drums keep pounding a rhythm to the brain
> La de da de de, la de da de da

Court dismissed!

REFERENCES

Associated Press (2007, November 17). Jeanine Pirro and husband end tumultuous marriage. Retrieved from http://www.nydailynews.com/news/jeanine-pirro-husband-tumultuous-marriage-article-1.258620

Black Doctor.org (2018) Blackdoctor.org (2018). Judge Lynn Toler: Putting Her Own Mental Health on Trial. Retrieved from https://blackdoctor.org/517454/judge-lynn-toler-mental-health/

Booker, Stephanie (2017, June 27). Couples Court With the Cutlers Starts Production on the First Season: New Syndicated Daytime Soap to Shoot in Atlanta. https://www.broadcastingcable.com/post-type-the-wire/couples-court-cutlers-starts-production-first-season-166854

Dawsey, Josh (2018, April 5). Trump's must-see TV: Judge Jeanine's show and her positive take on the president. **The Washington Post**. Retrieved from https://www.washingtonpost.com/politics/trumps-must-see-tv-judge-jeanines-show-and-her-positive-take-on-the-president/2018/04/05/626169a8-3902-11e8-b57c-9445cc4dfa5e_story.html?noredirect=on&utm_term=.4ca402df7822

Dillon, Nancy (2018, April 19). Witness reveals Fox news host Jeanine Pirro had affair with Texas cop who probed Robert Durst murder case. **New York Daily News.** Retrieved from http://www.nydailynews.com/news/crime/jeanine-pirro-allegedly-affair-robert-durst-case-article-1.3942442

Entertainment Studios, Inc. (2018)Entertainment Studios Signs Judge Karen Mills-Francis For Its Fourth Television Court Show. Retrieved from http://www.es.tv/entertainment-studios-signs-judge-karen-mills-francis-for-its-fourth-television-court-show/

Gartland, Michael (2012, December 23). 25 years after her rape claims sparked a firestorm, Tawana Brawley avoids the spotlight. **New York Post**. Retrieved from https://nypost.com/2012/12/23/25-years-after-her-rape-claims-sparked-a-firestorm-tawana-brawley-avoids-the-spotlight/

IMDb (1996). Judge Judy: Memorable quotes. Retrieved from http://www.imdb.com/title/tt0115227/quotes

Jordan, Christal. (2018, May 11). 'Couples Court' TV judges say having a prenup is like health insurance. Retrieved from https://rollingout.com/2018/05/11/couples-court-tv-judges-say-having-a-prenup-is-like-health-insurance/

Lombardi, Kate Stone. (2000, November 12). The Many Faces of Jeanine Pirro. Retrieved from https://www.nytimes.com/2000/11/12/nyregion/the-many-faces-of-jeanine-pirro.html

Millar, Chloe (2014, March 31). Order In The Court: 10 Secrets & Scandals Of TV's Judges. EXPOSED! Retrieved from http://radaronline.com/photos/order-in-the-court-10-secrets-scandals-of-tvs-judges-exposed/photo/638580/

Opfang, K. (2005, November 17). CJP orders Judge Kevin Ross removed from bench. **Metropolitan News-Enterprise.**

Pollack, A. (2009, August 17). DNA evidence can be fabricated, scientists show. **The New York Times.**

Reddit (2016. I was in the audience for The People's Court. AMA. Retrieved from https://www.reddit.com/r/IAmA/comments/bxkdq/i_was_in_the_audience_for_the_peoples_court_ama/

Spargo, Chris (2017, September 14). "Judge Judy reveals she left her first husband when he belittled her legal career and divorced her second when she got sick of catering to his demands (but remarried him a year later)." **Daily Mail**. Retrieved from http://www.dailymail.co.uk/news/article-4885270/Judge-Judy-opens-three-marriages-two-husbands.html

The People's Court. Com (2016). The People's Court. Retrieved from http://peoplescourt.com/cast/

Yasharoff, Hannah (2018, July 19). Whoopi Goldberg, Jeanine Pirro explain what happened during and after 'The View' shouting match. **USA Today**. Retrieved from https://www.usatoday.com/story/life/entertainthis/2018/07/19/whoopi-goldberg-shuts-down-jeanine-pirros-trump-comment-view/802049002/

Wikipedia (2016). Marilyn Milian. Retrieved from https://en.wikipedia.org/wiki/Marilyn_Milian

Woodson, C.G. (1933) *Mis-Education of the Negro*. Trenton, New Jersey: Africa World Press.